Contents

CW01507646

Colonial Origins of Democracy and Dictatorship

Why are some countries more democratic than others? For most non-European countries, elections began under Western colonial rule. However, existing research largely overlooks these democratic origins. Analyzing a global sample of colonies across four centuries, this book explains the emergence of colonial electoral institutions and their lasting impact. The degree of democracy in the metropole, the size of the white settler population, and pressure from non-Europeans all shaped the timing and form of colonial elections. White settlers and non-white middle classes educated in the colonizer's language usually gained early elections but settler minorities resisted subsequent franchise expansion. Authoritarian metropoles blocked elections entirely. Countries with lengthy exposure to competitive colonial institutions tended to consolidate democracies after independence. By contrast, countries with shorter electoral episodes usually shed democratic institutions and countries that were denied colonial elections consolidated stable dictatorships. Regime trajectories shaped by colonial rule persist to the present day.

ALEXANDER LEE is Associate Professor of Political Science at the University of Rochester. He earned his Ph.D. from Stanford University and his B.A. from Yale University. His research focuses on the factors governing the success or failure of political institutions, especially the historical evolution of state capacity, the political economy of South Asia, and the causes and consequences of identity politics. He is the author of *The Cartel System of States: An Economic Theory of International Politics* (2022), *From Hierarchy to Ethnicity: The Politics of Caste in Twentieth-Century India* (2020), and *Development in Multiple Dimensions: Social Power and Regional Policy in India* (2019).

JACK PAINE is Associate Professor of Political Science at Emory University. He earned his Ph.D. from University of California, Berkeley, and his B.A. from the University of Virginia. His research analyzes the origins of political regimes, how they survive, and when they break down into conflict. In addition to studying the colonial origins of national political institutions and states, he examines the strategic foundations of authoritarian power sharing, the guardianship dilemma, and democratic backsliding.

Colonial Origins of Democracy and Dictatorship

ALEXANDER LEE
University of Rochester

JACK PAINE
Emory University

CAMBRIDGE
UNIVERSITY PRESS

Shaftesbury Road, Cambridge CB2 8EA, United Kingdom

One Liberty Plaza, 20th Floor, New York, NY 10006, USA

477 Williamstown Road, Port Melbourne, VIC 3207, Australia

314–321, 3rd Floor, Plot 3, Splendor Forum, Jasola District Centre,
New Delhi – 110025, India

103 Penang Road, #05–06/07, Visioncrest Commercial, Singapore 238467

Cambridge University Press is part of Cambridge University Press & Assessment,
a department of the University of Cambridge.

We share the University's mission to contribute to society through the pursuit of
education, learning and research at the highest international levels of excellence.

www.cambridge.org
Information on this title: www.cambridge.org/9781009423533

DOI: 10.1017/9781009423526

First published 2024

Printed in the United Kingdom by CPI Group Ltd, Croydon CR0 4YY

A catalogue record for this publication is available from the British Library

A Cataloging-in-Publication data record for this book is available from the
Library of Congress

ISBN 978-1-009-42353-3 Hardback

Figures

Tables

Acknowledgments

The research culminating in this book project began with a straightforward premise: the period of Western colonial rule must have affected subsequent democratic trajectories. This critical juncture, which created new states and political institutions across the globe, was too widespread and disruptive to not matter. But how?

Academics routinely emphasize the benefits of collegiality, of which this project is a direct result. Informal conversations during office white-board sessions, holiday parties, and dinners established a baseline set of characteristics that required further analysis. In our initial research projects on how Western colonial rule affected subsequent regime trajectories, we examined individual colonial actors, namely, metropolitan officials (Lee and Paine 2019, *Journal of Comparative Economics;* Lee and Paine 2019 *International Studies Quarterly*), white settlers (Paine 2019, *Journal of Politics*), or both (Paine 2019, *World Politics*).

Carving off smaller slices enabled us to think about which pieces mattered and how they fit together to affect the big picture. Our varied interests on colonialism congealed into a book almost without us realizing it. We thank our friends and colleagues at the University of Rochester political science department both for their constant support and advice, and for creating the intellectual atmosphere that made this project possible. We particularly thank Gretchen Helmke, who encouraged us and provided excited feedback throughout the process while also serving as an invaluable mentor.

Outside Harkness Hall, we benefitted immensely from conversations with numerous colleagues. When the book was at an intermediate stage, Jim Robinson asked us what the main takeaway was (interesting facts about colonial elections are fine, but ...) and we realized that we needed to refocus on the advice we routinely give to our students. John Gerring's sharp comments on better integrating the case narratives with the statistical analysis provided the fuel needed to push the project over the finish line. We also thank seminar participants at Emory and UC Berkeley and panel members at ISA 2019, APSA 2020, and MPSA 2022; and in particular feedback from our discussants and other participants, including Brett Carter, Sean Gailmard, Jonathan Krieckhaus, Mike Miller, and Kunle Owolabi.

Jack thanks his wife Jessi, who put up with him while writing this, and his sons Malcolm (3) and Calvin (1), who have heard about this book literally their entire lives. Their support and encouragement (often to set the book down for a bit) was needed. Jack's parents read drafts throughout and were very excited that he would publish a book. Alex thanks his parents and his friends, especially Steven Stromberg, Matthew Melzer, Kimuli Kasara, Eric Vandenbrink, and Aatif Iqbal. Throughout, we each consulted with good friends and co-authors Avi Acharya and Anne Meng, who routinely express our own ideas better than we can ourselves.

1 | *Introduction*

A century ago, every democratic regime was in Western Europe or in a country settled by Western Europeans. The picture is now more varied. Non-Western countries such as India and Jamaica have been democracies for more than half a century, despite lacking many factors often cited as prerequisites for democracy. But stable democratic experiences are exceptional. In countries such as Uganda and Malaysia, democratic competition at independence gave way shortly afterward to military coups or autocratic consolidation by the incumbent. Many other countries, such as Angola, Kuwait, and Niger, were authoritarian at independence and did not establish democratic institutions until decades after independence, if ever.

Why some countries are democracies has long intrigued political scientists. The enormous literature on this topic almost exclusively examines variation in democracy levels *after independence*. However, these theories overlook the profound institutional restructuring that occurred under Western colonialism. The overall practice of colonial governance was unmistakably authoritarian. However, by the mid-twentieth century, most colonies had adopted hybrid political institutions with electoral elements. For *most* contemporary countries, mass electoral competition originated under external rule.

In this book, we provide a new theory and empirical evidence to answer two questions. First, why did colonies vary in their electoral experiences under Western rule? Electoral competition under colonialism was very common. Among 107 countries that gained independence from a Western power, all but eight experienced at least one national election under colonial rule.[1] However, colonial electoral institutions varied in many ways, including the timing of the first election, the scope

---

[1] Sample is all countries in the Varieties of Democracy (V-Dem) data set. Count of elections is based on our colonial elections data, both described later.

of the electorate, the role of elected versus appointed officials, and the powers of the legislature.

Second, did the colonial period matter for subsequent regime trajectories? Most contemporary regimes with electoral competition trace their roots at least in part to the colonial era. In 2022, ninety-nine non-European countries were democracies or electoral autocracies.[2] Of these, eighty-seven experienced their first election under Western colonial rule, and almost all the exceptions were not colonized by a Western power. We simply cannot explain postcolonial democracies or the broader importance of electoral competition in the non-European world without examining colonial origins.

Yet postcolonial democracy was not the only, or even the most frequent, product of colonial elections. Countries with lengthy episodes of colonial pluralism usually became durable democracies. However, the most common sequel to shorter episodes of colonial pluralism was military coups or electoral authoritarian regimes. Different facets of colonial electoral experiences are, as we demonstrate, highly correlated with democracy levels after independence. Colonial elections, *because* of their various flaws, put countries on divergent trajectories at independence that have largely reinforced themselves over time.

In contrast to our focus on colonialism, most leading theories of democratization focus solely on actors in sovereign states. Classic works analyze the interactions of various domestic social groups such as landed aristocrats, capitalist elites, military generals, the middle class, the working class, peasants, or the masses more broadly.[3] Causal factors posited to empower certain social groups at the expense of others include income growth,[4] asset mobility,[5] oil wealth,[6] and income inequality.[7] Many recent studies examine the role of elections within

---

[2] Calculated by authors using data from V-Dem and the Regimes of the World data sets.

[3] Moore 1966*a*; O'Donnell and Schmitter 1986; Rueschemeyer, Stephens and Stephens 1992; Collier 1999; Mahoney and Snyder 1999; Boix 2003; Acemoglu and Robinson 2006; Ansell and Samuels 2014; Miller 2021.

[4] Lipset 1959; Przeworski et al. 2000; Acemoglu et al. 2008.

[5] Bates and Donald Lien 1985; Boix 2003.

[6] Gause 1994; Ross 2001, 2012.

[7] Acemoglu and Robinson 2006; Ansell and Samuels 2014; Haggard and Kaufman 2012.

authoritarian regimes and the correlates of authoritarian stability.[8] These theories cannot explain how an external actor like a colonial ruler would affect prospects for democracy or dictatorship, nor whether institutions constructed under external rule should persist afterward. The democratization literature does not overlook external actors entirely, as some recent studies analyze attempts by the United States and Western Europe to promote democracy abroad.[9] However, these studies focus overwhelmingly on the post–Cold War period, when most of the world had already experienced some form of electoral competition.[10]

Scholars also neglect colonial political institutions when selecting cases for quantitative or qualitative empirical tests. Most authors sample postcolonial cases and most statistical tests use postindependence data. Many widely used cross-national measures of democracy, such as the Polity IV and Freedom House data sets, do not include colonized territories.[11] Thus, scholarship on democratization and electoral authoritarian regimes usually examines countries that had previously developed electoral institutions. However, because electoral institutions in most non-European countries date back to the colonial era, the standard approach overlooks the origins of these institutions.

Our book takes a broad historical and comparative approach to this problem. We collected a new global data set on colonial electoral institutions over the entire period of Western overseas rule. This wide scope enables us to study the origins and evolution of electoral bodies, as opposed to analyzing a snapshot of political institutions at a particular time or region. Colonialism was a critical juncture that resulted in most non-European countries gaining some form of Western-style elections, sometimes resulting in full-blown democracy. However, this finding neither requires nor supports a positive normative assessment

---

[8] Geddes 1999; Lust-Okar 2005; Brownlee 2007; Gandhi 2008; Blaydes 2010; Wright and Escribà-Folch 2012; Jensen, Malesky and Weymouth 2014; Miller 2015; Arriola, DeVaro and Meng 2021.

[9] Dunning 2004; Pevehouse 2005; Levitsky and Way 2010; Boix 2011; Gunitsky 2014; Hyde and Marinov 2014; Escribà-Folch and Wright 2015; Bush 2016; Haggard and Kaufman 2016; Miller 2020.

[10] Later, we engage in depth with the smaller number of studies that examine the effects of colonialism on democracy.

[11] Marshall and Gurr 2014; Freedom House 2022. The more recent V-Dem data, which we discuss later, is an exception.

of European colonialism overall. We demonstrate that the conditions under which external rule promoted democracy were historically rare and explain instead why colonial rule usually yielded postcolonial authoritarian regimes.

1.1 Overview of the Argument and Evidence

1.1.1 Origins of Colonial Electoral Institutions

To explain the timing, form, and rationale for electoral institutions across Western colonies, we develop a theory of electoral institutions that incorporates actors and motivations unique to the colonial context. We analyze the behavior of three policy-interested groups: metropolitan officials, white settlers, and non-Europeans (both native inhabitants and forced migrants). Metropolitan officials made the final decisions about constitutional form. However, both types of colonists could exert pressure through various options: lobbying and agitation, nonparticipation (e.g., withholding taxes, migration), and revolt. All three groups sought economic and other policies favorable to their group, which created a general preference for as much institutional control as possible. We explain how attributes of each actor structured key facets of colonial electoral institutions: the presence of any electoral body, its degree of policymaking autonomy, franchise restrictions, and democracy levels more broadly.

Competitive electoral institutions in the metropole were a permissive condition for colonial electoral bodies to emerge. Colonizers with pluralistic institutions (e.g., a strong parliament or a full-blown democratic regime) faced lower transaction costs to creating electoral institutions in their colonies. Officials and colonists alike from pluralistic metropoles had experience with such institutions, and these metropolitan institutions created a focal point for colonists' demands. By contrast, authoritarian powers feared that electoral institutions would stimulate rather than alleviate pressures for greater autonomy and would create damaging precedents for the metropolitan opposition. Additionally, elite groups who benefited from direct colonial rule were usually more influential in authoritarian metropolitan regimes. The influence of elite groups often led authoritarian colonizers to resist electoral concessions, even if the alternative was a colonial revolt.

Even metropoles with pluralistic electoral institutions resisted electoral concessions unless pushed. Who pressured the metropole, and how much pressure they exerted, should affect our outcomes: the degree of policymaking autonomy granted to colonists and who gained the franchise. This yields the general implication that the basic rules of colonial electoral competition and suffrage would usually be less democratic (often, much less so) than constitutional laws in the metropole.

White settlers, where they settled in large-enough numbers, were better able than non-white groups to push for electoral representation. Europeans with ties to the metropole had stronger lobbies, could cripple the economic productivity of the colony through non-participation, and sometimes posed a strong revolt threat. However, the actions of white settlers did not unambiguously promote democracy, especially in the long run. Settlers created representative institutions exclusively for themselves and repressed non-whites who sought political rights. How the dual effects of European settlers played out in practice depended on the size of the white settlement. Areas with a very large share of settlers could enfranchise most of the population without granting much political power to non-whites. However, white settler minorities eventually had to choose between non-white rule and continued mass disenfranchisement. Their predilection for the second alternative often weakened democratic institutions.

Although non-Europeans were usually less able to pressure the colonial state, they nonetheless could gain concessions in three distinct circumstances. First, a non-white middle class educated in the colonizer's language emerged in some major port cities and plantation islands. Campaigns by these groups often succeeded because they could lobby the colonial state using its own language and cultural idiom. It was normatively difficult for colonizers to justify excluding from voting those who met metropolitan voting criteria. However, because only a small segment of the non-white population exerted pressure, these efforts usually yielded small franchises and limited policymaking autonomy.

Second, non-Europeans sometimes had a credible threat to revolt. When the international system favored mass revolts in which anticolonial rebels could viably gain external support, as it generally did after 1945, mass franchise expansion became very costly to resist. However, the resulting elections often had shallow institutional roots.

Third, in some colonies (usually geographically small), a monarch had a plausible claim to national legitimacy. This created an option to perpetuate subnational policies of indirect rule by handing off power to a national monarch. Metropoles with a monarch at home were more willing to follow this decolonization path, which enabled traditional non-white elites to gain substantial autonomy under authoritarian rather than electoral institutions.

These theoretical implications explain much variation in colonial electoral institutions. In Chapter 3, we analyze early European colonies in the New World. In the eighteenth century, electoral assemblies were nearly universal in British colonies but almost entirely absent in other empires. However, by the nineteenth century, electoral representation was intermittently present in all colonial empires. Britain developed early parliamentary institutions at home and possessed an empire in which upper-class white men had strong options for lobbying and nonparticipation. These sources of pressure frequently yielded highly autonomous local assemblies, albeit with stringent economic, racial, and gender exclusions. By contrast, British officials delayed electoral reforms in later colonies whose white populations were predominantly Catholic – a disenfranchised group at home. Elsewhere, reforms across the continent stemming from the French Revolution made Britain less unique in its parliamentary constitution and led to electoral institutions in other colonial empires.

In Chapter 4, we analyze the entire colonial world from the mid-nineteenth century through 1945. Despite much smaller white settler populations and minimal threats of mass revolt, nearly half these colonies gained a national-level electoral body before 1945. The enduring influence of white settler minorities and the rise of non-white middle classes explain why. In some parts of Africa, whites settled in large-enough numbers to become politically ascendant. Like their eighteenth-century predecessors, they gained European-only elections. Where the white population was too weak to maintain hegemony, as in the British West Indies, elections were abolished before Blacks could gain a majority. Non-Europeans achieved representation only where they were part of a Western-assimilated middle class *and* white settlers were unimportant. Small groups of South Asian and African elites in the major colonial port cities gained electoral representation in the 1920s or earlier, as did Blacks in the British West Indies after the influence of white planters had waned.

World War II was a watershed for Western colonialism. Chapter 5 explains how weakened European powers confronted mass social movements that challenged colonial rule. To avoid costly rebellions, colonizers usually conceded mass-franchise elections and, eventually, independence to non-Europeans. However, the pace of reform and approaches to decolonization varied greatly because of differences in metropolitan institutions and the size of the white settler community. Although most colonizers preferred reform over confronting a rebellion, white settlers in Africa as well as Portugal refused to grant concessions that would diminish their economic and political power. Their intransigence fostered decolonization wars in which rebel movements gained control of the postcolonial state. Alternatively, colonial officials (often in the British empire) sometimes chose to grant power to unelected national monarchs.

1.1.2 Legacies of Colonial Electoral Institutions

This new theoretical understanding and empirical documentation of electoral competition under colonial rule helps to explain postcolonial democracy levels, as we show in Chapter 6. Experiences with nationally elected legislatures, which we refer to as colonial pluralism, and democracy levels at independence are each strongly positively correlated with democracy levels afterward.

Two types of countries had lengthy exposure to colonial elections, and consequently tended to remain stable democracies afterward. First, cases such as India and Jamaica in which a non-white middle class speaking the colonizer's language emerged in the nineteenth century and lobbied the metropole for electoral representation. Early concessions enabled non-European elites to form institutionalized parties with extensive electoral experience prior to gaining independence. Afterward, institutionalized parties acted as a buffer against possible military intervention. Second, Europeans developed early elections and comprised a majority of the colonial population in the historically unique neo-Britains (US, Canada, Australia, and New Zealand). In these countries, broad suffrage did not threaten the white political elite's hold on power, as it did in many other cases with smaller settler minorities.

However, relatively few colonies experienced lengthy periods of colonial pluralism. In most colonies, the first election occurred less than a decade (sometimes, only months) before independence; or, if elections occurred earlier, they were geographically circumscribed or the assemblies were virtually powerless. Parties tended to be weaker in these cases and elections were not perceived as the exclusive means of gaining and retaining power. Electoral institutions that existed at independence were often quickly swept away by military coups (e.g., Uganda) or incumbent consolidation (e.g., Ivory Coast), or used as an electoral authoritarian institution (e.g., Malaysia). Other colonial regimes forbade any (meaningful) elections. This usually yielded durable authoritarian regimes after independence governed by either a rebel group who fought the colonizer (e.g., Angola) or a national monarch (e.g., Kuwait).

Varying postcolonial experiences underscore the generic difficulties to establishing stable democratic regimes from above, even when the external power is democratic and exerts significant control over the institutional form. Two main contradictions prevented successful democracy promotion in most cases. First, the actors best positioned to set up representative institutions – white settlers – were also an elite landed class who sought to preserve their socioeconomic privileges. Thus, some cases with early colonial elections endured significant struggles to gain majority rule and to institutionalize non-European-led parties within the electoral system. Second, for metropolitan officials, establishing democratic institutions in their colonies was at best secondary to their goals, even if the home regime was a democracy. Manipulating elections to secure power for colonially aligned politicians or handing off power to a national monarch were often viable alternatives that would prevent conflict.

1.2 Sample, Concepts, and Data

To establish these claims, we use a multi-method approach. We collected an original data set of elections under colonialism that spans essentially all Western overseas colonies between the late fifteenth and early twentieth centuries, plus information on policymaking autonomy and franchise restrictions. Varieties of Democracy (V-Dem) provides additional democracy data for the twentieth century. We examine patterns and correlations through figures and tables of cases presented in the book, plus regressions analyzed in the Appendix. To provide more direct evidence of mechanisms, we consulted hundreds of primary and secondary historical sources that yield insight into how sources of colonist pressure such as lobbying, nonparticipation, and revolt influenced the decisions of metropolitan officials. Here we detail our sample of colonies as well as our conceptual and operational scheme for studying electoral institutions under colonialism.

1.2.1 Sample of Colonies

The ability of Western powers to establish noncontiguous, overseas empires was a product of improvements in maritime and military technology within Western Europe that had manifested by the late fifteenth century, which justifies our temporal focus. The three main scope conditions for our core sample are all colonies in which a *Western* power established *formal sovereignty* over an *overseas* dependency.

Western Colonies Only
European colonial rule was marked by violence, genocide, and (mostly) authoritarian rule. Early democratic institutions, in the sense of checks on the executive and popular forms of leadership selection and policy influence, were widespread across the precolonial non-European world.[12] In many cases, the initial European onslaught dismantled existing local participatory institutions by either decimating the population or coercively occupying territory. In that sense, looking to Western colonialism as an epoch that shaped contemporary democratic experiences may appear odd.

Nonetheless, institutions of "modern" democracy are undoubtedly European in their roots. Western Europe was unique in the development of institutions of *indirect* democracy, in particular parliaments with elected members and some formal prerogatives over levying taxes. Later developments of elected executives, responsible parliaments, political parties, and mass franchises within larger territorial states were also uniquely Western.[13] Western European powers, in large part

---

[12] Social scientists have only recently begun to scrutinize the democratic attributes of non-Western societies prior to colonization. For recent, primarily quantitative research, see Giuliano and Nunn 2013; Baldwin 2015; Bentzen, Hariri and Robinson 2019; Acemoglu and Robinson 2020; Ahmed and Stasavage 2020; Stasavage 2020; Bolt et al. 2023. All these contributions are indebted to the wealth of earlier historical and anthropological research on non-Western societies.

[13] Manin 1997; Stasavage 2020; Gerring et al. 2022, 27–35.

because they conquered much of the non-European world, were able to impose their institutional vision – regardless of the generic pros and cons of these institutions for promoting good governance relative to earlier institutions of direct democracy. Thus, there was indeed something distinctive about colonization by a Western power that should influence variation in "modern" democratic institutions. "Western" includes all countries in Western Europe and the neo-British offshoots. By contrast, we exclude all cases of colonization by non-Western powers, such as Russia, Japan, or China.[14]

Overseas Colonies Only
Separation between the rulers and the ruled is, implicitly, a crucial scope condition of our theory. Spatial separation usually created distinct interests between the metropolitan government and residents of the colony. This prompted demands for autonomous elected legislatures – a key outcome of interest in our theory. Consequently, we exclude all territories within Europe (e.g., Ireland) and all states/provinces in the four neo-Britains that were never under the formal colonial jurisdiction of a European power (e.g., the US state of Ohio).[15] We would need a distinct theory to explain why territorially contiguous dependencies were, usually, governed as integral parts of the imperial metropole; why some gained political rights commensurate to those of core residents; and why certain dependencies eventually broke away.

All Cases of Colonial Suzerainty
Among non-European territories colonized by a Western power, we take an expansive view of which to include in our sample. Western metropoles adopted varied administrative strategies in their overseas dependencies. These ranged from formal incorporation into the metropole (as in Algeria) to almost complete autonomy with the colonial power handling foreign policy only (as in Nepal or the Persian Gulf states).[16]

---

[14] All Russian and Chinese dependencies are also excluded by the *overseas* condition, discussed next.

[15] However, the original US states are in our sample because they were at one point governed as overseas colonies by a Western European power.

[16] Wight 1952 discusses legal distinctions among British dependencies.

Although it is commonplace to include cases such as Algeria, cases such as the British Gulf states are more controversial. Our justification for inclusion is that the choice over how much internal autonomy to concede was endogenous and strategic. Analyzing the effects of colonialism while excluding cases based on juridical relationships or degrees of administrative intervention will yield biased results. Colonial rule was significant not only because it invented certain new institutions, but also because colonizers strategically chose what to preserve. Many of the original protectorate treaties that Britain (and other powers) signed with local rulers throughout Africa were very similar in form to those signed with rulers in the Persian Gulf. Yet the powers decided to annex their African territories, thereby ignoring treaty stipulations that their sovereignty concerned external relations only,[17] whereas Britain continually permitted high internal autonomy in the Persian Gulf. The preservation of the Kuwaiti monarchy was, in this sense, as much a product of British colonialism as was the Indian parliament. The different approaches across European metropoles imply that France or Portugal, had they colonized Kuwait, likely would have abolished the monarchy. For this reason, we contend that the standard practice of excluding the Persian Gulf states from analyses of British colonialism tends to yield overly optimistic conclusions about the effect of British colonialism on democracy. However, we exclude cases in which Western powers did not establish formal suzerainty, such as in Iran, and concession cities with a built-in time limit, as in China.

Throughout the book, we mainly consider two distinct samples. For our analysis of colonies in the New World before 1850, our new measure of electoral institutions (see below) is coded at the level of the contemporaneous colony rather than modern country. This yields seventy-eight colonies for this region and period alone, a much larger number than we would obtain by anachronistically using the boundaries of modern countries. In the current US, we include not only the colonies that declared independence in 1776 but also earlier colonies such as Plymouth, New Haven, and West Jersey; temporary colonies such as East/West Florida; and colonies relinquished by another European power, such as New Netherland and New France. We also include colonies that never gained independence, such as Bermuda and

---

[17] Anene 1966; Alexandrowicz 1973.

Martinique. For later periods, we mostly use the sample of countries included in the V-Dem data set, which uses a more stringent population threshold and almost exclusively includes cases that eventually gained independence. We refer to later microstates only when they follow qualitatively distinct patterns from larger states.

To assess the robustness of our postcolonial results, we also conduct analyses with a full sample of non-European countries, including those colonized by a non-Western power (e.g., Taiwan) or uncolonized (e.g., Afghanistan). We have strong theoretical expectations that these cases should tend to be authoritarian. Non-Western colonizers were authoritarian and did not implant electoral institutions in their colonies. Most countries that avoided colonization entirely were historical empires with strong monarchies and militaries.[18] Even in cases that engaged in defensive modernization efforts that included the introduction of Western-style parliaments, electoral institutions were usually weak relative to authoritarian forces. The relatively low democracy levels in non-Western countries excluded from our core sample support our overarching claim that Western colonialism was a critical juncture for facilitating competitive political institutions, at least in the select colonies that gained lengthy exposure to electoral institutions.

1.2.2 Conceptualizing and Measuring Democratic Attributes

Conceptualization

Our ultimate outcome of interest is democracy. We follow Dahl's classic formulation, which stipulates that democracy requires competitive elections for the executive and legislature and a broad degree of participation among the populace.[19] Throughout history, sovereign countries and dependencies alike have often had some democratic pieces despite not meeting the standards for full democracy.[20] Countries that lack elections for the executive or to a national assembly, or that lack a national assembly entirely, are unambiguously *closed authoritarian* regimes. However, other regimes have a hybrid structure. The United Kingdom before the nineteenth century had an elected lower parliamentary house with strong powers; but a small franchise and corrupt

---

[18] Hariri 2012; Ertan, Fiszbein and Putterman 2016.
[19] Dahl 1971.
[20] Miller 2015.

and malapportioned elections. We refer to such regimes as *parliamentary* or *pluralist* to denote meaningful constraints on the executive despite small franchises, in contrast to closed authoritarian (or absolutist) regimes such as pre-Revolutionary France. More recently, many countries have become *competitive* or *electoral authoritarian* regimes with universal suffrage, but elections are highly tilted in favor of the incumbent.[21]

We apply this conceptual scheme to colonies, albeit with some notable alterations to match the colonial setting. Policymaking powers were always shared at least in part with metropolitan officials, in contrast to sovereign countries. Thus, the degree to which elections conveyed meaningful levels of policymaking autonomy to colonists was a key consideration in the colonial setting. We provide an operational scheme that enables us to systematically track key elements of Dahlian democracy across a broad temporal and spatial sample under Western colonial rule.

Existence of Electoral Institutions

Holding some form of election is the most basic element of democratic competition. Consequently, our core measure throughout the book is an indicator for whether colonists elect any seats to a territory-wide assembly or to the metropolitan parliament, the latter of which enables us to capture variation among French and Spanish colonies.[22] These electoral institutions varied in numerous ways and could be afflicted by a myriad of restrictions: a majority of seats on a council were appointed rather than elected, suffrage was limited, the elected assembly had advisory rather than legislative powers over finances, or only select localities elected representatives for the national assembly.

Our original data on colonial electoral institutions, supported by extensive qualitative historical sources, span a global sample from the first elections in Virginia's General Assembly in 1619 through the

---

[21] For operationalizations of related conceptual schemes, see Levitsky and Way 2010; Miller 2015; Lührmann, Tannenberg and Lindberg 2018.

[22] Electoral bodies were not the sole source of constraints on metropolitan crowns or colonial governors. Unelected bodies such as fully appointed councils or courts could also serve this purpose; see, for example, Franco-Vivanco 2021; Gailmard 2024. However, given our interest in electoral representation for colonists, we do not engage with nonelectoral sources of executive constraints.

twentieth century.[23] In most cases, periodic elections occurred between the first year in which an election occurred and the year in which the country gained independence. However, because our variable is measured annually, we also capture reversals, such as the creation of the Dominion of New England in the 1680s and the transition to direct crown rule across the British West Indies starting in the 1860s.

A practical advantage is that we can reliably track this variable across an expansive spatial and temporal sample. Given the objectivity of the operational criterion ("was there an electoral institution?") and our extensive sourcing, there are few concerns about measurement error, at least of a magnitude that would qualitatively alter any of the main patterns we highlight. Moreover, at least prior to 1945, colonies varied substantially simply in terms of whether any electoral institution existed.

We count only elections to national-level assemblies, not institutional bodies that governed specific localities such as municipalities or towns. We justify our focus on national-level institutions on two grounds, in addition to the difficulties of systematically collecting data on local institutions.[24] First, the disjuncture between the competitiveness of local and national institutions was small in many cases. The same developments that either restricted or expanded participation at the national level usually applied to the local level as well. Spanish *cabildos*, or town councils, were initially somewhat competitive institutions of local governance, in contrast to the absence of elections for higher-level political units such as *audiencias* or viceroyalties. However, by the seventeenth century, *cabildos* had become sites of venal office seeking, as opposed to a forum for popular participation.[25] The port cities in South Asia and Africa that became the earliest sites of popular participation in municipal councils were also the first localities that elected officials to territory-wide legislative councils or *conseils générales*.[26] Across British and French Africa, local elections were typically introduced at the same time as territory-wide elections.[27] In

[23] This builds on and expands an earlier data collection project in Paine 2019*a*.
[24] Collier 1982, 34–35, and Russell-Wood 1999, xxiv–xxvi, discuss limitations to compiling systematic data for local and municipal elections.
[25] See Chapter 3.
[26] See Chapter 4.
[27] Collier 1982, 34.

British North America and the West Indies, each distinct colony was geographically small enough that local and national institutions largely coincided.

Second, after independence, the national-level institutions of primary interest descended directly from territory-wide, rather than local, colonial institutions.[28] In most cases, the colonizer formally handed off power to the political party that won the final national-level election. These parties, even if regionally circumscribed in their electoral strongholds, usually formed for the purpose of competing in elections at the national level. In all cases, national-level competition eventually became the primary aim of the major political parties. The most relevant authoritarian institutions (victorious rebel groups, postcolonial monarchies, and militaries) also operated at the national level.

Policymaking Autonomy

The presence of any elected seats to a local or metropolitan assembly is but the most minimal aspect of democracy. Addressing the extent of colonists' policymaking autonomy is crucial for two reasons. First, colonial elections would not be a worthwhile outcome to study if they were always mere democratic "window dressing." We instead demonstrate that electoral representation constituted a concession that colonists usually considered to be meaningful.[29] Second, our theory carries expectations for the degree of autonomy that should accompany electoral concessions, depending on the identity and size of the pressure group. Therefore, capturing differences in autonomy is important for testing our theory.

Policymaking autonomy can range from no elections to highly circumscribed elections (e.g., minority of seats, indirect elections, lack of legislative powers) to representative government (majority of elected seats to a legislative body) to full autonomy over domestic affairs. In Chapters 3, 4, and 5 on the colonial period, we use distinct but related measures of autonomy, each of which correspond to the most important differences within the epoch.

---

[28] Local-level institutions were typically more important earlier in the colonial period. In other work, one of the authors casts doubt on accounts of postcolonial authoritarianism focused entirely on local-level colonial institutions; see Bolt et al. 2023.

[29] This complements Gandhi's 2008 argument about elections and legislatures in contemporary electoral authoritarian regimes.

Before 1850, we compiled original data on whether colonists had a fully elected lower chamber. Appointed governors and upper houses could, in principle, constrain the lower chamber. However, in practice, fully elected lower chambers in British North America and the West Indies amassed substantial legislative powers starting in the seventeenth century. After the Glorious Revolution, most of these colonies achieved a de facto equivalent to full autonomy over domestic policies, at least until the 1760s. Into the nineteenth century, we also track concessions of responsible government in British colonies, which corresponded with an elected executive council and full autonomy over domestic policies.[30]

Between 1850 and 1945, we collected original information on three restrictions on policymaking autonomy: (1) indirect elections, (2) non-representative government (i.e., a minority of seats were elected by colonists), and (3) a lack of power over finances. Any of these restrictions severely impeded the autonomy of colonists. By contrast, electoral institutions without any of these impediments, at minimum, constituted a form of representative government. We continue to track which cases had fully elected legislative councils or responsible government, although each was rare during this period.

After 1945, our main quantitative measure for autonomy is the timing of independence. By this point, representative government, full domestic autonomy, and jurisdictional sovereignty had become closely intertwined. Often, these events occurred consecutively (and sometimes simultaneously) in the span of less than a decade. Pressure from non-European colonists and the stance of the metropole and white settlers varied in ways that help to explain variation in the highest-possible level of autonomy, full independence.

Franchise Restrictions

Access to the franchise is another crucial element of the Dahlian conceptualization of democracy. We are interested both in who had the right to vote at different times and places and in the overall size of the franchise. Before 1850, we lack a systematic measure across cases.

---

[30] For all intents and purposes, we consider the achievement of dominion status to correspond with independence. The only exception is South Africa because colonialism persisted in the sense of local white settlers ruling over the African majority.

Instead, we draw from a large historical literature that documents aspects of the franchise qualitatively (who could vote) and quantitatively (rough estimates of the percentage of adults that could participate in elections). Although we lack information for each individual colony, similar franchise restrictions across groups of British colonies imply minimal loss of precision.

For 1850 to 1945, we collected original information on three types of franchise restrictions: (1) economic and educational restrictions, (2) racial restrictions, or distinctions based on communal rolls, and (3) geographic restrictions such that only a handful of areas of the colony elected representatives to a territory-wide assembly. Disaggregating the type of restriction is more directly meaningful for theory testing than measuring the size of the franchise because our core theoretical expectations pertain to *who* has the right to vote. Nonetheless, we also incorporate data from the V-Dem data set on the percentage of adults with the legal right to vote. This provides our primary measure of the franchise for the post-1945 period, when older voting restrictions were largely eliminated and the most theoretically relevant consideration became the timing of universal suffrage (both men and women).

Democracy Levels

The final outcome we examine is overall democracy levels, measured using V-Dem.[31] This data set measures thousands of attributes of democracy and covers a broad global sample of countries, in some cases going back to 1789. A key advantage for our purposes is that V-Dem improves upon earlier democracy data sets such as Polity IV by including information about nonsovereign territories. For colonies that gained independence after 1945, these data go back to 1900. Thus, the V-Dem data set enables us to track democracy levels during and after colonial rule. We analyze the Electoral Democracy Index, which combines five lower-level indices into an aggregate index that explicitly aims to capture the core elements of Dahl's conceptualization of polyarchy.[32] This index provides information about the quality of colonial elections, in particular elements such as the freeness and fairness of

---

[31] Coppedge et al. 2023*a*; Pemstein et al. 2023.
[32] Dahl 1971. The lower-level V-Dem indices are the size of the franchise, the presence of elected offices, the cleanliness of elections, freedom of association, and freedom of expression; see Coppedge et al. 2023*b*, 44, for details.

elections that are difficult to observe directly. Throughout the book, we discuss raw V-Dem democracy scores in relation to discrete regime types (closed authoritarian, electoral authoritarian, electoral democracy) to ease the interpretation of the scores. The Regimes of the World data set, a corollary of the V-Dem project, codes these discrete types.[33]

The temporal and spatial coverage of V-Dem is more circumscribed than our core measure of electoral institutions. V-Dem's colonial data starts centuries later, uses a more stringent population threshold that eliminates many smaller colonies, and excludes most territories that never gained independence. However, combining our data with theirs enables characterizing quantitative patterns for colonial electoral institutions that were not possible until now.

Colonial Pluralism

To connect colonial-era experiences with electoral institutions to postcolonial democracy levels, we measure the number of years of colonial pluralism for each colony, using our data and V-Dem. We code institutions as plural in any year a colony has electoral institutions with at least minimal legislative powers (i.e., not advisory) and national scope (i.e., elections are not restricted to a handful of specific areas). We additionally require a minimal V-Dem democracy score to rule out colony-years with very low levels of electoral autonomy or grossly distorted elections. Electoral institutions that meet this relatively low bar for pluralism should, if our theory is correct, meaningfully affect policy outcomes and create incentives for institutionalized national-level parties to emerge.

1.3 Colonialism and Democracy: Existing Research

Although many foundational studies on democracy overlook the colonial era, we are certainly not the first scholars to analyze political institutions under colonialism and their legacies. Our theory isolates the strategic interaction among specific actors by analyzing institutional constellations in the metropole and the relative power of each of white settlers and non-Europeans. The main explanatory variables are determined by deeper historical processes and nonpolitical causes,

---

[33] Lührmann, Tannenberg and Lindberg 2018 describe these data. The associated variable in the V-Dem data set is *v2x_regime*.

which make them endogenous. Some existing theories help to explain why the variables in our theory took certain values at certain times and places – for example, why white settlements varied in size. Such accounts are mostly *complementary* to our analysis. Other accounts are strictly *rival* to our theory because they address the same actors but propose opposing implications about their effects.

Overall, our core findings challenge many important existing ideas. (1) Unconditional arguments that Britain was better for democracy promotion have circumscribed empirical applicability. (2) Factor endowments offer minimal explanatory power for colonial-era electoral institutions. (3) European settlers were neither uniformly beneficial nor the only relevant colonial actor. We contribute to other, more complementary findings by characterizing big themes that affected colonial democratic institutions, hence broadening beyond monocausal explanations and individual regions or time periods.

Our findings also inform theories of democratization developed outside the colonial setting. Previous scholarship addresses the prodemocratic biases of middle-class groups, the antidemocratic biases of landed elites, the importance of sequencing democratic reforms, and the institutions of external powers. We engage with these ideas in Chapter 7.

1.3.1 Metropolitan Institutions

Many scholars claim that British colonialism left more beneficial democratic legacies than colonization by other European powers.[34] These arguments in part complement, and in part rival, our theory. We instead posit a conditional effect of British colonialism that depends on the size of the white settlement, the influence of a non-European middle class, and whether Britain is compared to less democratic colonizers.

Scholars posit various possible mechanisms for the thesis that Britain was better at democracy promotion. These include more competitive metropolitan institutions (our focus), promoting a political culture more consistent with democratic values, the use of common law rather than civil law, and capitalist rather than mercantilist economic

---

[34] As examples, see Huntington 1984, 206, Weiner 1987; La Porta et al. 1998, 1999; Abernethy 2000, 406; Treisman 2000, 418–427; Ferguson 2012; Narizny 2012, 362.

institutions. Some ex-British colonies did, indeed, consolidate long-lasting democratic rule after gaining independence, and these are the cases on which scholars often focus; for example, "Every country with a population of at least 1 million (and almost all the smaller countries as well) that has emerged from colonial rule since World War II and has had a continuous democratic experience is a former British colony."[35] Observations such as this, however, mask the extreme heterogeneity within the British empire by selecting on the dependent variable.

The empirical record supports our claim that the British empire was too heterogeneous across time and space and to make unconditional statements about the consequences of British rule. Seventeenth- and eighteenth-century British colonies in North America and the West Indies indeed developed electoral institutions more frequently than their peers governed by absolutist metropoles.[36] However, this initial British advantage largely disappeared during the nineteenth century. Later, in the twentieth century, British colonies had somewhat more competitive institutions in the years immediately preceding independence. However, much of this difference stemmed from more recent and superficial institutional reforms. The ex-British advantage largely dissipated in the decades following independence.[37] Whereas some British colonies gained lengthy experiences with elections during colonialism, many others did not.

Nor are we the only scholars to propose a conditional effect of British colonialism. One argument in this vein is that the impact of British colonialism depended on the directness of rule.[38] These theories in some ways complement ours, although they primarily focus on explaining economic development rather than democracy. We agree that only limited exposure to colonial elections would not produce post-colonial democracy. However, the presence of national-level elections

---

[35] Weiner 1987, 20.

[36] Gailmard 2024 complements our approach to this set of colonies by explaining the strategic incentives that induced the Crown to allow early assemblies as counterweights against exploitative colonial governors.

[37] In Lee and Paine 2019, we provide statistical evidence that the aggregate British advantage was stronger at independence than afterward. We also discuss why existing research reaches varying conclusions about the importance of British colonialism: it depends on which cases the researcher counts as a British colony and on the period analyzed.

[38] Lange 2004, 2009. See also Mamdani 1996; Lange, Mahoney and vom Hau 2006; Mahoney 2010.

(our focus) could coincide with practices of indirect rule (the predominant existing focus). Singapore, for example, was governed directly with minimal electoral participation, whereas India experienced more indirect rule but with a relatively long history of national elections.

1.3.2 White Settlers

Existing accounts of white settlers focus either on the settlers themselves (or other European actors such as Protestant missionaries) or on the geographical conditions that affected the size of white settlements. Certain aspects of these theories complement ours, in particular the claim that white settlers (could) promote democracy. But two other claims rival ours: (1) white settlers are unconditionally beneficial for democracy and (2) white settlers, Protestant missionaries, or factor endowments explain away the causal importance of metropolitan institutions.

Our pivot away from mainly highlighting the prodemocratic impulses of settlers yields conclusions in line with the relatively small body of social-scientific research on how emancipated persons spurred democratic reforms in many plantation colonies.[39] We build upon this idea by showing how the more general phenomenon of non-white middle classes – whether comprised of emancipated persons or European-educated elites in port cities – often promoted early electoral representation.[40]

European Cultural Diffusion

Many studies develop what we term the prodemocratic effect of settlers. Gerring et al. provide the most comprehensive theoretical discussion and empirical test of this thesis.[41] They argue that Europeans formed a democratic club; as Europeans conquered the world, they brought their ideas about political organization with them.[42] A core

---

[39] Ledgister 1998; Owolabi 2015, 2023.

[40] Wilkinson and Onorato 2013 also discuss the importance of early elections in a general sense for subsequent democratic legacies.

[41] Gerring et al. 2022. See Hariri 2012, 2015 for related statistical evidence on positive postcolonial democratic legacies. Many studies demonstrating positive development legacies of colonial European settlers posit colonial political institutions as a key intervening mechanism; see Acemoglu, Johnson and Robinson 2001; Engerman and Sokoloff 2011; Easterly and Levine 2016.

[42] Gerring et al. 2022, Ch. 8.

element of these ideas was the institutions of indirect democracy that Europeans had pioneered, which often displaced existing institutions of small-scale direct democracy. More Europeans meant more members of the club, which should yield higher democracy levels. Although the mechanism proposed in Gerring et al. is primarily one of cultural diffusion, the broad idea largely complements our focus on the advantages that settlers had at pressuring the metropole for political reforms. Gerring et al. support their thesis with empirical evidence that a higher fraction of the population with European ancestry is positively correlated with democratic institutions during the colonial era and afterward.[43]

Despite this point of agreement, our approach differs in two main ways. First, Gerring et al. stress the inherent similarity in core democratic ideas among all Europeans, regardless of metropolitan institutions. Throughout the book, we provide evidence that colonial elections occurred only within empires of pluralistic or democratic metropoles.

Second, Gerring et al. propose that the relationship between the fraction of the population with European ancestry and democracy should be positive and monotonic.[44] We instead demonstrate that settlers who made up a substantial minority (5 to 25 percent) of the population often dismantled earlier representative gains by accepting authoritarian British crown rule (West Indies) or provoking guerrilla wars (e.g., Rhodesia/Zimbabwe).[45] Besides the four historically exceptional neo-Britains, white settlers bequeathed clearly beneficial democratic legacies in relatively few cases.[46]

---

[43] Gerring et al. 2022, Chs. 10 and 11. In earlier chapters, they emphasize the importance of ports for facilitating European diffusion. As we discuss in Chapter 4, this idea helps to explain the rise of early non-white middle classes in select port cities.

[44] Although they discuss how small settler communities sought to restrict political rights to their group, they nonetheless suggest that the prodemocratic effects should tend to outweigh the antidemocratic effects (at least in comparison to cases with minuscule or no white settlements).

[45] Highlighting the countervailing, antidemocratic effects of settlers builds on our earlier work; see Paine 2019*a,b*. See also the discussion in Acemoglu and Robinson 2012, 2020 of how colonial settlers created conflicting legacies by establishing exclusive property-rights institutions.

[46] Fails and Krieckhaus 2010 offer a similar conclusion about white settlers and economic development legacies. The British West Indies, with intermediate-

Some scholars argue that the diffusion of Europe's democratic culture occurred through Protestant missionaries rather than settlers.[47] This idea in part complements our theory because, by promoting European-language education, Protestant missionaries help to explain the rise of non-European middle classes in some cases. However, we disagree with the stronger claim that Protestant missionaries explain away the importance of colonizer identity, in particular British colonialism.[48] In earlier work, we show that controlling for Protestant missionaries minimally affects the relationship between British colonialism and postcolonial democracy,[49] and we also use Protestant missionaries as a control variable throughout the present analysis. Others have established that the aggregate cross-national correlation between colonial Protestant missionaries and postcolonial democracy is in fact quite weak.[50]

Geographic and Precolonial Political Endowments
Another line of research complements ours by discussing which types of geographic and precolonial political endowments explain where European colonial settlements formed. Europeans settled en masse in areas where the disease environment was favorable to them and the native population had trouble resisting the European onslaught through a combination of low population density, the absence of states, and susceptibility to European diseases.[51] These theses help to explain why large white settlements arose in North America, Australia, New Zealand, and the Southern Cone of South America; as well as smaller white minorities in the West Indies and parts of Africa.

---

sized white settler populations that declined over time, did indeed become highly democratic after independence. However, a closer evaluation of these cases highlights the primary role of the *non-European* middle class in this outcome, rather than positive legacies of white settlers.

[47] Lankina and Getachew 2012; Woodberry 2012.

[48] Woodberry 2012, 254; Hadenius 1992, 133.

[49] Lee and Paine 2019.

[50] Nikolova and Polansky 2021.

[51] For statistical evidence, see Acemoglu, Johnson and Robinson 2001, 2002*b*; Sokoloff and Engerman 2000; Engerman and Sokoloff 2011; Hariri 2012; Easterly and Levine 2016; Paine 2019*b*. For related research on colonial factor endowments, see Frankema 2009*a*; Bruhn and Gallego 2012; Arias and Girod 2014.

Some scholars go farther and contend that variance in local economic factor endowments can fully account for any differences across European empires. This argument is incompatible with our theory because it implies that metropolitan institutions did not matter. Engerman and Sokoloff argue that the early British North American colonies gained representative institutions not because they were British, but instead because factor endowments in North America were more conducive to family farms and local democracy. By contrast, climates and geologies favorable to mining and sugar plantations in Cuba and Peru facilitated coercive labor institutions and authoritarian governance.[52] However, even in the historical context for which this argument was developed, factor endowments do not help to explain variation in political institutions. Representative institutions became widespread across the British West Indies in the seventeenth century despite factor endowments that encouraged coercive labor institutions to produce sugar on plantations. Conversely, Spanish Southern Cone colonies and French Canada did not gain representative institutions despite factor endowments that made family farms economically viable.

1.4 The Road Ahead

In this book, we establish that political representation under colonialism emerged and was sustained by the interaction among metropolitan political institutions, the size of the white settlement, and the pressure exerted by non-Europeans. The ways in which these factors varied across time and space yielded varying patterns of political institutions and divergent inheritances that continue to heavily influence regime trajectories to the present day. After presenting a theoretical framework for electoral competition under colonial rule in Chapter 2, Chapters 3 to 5 provide empirical evidence for different colonial time periods. Chapter 6 discusses postcolonial legacies. Chapter 7 summarizes the arguments thematically and discusses our contributions to broader research on democratization.

---

[52] Engerman and Sokoloff 2011, 44–46, 218. For similar arguments, see Acemoglu, Johnson and Robinson 2001, 1388, and Hariri 2012, 474. Owolabi 2014 describes the broader turn away from colonizer identity in recent research.

2 | A Theory of Colonial Electoral Institutions

In this chapter, we present a theoretical framework that structures our analysis in Chapters 3 to 5. Colonial politics featured three main actors: metropolitan officials, white settlers, and non-Europeans living in the colonies. Metropolitan officials preferred to concentrate decision-making power in their hands. However, colonists sought political representation to gain influence over colonial policy. When facing pressure from colonists (either white or non-white), metropolitan officials could respond by offering electoral concessions. Colonists could pressure the colonial state through three main means. They could *lobby* or *agitate* to raise the cost for metropolitan officials to not grant concessions. They could engage in *nonparticipation* by refusing to pay taxes, forgoing valuable economic investments, relocating to a different colony, or simply remaining in the metropole. And, as an option of last resort, colonists could *revolt*.

Attributes of each of the three main actors structured colonial electoral institutions. Metropoles with pluralistic institutions at home should be more responsive to demands by colonists for electoral representation. By contrast, authoritarian metropoles should strongly resist electoral concessions, even if the alternative was to combat anticolonial insurgents.

We anticipate white settlers to have a dual effect. Sizable white settlements should trigger early electoral institutions (the prodemocratic effect). However, white settlers should not unambiguously improve democracy. Smaller settler minorities faced incentives to repress demands for franchise expansion, which could undermine the democratic foundations created by early elections (the antidemocratic effect).

Where white settlers were less influential, we highlight three constellations of the non-European population. Where local elites were weak, non-Europeans should not gain early elections. Instead, they would move rapidly to mass-franchise elections with high autonomy after World War II, when the threat of revolt spiked. In cases with a large non-white middle class, we expect early elections with small franchises and low autonomy, which should broaden peacefully over time. Finally, cases with a national monarch should correspond with high autonomy without meaningful electoral bodies.

2.1 Divergent Preferences over Political Institutions

2.1.1 Actors and Goals

Metropolitan officials encompassed the key decision-makers in Europe (e.g., the Prime Minister and Colonial Ministers) and officials in the colonies recruited from the metropole (e.g., Governors and Under Secretaries). Depending on the structure of home institutions, nonofficial metropolitan actors such as voters and the press could influence colonial policy, but only indirectly.

Metropolitan officials gained economic rents from colonial rule. Europeans seized physical goods and forced indigenous persons to produce for them, as with Spanish plunder of the Aztec and Inca empires.[1] Europeans coerced enslaved persons to produce export goods at low prices, as with sugar plantations fueled by the Atlantic slave trade. A less coercive way to produce rents was to create trade barriers that generated privileged access to the colonial market for manufacturers in the metropole. Examples include the British Navigation Acts, the Spanish *flota* system, and tariff barriers imposed by the Third French Republic.

Europeans also gained noneconomic benefits. Some colonial possessions housed military bases that enhanced the European power's strategic influence. For example, outposts along the coasts of Africa served as coaling stops on routes to India and the Far East. Colonial possessions could also provide prestige rents that transcended their economic importance. For example, the French empire is usually thought to have been acquired primarily to enhance France's status as a great power, rather than for economic reasons.[2]

Absent constraints, metropolitan officials sought to concentrate decision-making power in their own hands. This would ensure the

---

[1] Elliott 2007, 20; Taylor 2002, 57.
[2] Abernethy 2000, 216; Pritchard 2004, 234; Stearns, Gosch and Grieshaber 1988.

most favorable distribution of economic rents and unilateral control over decisions that affected their strategic position and prestige rents. However, this goal came into tension with the aims of individuals living in the colonies.

Officials from the metropole constituted a tiny minority of the over-seas population.[3] However, they were not the only Europeans in the colonies, where "unofficial" European settlers also resided. In some colonies, white settlements came to comprise either a sizable minor-ity or an outright majority of the population. Wherever this occurred, white settlers were the colonial upper class. Europeans typically seized the most productive agricultural land for themselves and exploited the native or enslaved population as a cheap labor force.[4]

White settlers shared certain core goals with the metropole. Retain-ing the colonial connection provided insurance against threats posed by non-white revolts and other European powers. However, the goals of white settlers also diverged from those of metropolitan officials in important ways that encouraged them to seek as much autonomy as possible. Most important, white settlers competed with metropolitan officials and firms to control the flow of colonial rents. Settlers sought to block attempts to redistribute surplus to the metropole via trade re-strictions or direct taxes; for example, the American Revolution began as this type of protest. Similarly, white settlers sought to monopolize the benefits of exploiting non-whites through institutions such as the encomienda and slave plantations.[5]

In most colonies, the majority of the population was not white.[6] Of-ten, the bulk of the non-white population was native to the territory upon which Europeans intruded. Where the indigenous population was originally small and/or decimated by European diseases and coercion, Europeans usually forcibly imported laborers. Non-whites faced pervasive discrimination and the denial of basic civil and eco-nomic rights. Even in colonies with "inclusive" economic institutions,

---

[3] Kirk-Greene 1980.

[4] Mosley 1983; Paine 2019*a,b*.

[5] Abernethy 2000, 286–289, 298–299; Will 1970, 1; Franco-Vivanco 2021.

[6] All colonial societies recognized white Europeans as a socially and economically distinct group. However, the dividing line between whites and non-whites varied across time and space; see Loveman 2014. We abstract away from these differences and use the term "whites" to describe individuals socially classified as such, regardless of skin color.

non-whites were typically excluded from such arrangements.[7] Non-whites often enjoyed local autonomy under indigenous chiefs or princes, but as part of bifurcated states that confined most non-Europeans to secondary legal status.[8] Economically disfavored, the non-white majority viewed political inclusion as one route to secure basic rights.

2.1.2 *Why Electoral Representation Mattered*

Political science research on regime transitions has established that political institutions create distributional consequences and are path dependent. Political institutions create distributional consequences because they alter the relative ability of political actors to influence policy choices. Political institutions are path dependent because, once created, they are costly to alter or overturn.[9] For instance, a group with representation in a legislature can capitalize on its position in state institutions to tax itself lightly and others heavily, or to expropriate the land and labor of unrepresented groups. Groups prefer institutional representation to one-off policy concessions because governing actors cannot fully commit to promises they make about future policies.[10]

Colonial assemblies varied in their membership and scope of policy responsibility. In some, colonists controlled all major economic policies. Early British settler colonies adopted the Old Representative System, in which a fully elected lower assembly initiated all spending bills. In later British colonies, representative government meant that colonists comprised a majority in the legislative council. Colonies with responsible government were even more autonomous because the legislative council consisted entirely of elected, self-governing colonists and had more direct power over the executive. This degree of autonomy was characteristic of British dominions and of the French Union in the late 1950s. In all these cases, the power of the metropole was mostly limited to foreign and defense policy.

In many other colonies, metropolitan-appointed officials were the most important voice in policymaking, even if an elected assembly

---

[7] Acemoglu and Robinson 2012.
[8] Mamdani 1996.
[9] We develop this idea in detail when discussing postindependence persistence; see Chapter 6.
[10] Acemoglu and Robinson 2006; Meng, Paine and Powell 2023.

existed. One technique to curb colonial autonomy was to grant colonists control over only a minority of seats in an assembly, which contained a majority of official members who were legally bound to vote for government-approved policies. In such cases, the council served more as a sounding board for colonists' grievances than as an arena for autonomous policymaking.[11] An alternative form of partial representation, used at various times in the French and Spanish empires, was to permit colonists to elect members to the metropolitan legislature. In these cases, colonists could not directly determine policy because they comprised only a small fraction of the metropolitan assembly. Other ways in which metropolitan officials could limit the policymaking autonomy of colonists included restricting the franchise to social groups perceived as sympathetic to its policies, interfering in elections to promote favored candidates and parties, and creating constitutional limits on the authority of the elected assembly (e.g., denying control over finances).

Even where autonomy was limited, colonists benefited from electoral representation. Positions in metropolitan legislatures were not merely symbolic, as colonists could sometimes achieve major objectives when they allied with metropolitan parties. For example, in 1946, Félix Houphouët-Boigny of French West Africa gained a seat in the French Parliament and convinced the assembly to ban forced labor in the colonies. Similarly, in cases such as Kenya, the minority of white-elected seats on the legislative council created an institutional channel through which settlers pressured British officials for policy concessions.

Limited institutional concessions have parallels outside the colonial setting. Early European parliaments' main function was to legitimate extraordinary taxation.[12] Only later did parliaments gain responsibility over expenditures or move to universal suffrage.[13] In many contemporary authoritarian regimes, legislatures exist despite neither controlling the budget nor exercising ministerial responsibility. Even when entirely unelected, legislators can propose, amend, or obstruct bills favored by the government and can influence outcomes more directly when officials in the executive branch are divided.[14]

---

[11] Wight 1946*a*, 100.
[12] Stasavage 2011; Van Zanden, Buringh and Bosker 2012.
[13] Cox and Dincecco 2021.
[14] Gandhi, Noble and Svolik 2020.

2.2 Metropolitan Political Institutions

Given the conflicting goals of the main actors over representation in electoral bodies, what factors influenced outcomes? One important dimension was metropolitan political institutions. More pluralistic institutions at home made electoral concessions in the colonies more tolerable than in empires with authoritarian metropoles for two reasons. First, institutional similarity lowered the associated transaction costs. Second, their domestic constituencies gained fewer benefits from colonialism.

2.2.1 Institutional Similarity and Transaction Costs

Elected Legislatures

All European powers had the institutional know-how to construct some form of authoritarian rule. British officials – despite parliamentary institutions at home – had no qualms about installing military rule or all-powerful colonial governors throughout Southern Nigeria upon conquest at the turn of the twentieth century.[15] However, only some colonizers had previous experience with elected institutions, and institutional similarity lowered the transaction costs of implementing such institutions in the colonies. Elections, parliaments, and legal systems require some knowledge to operate efficiently. For example, early English colonists used the parliamentary rules and procedures from the British Commons as a starting point, rather than inventing rules from scratch.[16] These continuities made their proceedings easier for colonists and metropolitan officials alike to understand, and lowered the transaction costs of introducing them.[17]

Metropolitan parliaments also created a focal point for colonists' demands. When pressing the imperial center for reforms, colonists had to coordinate around appropriate institutional objectives. Metropolitan institutions created a focal point because settlers born in the

---

[15] Anene 1966; Tamuno 1972; Lugard 1922; Afigbo 1972.
[16] Squire 2012, 71.
[17] When constructing rules and bureaucracies in the colonial setting or more generally, states often force citizens to adopt social practices that are legible to central bureaucrats because the alternative of adopting a new institutional form for each community would create administrative difficulties; see Abernethy 2000, 279; Scott 1998.

metropole were most familiar with those rules. Nor could metropolitan officials – themselves chosen by that political system – easily criticize the demand as unreasonable or impractical.[18] For example, English settlers often argued that they should not lose any political rights simply because they migrated overseas.[19]

By contrast, colonists from authoritarian metropoles lacked such a focal point for their demands. They could propose only foreign institutions, yielding debates about which were most appropriate.[20] Moreover, the lack of institutional similarity made autocratic officials suspicious of parliaments. The consolidation of European absolutism in countries such as France and Spain had involved suppressing medieval assemblies, and residual assemblies in places such as Brittany and Aragon remained obstacles to authoritarian rule into the eighteenth century. Consequently, autocratic officials viewed parliaments as coordination mechanisms for revolt rather than as responsible governing institutions. They did not believe that parliaments would satisfy grievances or fix other colonial governance problems, and parliaments overseas could also have stimulated such demands at home.[21]

Franchise Size

When the metropole granted political representation, its officials sought to restrict the franchise to those who could vote at home. Early arguments to restrict voting rights to property-owning men, for example, were that only they possessed sufficient "independence" and a stake in society to exercise the franchise responsibly.[22] Beliefs about which groups possessed a large-enough social stake stemmed from officials' own social position, which was itself a function of the structure of metropolitan institutions. They applied these same rationales to restrict the franchise overseas.

---

[18] Abernethy 2000, 287.

[19] Greene 2010*b*, 54–57.

[20] North, Summerhill and Weingast 2000 propose a similar mechanism to explain democratic instability in the late colonial and early postindependence periods in Spanish America. Most of these countries, despite divergent colonial experiences, closely modeled their constitutions on that of the United States.

[21] Simpson, Griffiths and Borah 1956, 252–253; Góngora 1975, 103–104; Maguet 1911, 10.

[22] Keyssar 2009, ch. 1.

Monarchies

The principle of institutional similarity structured metropolitan officials' perspectives not only on electoral institutions. In metropoles with a monarchy, it was easier to justify monarchies in its colonies, even if the monarchies in question were much more authoritarian than the contemporary European version. We return to this theme when discussing the use of local dynasties for subnational indirect rule.

2.2.2 Domestic Political Constituencies

Metropolitan institutions determined which actors within the metropole exercised political power. Elites who favored colonialism tended to exert more influence in more authoritarian polities. By contrast, classes indifferent to or actively opposed to empire were more powerful in democracies.

Elites within the metropole reaped a disproportionate share of the benefits of colonialism. Officials in colonial bureaucracies and armies often owed their salaries and prestige to colonial rule, whereas businessmen who traded with the colonies or owned overseas assets enjoyed favorable terms of trade and other forms of rents from participating in uncompetitive markets.[23] Nor were the benefits concentrated only among upper-strata elites. High-ranking officials living in the colonies were generally drawn from lesser nobility and other more marginal elites, who viewed the colonies as a vocation and a source of social mobility. British MP John Bright famously called the British Empire a "gigantic system of out-door relief for the aristocracy of Great Britain."[24] Administrators and officers often served in the colonies to gain a higher standard of living than in the metropole. George Orwell, himself a former colonial official, commented that soldiers and officials went to India because "with cheap horses, free shooting, and hordes of black servants, it was so easy to play at being a gentleman."[25] The traditional image of administrators in Spanish America was the "down-on-his luck hidalgo whose pride and sense of honor propelled him to the Indies in hope of improving his fortunes."[26]

---

[23] Fieldhouse 1986.
[24] Quoted in Trevelyan 1913, 274.
[25] Quoted in Symington and Symington 2002, 16.
[26] Altman 1987, 323; see also Burkholder and Chandler 1977, 7.

By contrast, members of the working class and sections of the middle class with no links to the state or the tradable sectors were, in general, less aware of the empire and more sensitive to its costs from higher taxes. All taxpayers in the mother country bore the costs of suppressing revolts whether or not they personally benefited from colonialism, and protected imperial markets raised consumer prices. Reflecting this perspective, US presidential candidate William Jennings Bryan remarked during the debate on annexing the Philippines that "the very people who receive least benefit from imperialism will be injured most by the military burdens which accompany it."[27] Suppressing revolts entailed restrictively high costs, analogous to the high expenditures incurred by sovereign states when fighting wars.[28] Even failed revolts were very costly for the metropole.[29] Combating a widespread rebellion was an order of magnitude more expensive than the ordinary expenses and profits of colonialism. For example, in 1905, the government of German South West Africa (Namibia) spent 4.5 million marks in its ordinary budget, 40 percent of which was a subsidy from German taxpayers. During this same period, the metropolitan government spent 600 million marks over five years to suppress the Herero rebellion in South West Africa.[30] From 1961 to 1974, Portugal spent 22 percent of state expenditures on combating anticolonial insurgencies.[31]

When the costs of empire were perceived to be low, the concentrated interests of a small metropolitan elite could win out over the diffuse interests of the metropolitan mass electorate, even in democracies. However, when colonists could credibly threaten a major revolt, consensus within the metropole's political class could dissipate rapidly unless the political class was very narrow. Consequently, democratic domestic institutions that empowered workers or other nonelites lowered the willingness of metropolitan officials to pay the military costs of counterinsurgency, even if the political concessions needed to avoid insurgency reduced the flow of colonial rents or required severing the colonial connection entirely. By contrast, authoritarian regimes usually

---

[27] Arnold and Wiener 2015, 341.

[28] We review this voluminous literature in Lee and Paine 2023.

[29] In human terms, revolts were almost always more costly for the colonists who fought them. However, metropolitan officials were usually indifferent to these costs, especially if the combatants were not white.

[30] Keltie 1905; Hull 2013, 88.

[31] Ferraz 2022.

empowered the bureaucratic and military sections of the upper class over the masses.

However, variation among metropolitan democratic institutions could also affect the timing and form of colonial reforms. Even democratic home institutions were vulnerable to capture by special interests who gained concentrated benefits from colonial rule. Government coalitions in France, for example, were notoriously unstable during the Third and Fourth Republics, which created opportunities for colonial sympathizers to hold the balance of power.[32] Left-wing parties should also be more permissive of colonial institutional reforms. Compared to conservatives, these parties were less electorally dependent on elites and were usually more skeptical of imperialism and extra-European military entanglements. Empirically, left-wing parties became ascendant late in the colonial period; no left-wing party governed a colonial power for more than five years until after 1945, when such governments were formed in Britain, Belgium, and the Netherlands.[33] In Spain and Portugal, authoritarian regimes kept the left out of power until the 1970s.

2.3 Size of the White Population

Pluralistic metropolitan institutions created a permissive condition for colonial representation. However, we anticipate that even democratic colonizers would not willingly grant institutional concessions absent a push from colonists. Compared to non-Europeans, white settlers had policy preferences more closely aligned with those of the metropole, which increased its willingness to offer concessions to this group. Settlers also had advantages over non-whites in their ability to lobby, to hinder economic output by withholding participation, and (sometimes) to revolt. These tactics increased the costliness to the metropole of not offering concessions. Consequently, we expect that colonies with sizable white settlements should frequently gain representative institutions and, where the white population was particularly large, high policy-making autonomy.

However, we also anticipate that the elite economic position of white settlers should lead them to create representative institutions for

---

[32] Spruyt 2005.
[33] Data from Brambor and Lindvall 2018.

themselves only. The same factors that empowered white settlers to push for institutional concessions would enable them to exclude non-Europeans from the political community. For these reasons, sizable white settlements should exert dual effects on democratic development. We expect that the antidemocratic effects would be amplified in settler-minority colonies, in which the white population was large enough to constitute a landed elite despite comprising only a small fraction of the overall population. Settler minorities could preserve their political and economic dominance only by exerting heavy repression.

2.3.1 Prodemocratic Effects

Closer Preference Alignment

Metropolitan officials usually were more sympathetic to the interests of white settlers than of non-Europeans because of closer-aligned policy preferences and perceived loyalties.[34] Settlers and metropolitan officials vigorously disputed how economic rents should be distributed. However, settlers nonetheless generally favored strong political and economic ties with the metropole, with whom they shared a language and on whom they depended for military backing against non-whites. Although a colonial legislature might reject some metropolitan-favored policies, it would usually allow the imperial center to retain its naval bases, trade ties, and international prestige. By contrast, non-Europeans were more often perceived as harboring aims fundamentally opposed to those of the colonial state. This made colonizers more willing to repress such groups rather than to grant concessions.

Not all white settlers had closely aligned preferences and loyalties, however. In colonies where white colonists came from European countries other than the metropole, they were outsiders despite a common European heritage. For example, Catholic settlers were considered a potential threat in the West Indian and Canadian colonies that Britain conquered from France and Spain in the eighteenth century, as were the Afrikaners of South Africa.

Lobbying and Agitation

White settlers (who descended from the metropole) enjoyed social, linguistic, and educational ties to the metropole that helped them to

---

[34] Abernethy 2000, 286–289, 298–299.

pressure the colonial state, often through organized bodies. American colonists sent permanent agents to London to exploit political divisions and undermine attempts by the Board of Trade to develop discriminatory economic plans.[35] The West Indian lobby was powerful in London throughout the eighteenth century.[36] Spanish settlers successfully lobbied the metropole to impose formidable requirements for obtaining permission to travel to the New World.[37] In the twentieth century, French colonists in Algeria maintained tight ties with colonial sympathizers in the French Parliament. British colonists in Kenya and Rhodesia set up offices to promote their interests in London.[38]

Lobbying and agitation imposed costs on autocratic officials despite not posing a direct threat of mass violence, similar to contemporary prodemocracy protests and civil resistance movements.[39] European officials sought to avoid developing a reputation for bad governance or tyranny that could hinder prospects for keeping their office at home or gaining promotion. European officials living among sizable white settler populations also feared social exclusion. For example, in Kenya: "It is with the whites that the civil servant must live during his term of service in the colony. The threat of ostracism ... is a very real one ... if this 'cutting' fails to daunt the official there is always a powerful lobby of Kenyan settlers waiting on the secretary of state in London."[40]

Nonparticipation

White settlers could passively undermine the colonial state in various ways. Where they settled in large-enough numbers, white settlers controlled the best land and were the wealthiest group of colonists. Ensuring their economic participation was vital for development because settlers could cripple the colonial state by refusing to pay taxes or by forgoing investments to upgrade production technology.[41] The possibility of nonparticipation was especially threatening in colonies

---

[35] Elliott 2007, 222–223.
[36] O'Shaughnessy 2000, 15.
[37] Engerman and Sokoloff 2011, 53.
[38] Cohen 2009.
[39] Chenoweth, Stephan and Stephan 2011; Brancati 2016.
[40] MacRae 1937, 29.
[41] This source of pressure has analogs to mobile, tradable forms of production, which Bates and Donald Lien 1985 link to the emergence of medieval parliaments throughout Europe. Our lobbying/agitation and nonparticipation

founded by corporations or by proprietors with a personal financial stake in the colony's development.

Colonial officials also needed to attract settlers and prevent them from moving away. Elected assemblies could solve the generic hold-up problem of the colonial state by extracting rents after colonists had sunk costs by traveling overseas. In the early British empire, the Crown and corporations/proprietors perceived local assemblies as an effective means to encourage settlement and economic production.[42] Political representation offered a means to help enforce indentured servitude contracts, and hence to encourage colonists to take long and expensive journeys across the Atlantic.[43] In Southern Rhodesia (Zimbabwe), one goal of introducing and deepening electoral concessions between the 1890s and 1920s was to attract European settlers.[44]

Revolt

When lobbying/agitation and nonparticipation failed to gain the desired concessions, white settlers could revolt as a last resort. Settlers usually participated in the colonial militia or military and could access European military technology.[45] Moreover, they were better positioned than non-white rebels to gain international support within the context of a European-dominated international system. For example, European nations immediately recognized the United States after its war of independence but did not extend diplomatic relations to Haiti for decades, and then only after Haiti paid a large indemnity to France.

For colonies with large European populations, the ongoing threat of revolt created a latent source of instability. On the one hand, large settler communities were well positioned to push for high levels of autonomy. On the other hand, the colonies were not valuable to the metropole if settlers monopolized the sources of rents. This tension made it difficult to calibrate the optimal degree of autonomy. The metropole and settlers were uncertain about each other's resolve; and

---

options also have analogs to Hirschman's 1970, 1978 concepts of voice and exit, respectively.

[42] Gailmard 2024.

[43] Engerman and Sokoloff 2011, 225–226; Nikolova 2017.

[44] Lee 1975.

[45] Abernethy 2000, 318–321. This was true even in many cases in which settlers lacked electoral representation, such as Spanish America; see Lynch 1992, 79–80.

wars, regime instability, and fiscal crises could suddenly undermine previously viable arrangements. Consequently, settlers might demand more autonomy than the colonizer was willing to grant or the metropole might restrict autonomy in ways that settlers found unacceptable. In light of these tensions, Abernethy comments that the puzzle is not why Spanish and British American countries eventually gained independence, but instead "why settlers remained formally dependent on metropoles for as long as they did."[46]

2.3.2 Antidemocratic Effects

White settlers sought to create representative institutions exclusively for themselves and had strong economic and racist incentives to jealously guard their monopoly over voting rights. Europeans seized control of the best land, used coercive methods to recruit labor, and worried that majority rule would lead to massive redistribution of land.[47] Racial differences reinforced these views and contributed to a siege mentality among whites anxious to guard their rents and elevated social status.

The size of the white settlement should condition how the competing prodemocratic and antidemocratic forces would play out in practice. In the neo-Britains (colonies comprising the future United States, Canada, Australia, and New Zealand), white settlers were an overwhelming majority of the population. These demographics reflected a combination of low population densities in North America and Oceania prior to European settlement and the decimation of native communities by diseases and war. These cases could qualify as minimalist democracies simply by enfranchising most of the white population. White political control could be secured even without harsh repression of the mass population, yielding relatively beneficial democratic legacies.

The West Indies, South America, and parts of Africa were more typical of colonies dominated by settlers. European communities in these regions were large enough to be economically dominant and politically influential. However, they comprised a minority of the colonial population and, in many cases, only a tiny minority. White elites perceived

---

[46] Abernethy 2000, 319.
[47] Mosley 1983; Paine 2019*b*; Gann and Duignan 1970, 161.

that a transition to majority rule would extinguish their economic and cultural privileges, which created strong incentives to cling to power through repression. Successful repression could entail either gaining metropolitan support to maintain authoritarian control over the non-white majority or declaring independence to fight non-whites without external interference.

Overall, we have clear theoretical expectations that settler minorities should gain early electoral representation with medium levels of autonomy and highly restrictive franchises. However, the same tools that made white settlers effective at gaining representation for themselves could also be used to deny representation to others. This renders ambiguous our theoretical expectations about overall democracy legacies.

2.4 Pressure from Non-Europeans

Non-Europeans in the colonies, unlike white settlers, had limited means to influence the political process. Instead, they often had to rely on white actors such as missionaries to lobby the metropole to stem gross abuses. Migration was difficult for natives and nearly impossible for enslaved persons.[48] Nor did metropolitan officials usually face audience costs at home from repressing non-whites, in contrast to harsh reactions against repressing white settlers.[49] For example, during the 1899–1902 Boer War, uproar over the confinement of white Afrikaners in concentration camps contrasted with tepid responses to the subjugation of thousands of Black Africans in those camps or to broader restrictions on African civil rights.

Nevertheless, non-Europeans could occasionally pressure the colonial state for electoral concessions. We highlight the two situations where this could occur as well as a third set of cases in which the indigenous elite lobbied for authoritarian institutions rather than elections.

2.4.1 Western-Educated Middle Classes

Non-Europeans with Western education occasionally became effective lobbyists, in particular when they did not have to compete with

---

[48] Typically, the best nonparticipation option for non-whites was internal: hiding from the colonial state or otherwise making themselves illegible to European officials; see Abernethy 2000, 303–306; Gardner 2012.

[49] Abernethy 2000, 288.

an influential settler population. This middle class, referred to as the comprador or *évolué* class, consisted of local merchants, professionals, and bureaucrats clustered in the colonial capital and major urban areas. Port cities had long-standing trading relations with European states and early exposure to missionaries, which facilitated higher levels of education.[50] In many areas with large enslaved populations, the colonizer's language was imposed as the lingua franca and, after emancipation, the colonizer bestowed metropolitan legal rights upon the entire population.[51] In other cases, individuals elevated their social position by serving as intermediaries between the colonizers and the broader population and by gaining familiarity with the colonizer's language, culture, and political system.[52]

Non-white elites did not belong to the same social networks as settlers, but they could use the same rhetorical technique of portraying colonial regimes as tests of the colonizer's stated ideals. It was difficult for colonizers to justify denying representation for educated elites who met the qualifications for voting at home, even if their skin color differed. Activists such as Dadabhai Naoroji in India expounded the gap between the metropole's announced principles, which he professed to revere, and the "un-British" or repressive reality of colonialism in practice.[53]

Many organizations that would later become political parties, such as the Indian National Congress, originated as associations of elites who lobbied the colonial state. These elite actors often positioned themselves as moderate alternatives to radical groups less aligned with metropolitan objectives. Metropolitan officials skeptical of the colonial project often proved sympathetic to these appeals. For example, associations of elite Indians who proclaimed their loyalty and avoided civil disobedience shaped the views of Liberal governments, who passed the Indian Councils Acts of 1861 and 1909. Reforms in 1935 sought to empower Indian men whose views were perceived as moderate. Supporters argued that "if you wish your Indian public men to act in a responsible manner you must give them responsibility" and

---

[50] Lankina and Getachew 2012; Woodberry 2012; Gerring et al. 2022; Ricart-Huguet 2022.
[51] Owolabi 2023.
[52] Lee 2017.
[53] Naoroji 1901.

that "it is better that the agitator should be in the Assembly [than] in the street."[54]

2.4.2 Mass Nationalist Movements and Revolt

Revolt was always the option of last resort for the colonized, but prospects for success changed over time. Prior to the twentieth century, the empowerment of non-elite Africans, Arabs, and Asians seemed unattainable. After World War II, changes in the structure of the international system and the rise of mass nationalist movements gave mass revolts an aura of inevitability.

Before the twentieth century, non-white colonists faced nearly insurmountable impediments to overthrowing the colonial state. This reflected Europeans' technological and organizational advantages over indigenous inhabitants of the Americas and the enslaved population. In the New-World colonies, the indigenous population was less dense than in Eurasia and was weakened by epidemics.[55] The delayed onset of the Neolithic Revolution throughout the Americas also meant that military technologies were less advanced than in the Old World. Although a handful of major revolts threatened colonial rule, imperial troops and European settlers usually crushed these uprisings.[56] Nineteenth-century industrialization reinforced these technological advantages. As Hilaire Belloc infamously declared, "Whatever happens, we have got the Maxim [machine gun], and they have not."[57] Even in Africa and Asia, where the biological and technological advantages of Europeans were less profound, colonial states nonetheless were usually able to defeat revolts while inflicting massively asymmetric battlefield casualties. The 1857 rebellion in India, for instance, resulted in the deaths of roughly 6,000 British soldiers and civilians compared to 800,000 Indians.[58]

Enslaved Africans faced equally difficult challenges. Intensive surveillance of plantation societies undergirded by the threat of brutal white repression made widespread slave revolts unlikely to succeed,

---

[54] Zetland 1934; Hansard 1935.
[55] Diamond 1998.
[56] Abernethy 2000, 307–312.
[57] Belloc 1898.
[58] Peers 2013.

even if the social position of enslaved people was so desperate that they occasionally risked such attempts. The Haitian Revolution created fear among whites throughout the hemisphere, but this was the only successful anticolonial revolt led by non-whites before World War II.

Structural conditions for mass revolts improved over time. In the interwar period and accelerating after World War II, the balance of power tilted decisively toward colonists. Western technologies such as automatic weapons became ubiquitous, while European powers became less able to resist armed anticolonial movements due to the disruptions of World War II.

Changes in the international system also encouraged aspiring revolutionaries. Prior to World War II, Europeans generally colluded to prevent anticolonial rebellions, which disabled rebels from gaining cross-border bases. After World War II, the rise of anticolonial superpowers meant that pressure flowed in the opposite direction. For both ideological and practical reasons, the Soviet Union supported the replacement of colonial rule with sympathetic sovereign states and offered aid and arms to many anticolonial rebels. The other superpower, the United States, was more ambivalent in private but usually professed anticolonial attitudes in the context of the Cold War. Once the end of European rule was viewed as inevitable, a gradual and participatory decolonization seemed desirable to prevent groups with Soviet ties from taking power.

2.4.3 Traditional Elites and National Monarchies

Urban professional classes arose only in a few places and mass nationalist movements arose late. For most of the colonial period, traditional elites in rural areas were the most politically important group of colonized non-Europeans. Colonizers relied on traditional rulers for governance purposes because they could use existing infrastructure to cheaply govern vast territories, a practice often referred to as indirect rule.[59] Thus, in contrast to the typical exclusion of non-Europeans from the *central* colonial institutions, favored non-Europeans dominated *local* institutions that were often granted substantial autonomy. Favoritism toward native authorities yielded bifurcated states in which

---

[59] Lugard 1922; Berry 1992. For evidence on the institutional makeup of British Native Authorities, see Bolt et al. 2023.

native law prevailed in rural areas, whereas Europeans and select privileged non-whites were subject to Western law.[60]

The broad goals of rural elites resembled those of urban elites – to gain autonomy from the metropole with themselves in control. However, their specific aims differed. Urban elites appealed to the political principles of the metropole to gain representation in national legislative bodies. By contrast, their aristocratic rivals sought to bolster traditional institutions, often by actively supporting the colonial project.[61]

Out of necessity, all colonizers relied on traditional elites to some extent. However, metropolitan institutions and the principle of institutional similarity (discussed earlier) affected their stance on which traditional institutions could be justified as legitimate. Metropoles with a monarchy at home, such as Britain, viewed traditional elites as sympathetic actors through which to construct systems of indirect rule and perhaps as options for handing off power when devolution became necessary. For example, the 1919 and 1935 Government of India Acts included special quotas for large landowners and princes in the colonial legislature.[62] One peer commented during the 1935 debate, "I found that many of these [Indian] landowners outdid me in their Conservative views . . . in those landowners we have got a potential reservoir of leadership and of sound, solid common sense."[63] By contrast, monarchs contradicted the ideals of republican polities such as France, who viewed monarchy as threatening and archaic. As Crowder contends, "Most of the French administrators who came out to French West Africa were Republicans, and distrusted monarchy and aristocracy in principle."[64] At the onset of colonial rule, France often deposed monarchs and broke up former kingdoms, in contrast to the standard British practice of preserving local dynasties.[65]

After 1945, reliance on traditional rulers became harder to sustain. In colonies such as the Gold Coast, urban elites formed the base of

---

[60] Mamdani 1996.
[61] Crowder and Ikime 1970.
[62] Lee 2018.
[63] Hansard 1934.
[64] Crowder 1968, 188.
[65] Müller-Crepon 2020. For broader quantitative comparisons of the directness of rule in British and French colonies, see Gerring et al. 2011; Lee and Schultz 2012; Letsa and Wilfahrt 2020.

nascent nationalist organizations, which directly challenged the status of traditional rural rulers.[66] Given the rising threat of revolt, colonizers faced unprecedented pressure to delegate more authority to a broader set of actors in most colonies.

However, in some special cases, the elites favored under older institutions of indirect rule could plausibly inherit the postcolonial state. In cases such as Kuwait and Swaziland, a single monarchy had jurisdiction over the entire (or a majority of) the colony's territory. In such national monarchies, there was no opposition between a colonially run center and a non-white periphery. The monarch was necessarily involved in national affairs, although colonial authorities could nonetheless circumscribe his power in various ways. As decolonization became inevitable, delegating control to national monarchies offered a possible substitute to handing off power to mass-elected non-Europeans.[67] The virtues of institutional similarity should make metropolitan (constitutional) monarchies more willing to hand power off to national monarchies than republican metropolitan regimes.

2.5 Summary of Theoretical Implications

We summarize our main theoretical implications in Table 2.1. When facing pressure from colonists, political institutions at home influenced the response of the imperial center. *Authoritarian metropoles* should generally resist electoral representation or policymaking autonomy for colonists. Wherever the colonizer was autocratic throughout a territory's history, the colony should be undemocratic at independence. If metropolitan institutions fluctuated over time, we expect (a) electoral institutions will be more prevalent in its colonies during more democratic periods at home and (b) the ultimate legacy at independence would depend on the balance of pluralist versus authoritarian institutions during colonialism.

Given the reluctance of authoritarian colonizers to concede electoral representation, we anticipate that more pluralistic institutions

---

[66] Boone 2003, 159–174.

[67] In other cases, such as Nigeria and Sierra Leone, members of traditional lineages developed successful political parties that won elections to gain control of the state at independence. Even in cases where traditional rulers were displaced after independence, local dynasties often survived and constitute relevant political actors to the present day; see Baldwin 2015.

Table 2.1 *Summary of theoretical implications*

Colonial category	Early elections	Early autonomy	Peaceful franchise expansion	High democracy at independence and afterward	Examples
Authoritarian metropole	✗	✗	✗	✗	Mexico, Angola
Pluralistic metropole					
Settler dominant	✓	✓	✓	✓	United States, Australia
Settler minority	✓	Medium	✗	Ambiguous	Algeria, South Africa
Weak elites/late revolt threat	✗	✗	✓	✗	Niger, Malawi
Non-white middle class	✓	✗	✓	✓	India, Jamaica
National monarchy	✗	✓	n/a	✗	Kuwait, Swaziland
Empirical tests	Chapters 3 and 4		Chapter 5	Chapter 6	

at home would create a permissive condition for colonial representation. However, all else equal, even metropolitan officials in democratic polities preferred to concentrate policymaking power in their own hands. Thus, we expect that parliamentary or fully democratic metropoles will permit representative institutions only when facing pressure from colonists. The precise institutional constellation should depend on the strength of European settlers and of non-white colonists.

White settlers were well positioned to pressure the metropole with lobbying/agitation, nonparticipation, and revolt options; and, generally, they held preferences more closely aligned with those of metropolitan officials. This should yield early electoral representation. In *settler-dominant* colonies, which we operationalize as those with a white population share of at least 25 percent, we expect two consequences. First, they could carve out substantial policymaking autonomy for themselves, perhaps coming into conflict with restrictions preferred by the metropole. Second, they should create a mass franchise, albeit confined mostly or entirely to the white community. This should yield high levels of democracy at independence, even if the democracy was racially restrictive.

Settler-minority colonies (in which whites were roughly 5 to 25 percent of the colonial population) had similar advantages for pressuring the metropole. However, settlers not only would gain lesser autonomy in these cases, but should more vigorously resist pressure to expand the franchise. It is theoretically ambiguous whether developing early elections or resisting franchise expansion would be the more important legacy for democracy levels at independence.

Many colonies without a notable white settler population had *weak elites* who could not effectively pressure the metropole for concessions, typically resulting in no early elections. After 1945, we anticipate that the rising threat of revolt will yield elections with mass franchises. However, as we show in Chapter 6, these hasty concessions did not create strong parties and norms of executive turnover via free and fair elections. This resulted in low democracy levels at independence, albeit higher than in countries with authoritarian metropoles or national monarchies.

We anticipate that colonies with European-educated *non-white middle classes*, whether comprised of emancipated slaves or professionals in port cities, will follow a distinct path. These classes of non-

Europeans had better ability to lobby and agitate. This should yield early electoral representation, albeit with a small franchise and low policymaking autonomy – which would reflect the small segment of the population making such demands. Unlike in settler-minority colonies, those privileged by early elections should not strongly oppose larger franchises, at least not to the point of supporting repression. Peaceful expansion of early competitive institutions should yield high levels of democracy at independence.

Finally, in some exceptional cases, a *national monarch* existed who could plausibly be assigned to rule the entire territory. Here, policies of indirect rule designed for subnational governance would in fact yield high autonomy for a national government led by indigenous actors, albeit without elections. We expect that such outcomes would occur more frequently among colonizers with a constitutional monarchy at home, following the principle of institutional similarity.

In the following chapters, we show that these theoretical implications help to understand patterns of electoral institutions across four centuries of Western colonial rule. The three chapters with evidence on electoral institutions under colonialism are organized temporally, albeit with a theoretically rooted distinction for each time period. In Figure 2.1, we demonstrate how the types of colonies changed over time. Until the nineteenth century, settler populations tended to be large and metropolitan institutions were the main source of theoretically relevant variation (Chapter 3). Settler-dominant and settler-minority colonies each comprised more than a quarter of the total of all colonial cases between 1600 and 1850, as shown in Figure 2.1(a). Colonies with an authoritarian metropole constituted roughly another third.[68] Colonies that lacked notable white settlements, all of which were in the Old World, were a small fraction of the total.

These trends flipped over the next century as the white population became smaller throughout the colonial world (Chapter 4). Settler-dominant colonies became nearly nonexistent, and settler colonies shrank to 6 percent of the total. Authoritarian metropole colonies also became less prevalent, reflecting democratization in France and the end

---

[68] All these cases also met our 5 percent European population threshold for settler minorities, again underscoring the prevalence of relatively large settler populations in early colonies.

1600–1850   1850–1945

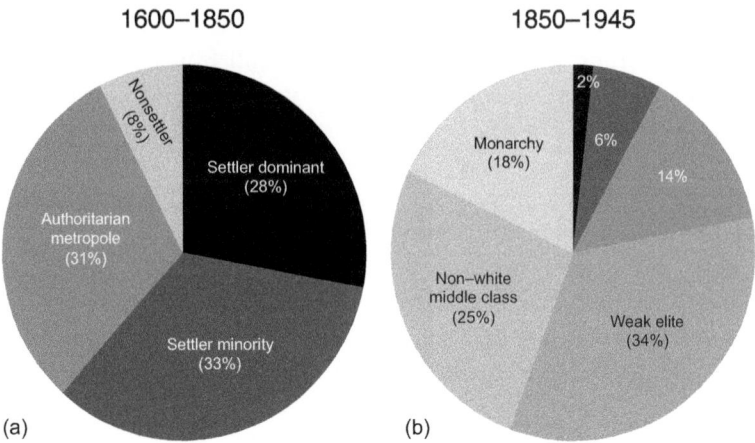

(a)   (b)

Figure 2.1 Categories of colonies over time

General notes: The pie charts depict the percentage of colonies in each category, averaged over all years that each territory was under Western colonial rule (within the specified time period for each panel). The percentages shown for the two time periods are not strictly comparable because of different sampling schemes for the pre-1850 and the post-1850 cases. Nonetheless, the figure conveys the qualitative shift in the types of colonies over time.

Notes for (a): The sample contains every New-World colony in Chapter 3 plus any Old-World colonies (from the sample in Chapters 4, 5, and 6) that came under Western rule before 1850. Among the New-World colonies, we code as authoritarian metropoles all colonies within the following empires and years: France until 1789 and then 1799–1848; Portugal in all years except 1820–1822; Spain in all years except 1808–1813; and the Netherlands from 1796 to 1814. Settler dominant are the following colonies in years in which the metropole had pluralistic institutions: all US colonies, all Canadian colonies, all Australian colonies, New Zealand, Bahamas, Dominican Republic, Argentina, Bermuda, Cuba, Puerto Rico, and Chile. All other New-World colonies are settler minority. The early Old-World colonies are a mixture of nonsettler colonies and settler minorities.

Notes for (b): The sample includes every colony from the V-Dem sample in Chapters 4 through 6; Appendix Table A.9 lists the cases and categories. We also add two setter-dominant cases: Australia until 1901 and New Zealand until 1907. Due to rounding, the percentages in Panel B do not add up to exactly 100.

of the Spanish American empire. Instead, colonies with small settler populations and pluralistic metropoles predominated, with weak elite and non-white middle-class colonies collectively comprising 59 percent of the total. The composition of colonies stayed largely the same after 1945, but the newfound threat of revolt yielded mass franchise expansion in colonies without vested interests to hold on (Chapter 5). In Chapter 6, we assess how different experiences under colonialism affected democracy levels at independence and afterward.

3 | Representation in Settler Colonies through 1850

Before the nineteenth century, most European colonies were located in the New World. Although European powers sailed across the world and established trading relations throughout parts of Asia and Africa, only in the Americas and West Indies were they able to overwhelm and decimate the indigenous population to gain expansive territories. Consequently, white settlers became the most politically influential group of colonists in the New World. They comprised a majority of the population in most of North America, Oceania, and the Southern Cone of South America and a small but influential minority in the West Indies and Peru.[1] Europeans also enjoyed technological advantages in coercion that made it nearly impossible for non-whites to successfully overthrow the colonial state.

Within the New World, variation in metropolitan political institutions was the main determinant of electoral institutions between the seventeenth and mid-nineteenth centuries. As anticipated in Chapter 2, pluralistic institutions in the metropole should facilitate electoral bodies in the colonies. We expect white settlers to push for representation and to gain high levels of policymaking autonomy, with the franchise restricted to those who met metropolitan voting requirements. By contrast, we expect authoritarian metropoles to block electoral representation in their colonies.

Three empirical patterns support these theoretical expectations. First, the predominant pattern across the entire period is that British colonies experienced more electoral competition. The British metropole, although not democratic by contemporary standards, had a stronger parliament and better-established rights of representation

---

[1] Every colony in the sample for this chapter meets the population thresholds we use for settler-minority (Europeans at least 5 percent of the population) or settler-dominant colonies (at least 25 percent). Therefore, using the terminology from Chapter 2, every colony was either *settler-dominant/minority* or *authoritarian metropole*, depending on metropolitan institutions. The end of Chapter 2 describes how we classified each colony.

than did the other imperial centers. Prior to the French Revolution, colonists in the French, Spanish, and Portuguese empires lacked electoral representation beyond the municipal level. Their rulers feared that electoral bodies would stimulate rather than quell pressures for revolt.

Second, British colonies varied in ways that our theory anticipates. British-settled colonies in North America, the West Indies, and Oceania routinely gained fully elected assemblies shortly after settlement. In these colonies, white colonists leveraged their lobbying and nonparticipation options to pressure the colonial state for significant policymaking autonomy. However, these colonies were not democratic by contemporary standards. Shaped by restrictions at home, voting rights were confined to white property-owning men. Moreover, when actions by colonists adversely affected the interests of the metropole, London sought to restrict local autonomy and ignored settler interests. Such actions prompted the American Revolution. As the British empire expanded, the demographic composition of its white population changed in ways that reduced their lobbying and nonparticipation options. Colonies with putatively disloyal Catholic or convict populations experienced long delays before gaining electoral representation. Settlers in Canada and Australia gained representation and high autonomy only after the demographic makeup of their white population changed.

Third, Britain was not the only parliamentary metropole during this period. The Netherlands, the only other colonizer with even reasonably strong parliamentary institutions before 1789, permitted limited electoral institutions in some colonies that echoed the oligarchic cast of metropolitan Dutch politics. After the French Revolution, political transformations in authoritarian metropoles triggered reforms to colonial institutions. This pattern was most apparent in France, which fluctuated between democratic and authoritarian institutions after the French Revolution, and whose colonial institutions closely tracked metropolitan patterns. Spain and Portugal engaged in abortive electoral reforms in their colonies, which preceded the dissolution of their American empires.

3.1 Main Patterns

Existence of Electoral Institutions
Electoral institutions were more common within the British empire than elsewhere, as shown in Figure 3.1. Within twenty years of

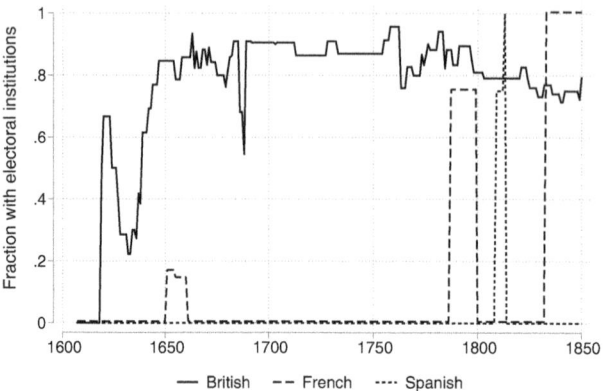

Figure 3.1 Electoral institutions: 1607–1850
Notes: The outcome variable indicates whether a colony has any elections
to a territory-wide political institution or to a metropolitan parliament, averaged across the British, French, and Spanish empires. The sample consists of
colonies within these empires listed in the tables throughout the chapter.

the initial colonial settlement, thirty-six of fifty (72 percent) British
colonies began to hold regular elections for an assembly, compared
to one of twenty-eight colonies in other empires.[2] Across the entire
temporal sample, starting with the Dominican Republic in 1492 and
ending for all colonies in 1850, electoral institutions existed in 82 percent of colony-years among British colonies compared to 5 percent of
colony-years among non-British colonies. Thus, the discrepancies are
large in magnitude and, as we show with the regression analysis in the
Appendix, statistically significant.[3]

Although British colonies tended to hold elections earlier and
for a longer period than other colonies, not all British colonies
gained representative institutions shortly after the colony was established. Neither factor endowments, the legal form of the original colonial charter, nor settlement by religious minority groups
can explain intra-British variation.[4] The more important difference
was the political strength of the white settlers. Generally, the white

---

[2] See Appendix Table A.1.
[3] See Appendix Table A.2. As we discuss later, alternative explanations such as
factor endowments cannot explain these interimperial discrepancies.
[4] See Appendix Table A.4.

community was stronger in colonies founded by English settlement, except where dependent Englishmen were deported overseas such as convicts (New South Wales, Tasmania, and Western Australia) and the poor (Georgia). Excluding these four, twenty-one of twenty-six (81 percent) of the settled colonies gained representation within twenty years of settlement. Another twenty colonies were conquered from other powers. Britain was more inclined to deny representative institutions when the white population was predominantly Catholic, and therefore deemed to have less-aligned preferences with the metropole. This was true in many former French and Spanish colonies. Among conquered colonies, all five captured from the (Protestant) Dutch held elections within twenty years compared to only nine of fifteen (60 percent) colonies conquered from France and Spain.[5]

Prior to 1789, the Netherlands was the only other colonizer with parliamentary institutions at home. Electoral institutions were more common in the Dutch empire than in absolutist empires, but less prevalent than in the British empire.[6] The French Revolution yielded political reforms in France, Spain, and Portugal, all of which temporarily established parliamentary regimes. Consequently, after 1789, British colonies became less distinctive in the existence of electoral institutions, as shown in Figure 3.1. British colonies are statistically distinct from French colonies only during periods when France had authoritarian institutions at home.[7]

More generally, electoral institutions were nearly exclusive to colony-years in which the metropole had relatively strong parliamentary institutions, as opposed to authoritarian institutions.[8] Representative assemblies existed in 72.7 percent of colony-years with

---

[5] Britain was more permissive of electoral institutions in former French/Spanish colonies where the pre-existing population was very small, and therefore English settlers could more easily overwhelm the existing French population. In general, English inhabitants of settled colonies were guaranteed certain English legal rights, whereas the Crown had greater prerogative in conquered colonies; see Wight 1946a, 28.

[6] See Appendix Table A.5.

[7] See Appendix Table A.6.

[8] As authoritarian institutions, we code France until 1789 and then 1799–1848 and 1852–1870; Portugal in all years except 1820–1822; Spain in all years except 1808–1813; and the Netherlands from 1796 to 1814.

parliamentary metropoles compared to 1.5 percent for authoritarian metropoles, a statistically significant difference.[9] We also compare colonies to themselves over time by adding unit fixed effects to the regressions. These specifications hold constant any colony-specific factors that do not change over time. The coefficient estimate for parliamentary metropoles in the fixed-effect models is large in substantive magnitude (an additive increase of 41 percent to the incidence of electoral institutions) and statistically significant despite dropping all British colonies, which were governed by a parliamentary metropole in all years.

Policymaking Autonomy

Electoral concessions in the British colonies delegated meaningful policymaking autonomy to colonists. Under institutions known as the Old Representative System, colonists gained fully elected lower chambers with rights to levy taxes and to initiate legislation. Over time, Britain introduced the crown colony system to reduce settler autonomy. Consequently, many colonies with electoral bodies in the nineteenth century had less autonomy than their predecessors, although colonies in Canada, Australia, and New Zealand eventually gained greater autonomy through responsible government and dominion status. Autonomy was highly circumscribed in other empires. In many cases, territory-wide elections were to the metropolitan parliament, where metropolitan representatives always predominated. French local assemblies, even when elected, lacked the autonomy of their British counterparts.

Suffrage

Franchise rules closely mimicked those in the home countries. As in England itself, colonial laws restricted the franchise to white men who met property requirements. The franchise was larger in the US colonies

---

[9] See Appendix Table A.7. The percentage for parliamentary metropoles is lower than that for British colonies because of the fairly low prevalence of elected assemblies among Dutch colonies. Moreover, the percentage for authoritarian metropoles is not zero because of early, short-lived elections in French Canada and later colonial elections during semi-authoritarian periods in France.

only because lower land inequality yielded a higher fraction of the population that met property requirements. Suffrage was, nominally, large throughout the French and Spanish empires in their post-1789 pluralist periods, which reflected broad male franchises at home.

Democracy Levels

The handful of available data points on V-Dem's democracy index in 1789 demonstrate interimperial differences as well as the overall low levels of democracy in the eighteenth century. The score for the United States (0.35) is roughly the average score among regimes classified as electoral authoritarian in 2022. Scores were even lower elsewhere; by a modern comparison, they would rank with Saudi Arabia, the least democratic country in the world in 2022. The average score in six Spanish American colonies (Chile, Cuba, Dominican Republic, Guatemala, Mexico, and Venezuela) was 0.03, Portuguese Brazil was 0.01, and French Saint Dominigue (Haiti) was 0.04. Even after electoral reforms in the Spanish empire, democracy scores remained uniformly low. Between 1789 and 1820, none of these non-British colonies attained a democracy score that exceeded the average score among closed authoritarian regimes in 2022 (0.16).

3.2 Comparing Authoritarian Metropoles to Britain

Across the entire period covered in this chapter, the strongest correlate of having electoral institutions is British colonialism. We attribute this to differences in metropolitan institutions. Qualitative evidence from colonies with authoritarian metropoles demonstrates more directly that their metropoles feared (1) the repercussions of permitting elected bodies and (2) were willing to tolerate the associated costs of denying representation. Alternative explanations, such as factor endowments, cannot explain away this effect.

3.2.1 Differences in Metropolitan Institutions

Differences in metropolitan institutions explain the affinity between British colonialism and early electoral representation. English settlers established the country's first successful overseas colonies in the early seventeenth century. By this time, the English Parliament had established itself as an important political institution. Although national estates existed in many European countries at the time,[10] the English Parliament's central role in legislation and approving taxes outpaced its peers.[11] During the sixteenth century, members of the House of Commons protected their existing role in granting taxes for war and demanded new rights and immunities. The House of Commons grew in power relative to the House of Lords and a higher fraction of elections for the Commons were contested.[12] By the end of the sixteenth century, it became a fixed principle of English law that only a representative legislature could control finances.[13]

The early foundation of parliamentary privileges precipitated the confrontations between Parliament and the Stuart kings in the seventeenth century. The disputes between James I and his parliaments over sovereignty, money, and foreign policy foreshadowed the disputes in which his son, Charles I, engaged. In 1640, Charles I reluctantly called parliament into session after a lengthy period of raising revenue by other means. This confrontation eventually degenerated into a civil war that ended with the execution of Charles and a period of political instability and military rule. In 1688, Parliament reinforced its position by deposing Charles' son, James II, in the Glorious Revolution. Post-revolution legislation permanently entrenched the principle that a "King in Parliament," rather than the King alone, governed England. Parliament reaffirmed privileges they had claimed traditionally (e.g., the 1688 Bill of Rights) and passed new statutes that prevented the Crown from gaining funds independent of Parliament.[14]

Thus, during the seventeenth and eighteenth centuries, Parliament usually played a key role in policymaking and many seats for the Commons were chosen by competitive elections (although rotten boroughs persisted into the nineteenth century). However, the franchise was small as nearly all nonproperty holders, women, and Catholics were believed unfit to vote. As of 1831, only about 3 percent of the

---

[10] Marongiu 1968; Stasavage 2011; Van Zanden, Buringh and Bosker 2012; Abramson and Boix 2019; Kenkel and Paine 2023.
[11] Koenigsberger 1995, 302.
[12] Rabb 2002, 43–44.
[13] Keith 1912, 1–2; Sacks 1994, 58–59; Congleton 2010, 307–310.
[14] Pincus and Robinson 2014, 197–201; Cox 2016.

population was enfranchised.[15] The franchise increased gradually during the nineteenth century, but suffrage did not become universal until after World War I.

In contrast to England, parliaments were weak in Spain, Portugal, and France. Parliaments arose across the Iberian Peninsula in the twelfth century.[16] However, as the English Parliament increased its powers vis-à-vis the Crown in the sixteenth and seventeenth centuries, the Castilian *Cortes* tended to decline in status.[17] A key event in the consolidation of stronger powers for the monarchy was the Revolt of the Comuneros (1520–1521), which resulted in a decisive royal military victory over the cities represented in the Castilian *Cortes*. Over the next half century, the *Cortes* was rarely in session. Fiscal exigencies in the late sixteenth century temporarily made the Crown reliant on taxes raised by the *Cortes*. However, by the mid-seventeenth century, Habsburg kings ceased to call the *Cortes* and instead raised funds through nontax means or by negotiating directly with individual towns. Even at its height, the *Cortes* was used exclusively for tax-raising purposes and never for legislating.[18] The Spanish Crown imposed various arbitrary fiscal measures in the seventeenth century, none of which triggered the type of legal-constitutional crises that occurred periodically in Stuart England.[19]

Parliaments in Portugal and France were even weaker and met rarely. Despite medieval roots, the Portuguese *Cortes* met only three times when Habsburg Spain governed Portugal (1580–1640), sporadically over the next half century, and not at all from 1698 until the nineteenth century. Kings regularly revoked or altered by decree laws passed by the *Cortes*.[20] The Crown was sufficiently unconstrained that in the 1750s, the Marquis of Pombal engaged in broad repression and

---

[15] V-Dem reports a figure of 2.5 percent of adults with the legal right to vote in all years between 1789 and 1831. Numbers provided in O'Gorman 1986, 37, yield an estimate of approximately 3.1 percent of the total population in 1831.

[16] Marongiu 1968.

[17] At the beginning of Spain's colonial period, the "Spanish" Crown was a composite monarchy that reflected the marital union of the Queen of Castile (Isabella I) and King of Aragon (Ferdinand II). We focus on Castilian institutions because Spanish territories were legally part of Castile; see Elliott 2007, 121.

[18] Thompson 1994*a,b*; Gelabert 1999.

[19] Thompson 1994*a*, 215.

[20] Disney 2009*a*, 240–242.

executions of the higher nobility, breaking up major houses that had constituted the upper-class elite for over a century.[21] France's Estates-General failed to establish veto power over extraordinary taxes during the Hundred Years' War,[22] leading to centuries of royal supremacy. The Crown called the national Estates-General for a total of only twelve years in the sixteenth century, two years in the seventeenth century, and none in the eighteenth century before 1789.[23]

3.2.2 Authoritarian Colonial Institutions

When confronted with settler demands for representative institutions, metropolitan officials responded with rationales that mirrored their justifications for authoritarianism at home. Consequently, colony-wide elections essentially never occurred in the colonies of authoritarian metropoles. Table 3.1 summarizes the cases.[24]

Iberian America

The European population was relatively large throughout the Spanish American empire.[25] However, despite the presence of settlers, no political institutions above the municipal level had an electoral component until the nineteenth century. Spain replicated political institutions from home, including viceroys (royal governors), *audencias* (high courts), *cabildos* (town councils), and the legal system (codified in the *Recopilación de las leyes de Indias* in 1680).[26] However, the

---

[21] Opello Jr. 1994, 39–41; Disney 2009a, 292–298.

[22] Henneman 1999.

[23] Data from Abramson and Boix 2019.

[24] Minor European empires with authoritarian metropoles in the seventeenth century, such as Sweden (New Sweden) and Denmark (Danish West Indies), also did not establish representative institutions in their colonies.

[25] Using data from Gerring et al. 2022, the average European population share among colonies in the empire in 1800 was 29 percent. This ranged from 13 percent in Peru to more than 40 percent in Argentina, Cuba, Puerto Rico, and Chile.

[26] By the end of the sixteenth century, Spanish America consisted of two viceroyalties, New Spain and Peru, which collectively comprised eleven *audiencias*. Each consisted of a council whose primary duties were judicial but with additional executive and legislative responsibilities; see Burkholder and Chandler 1977, 2. During the sixteenth century, the Habsburgs had centralized the empire by displacing the autonomous *encomiendas* of conquistadores with salaried state agents, *corregimientos*; see Garfias and Sellars 2021.

Table 3.1 *Pre-1850 electoral institutions: Authoritarian metropoles*

Colony	Colonial years	First election	Reversals
Spanish empire			
Santo Domingo (Dom. Rep.)	1492–1821	1813	1814
New Spain (Mexico)	1521–1824	1809	1814
New Granada (Colombia)	1525–1819	1809	1814
Peru	1531–1821	1809	1814
Puerto Rico	1580–1898	1809	1814
Cuba	1607–1898	1809	1814
Guatemala	1609–1821	1809	1814
Yucatan (Mexico)	1619–1824	1813	1814
Provincias Internas (northern Mexico, US)	1776–1824	1813	1814
Rio de la Plata (Argentina)	1776–1816	1809	1814
Venezuela	1777–1823	1809	1814
Chile	1789–1818	1809	1814
Portuguese empire			
Brazil	1533–1822	1820	None
French empire			
Acadia (Nova Scotia)	1605–1713	None	n/a
Canada (Quebec)	1608–1763	1651	1661
St. Christopher and neighbors	1623–1763	None	n/a
Guadeloupe and Marie Galante	1635–Present	1787	1800, 1852
Martinique and Grenada	1635–Present	1787	1800, 1852
French Guiana	1643–Present	1833	1852
Placentia-Île Royale (Newfoundland, Cape Breton)	1655–1763	None	n/a
Saint Domingue (Haiti)	1665–1804	1787	1800
Louisiana-Illinois	1683–1763	None	n/a

Notes: For the Spanish empire, this table lists each viceroyalty, captaincy general, and commandancy general within the pre-Napoleonic Spanish empire in the New World. For most cases, we code the onset of colonial rule as the first year of Spanish settlement/conquest; although for cases previously governed by another colony within the empire, we code the onset of colonial rule as the year in which it became a distinct political unit. The Philippines followed a similar institutional trajectory as the American colonies, although we do not list this case because it is not located in

Table 3.1 *(cont.)*

the New World. For the Portuguese empire, we include a single entry for Brazil. For parts of the sixteenth century, it was disaggregated into captaincies, and for centuries into the State of Maranhão in the north and the State of Brazil in the south. However, in 1775, the two states were merged into one. For the French empire, this table replicates the list of colonies from Pritchard 2004, 423–424. Note that France ceded Grenada, but not Martinique, to Britain in 1763. The sources for representative institutions are listed later in the chapter. No colony had a fully elected chamber of an assembly before 1850, which we list in the British tables, and therefore we omit this column from the present table.

Crown deliberately chose to not allow for parliaments, or *cortes*.[27] When confronted with settler demands for representative institutions, metropolitan officials responded with rationales that mirrored their justifications for authoritarianism at home. The Revolt of the Comuneros in 1520–1521 and a rebellion in Peru in the 1540s prompted their fear that convening a *cortes* would stimulate rather than prevent revolts. In 1559, Philip II contemplated convening a *cortes* in the Americas to secure new tax grants after a royal bankruptcy, but ultimately rejected the idea upon advice from Peruvian commissioners that conditions were too turbulent. In Mexico in 1567, the council of Mexico City agreed to have a proposed *cortes* vote funds for the king, but in return for redressing grievances. Philip II rejected this proposal from a realm then under investigation of rebellion. In 1611, Philip III made a similar inquiry about Peru, but Viceroy Montesclaros in the Americas feared that representative institutions would be dangerous in "provinces subject to such disturbances."[28]

Intimidated by a fear of settler revolts, the Spanish crown favored Spanish-born *peninsulares* over potentially disloyal American-born whites (creoles), despite their agitation for representation.[29] Representation in provincial *audiencias* was the "ultimate goal of creole ambition."[30] However, as of 1687, creoles held less than one quarter of all *audiencia* seats, and all but one were not "native sons";

[27] Haring 1947, 6; Parry 1966, 205; Elliott 2007, 127; Burbank and Cooper 2010, 147.
[28] Simpson, Griffiths and Borah 1956, 252–253; Góngora 1975, 103–104.
[29] Burkholder and Chandler 1977, 5–6.
[30] Lynch 1992, 76.

that is, their *audiencia* seat did not correspond with their place of birth.[31] Creole fortunes improved somewhat in the next half century when fiscal desperation and the War of Spanish Succession compelled the Crown to auction off *audiencia* seats.[32] In the average year between 1690 and 1750, native sons held 14 percent of *audiencia* seats and creoles as a whole held 42 percent of seats. However, the consolidation of the Bourbon dynasty in the mid-eighteenth century led to a renewed drive to centralize control over its empire.[33] By 1808, native sons held 6 percent of seats and creoles as a whole held 19 percent.

The only elected institutions in Spanish America were town governments, but even this form of representation was eliminated over time. The *cabildo* was the core unit of local governance for urban-oriented Spaniards. Although many American *cabildos* began with an electoral component, the memory of the Revolt of the Comuneros at home made the Spanish Crown "intensely suspicious" of these bodies exercising autonomous authority.[34] By the early seventeenth century, most municipal offices had become proprietary and hereditary,[35] although unelected *cabildos* in some areas (e.g., Lima) began to revive in importance in the late eighteenth century.[36]

Authoritarian policies were economically costly. The metropole struggled to raise revenue without local assemblies to legitimize taxation. Mimicking the bargain struck with nobles in Spain, American creoles were exempt from paying taxes. This left indigenous persons, mining, and consumption as the tax base, which the Crown often supplemented by selling offices.[37] Spain purposely limited European migrants to block individuals the metropole deemed to be disloyal. The Spanish Crown prohibited not only citizens from other

---

[31] Burkholder and Chandler 1977, 5–9. Creoles specifically sought to hold office within their own district, and therefore the percentage of *audiencia* seats held by native sons is the best measure of how Crown policies responded to settler demands. All the figures for *audiencia* seats draw from Burkholder and Chandler 1977, Appendix VI.

[32] Burkholder and Chandler 1977, 15–80.

[33] Burkholder and Chandler 1977, 83–135; Lynch 1992, 77.

[34] Parry 1966, 205.

[35] Haring 1947, 164–167; Moore 1954, 265–284.

[36] Moore 1966*b*, 173–196; Fisher 1969.

[37] Elliott 2007, 139, 170; Guardado 2022.

countries to move to its colonies, but also prevented Spaniards from any kingdom except Castile from emigrating without a special license. In particular, for centuries, the Crown sought to prevent the spread of "Aragonese liberties" in its overseas territories, as the *Cortes* of Aragon was strong.[38] This policy was economically inefficient because the areas controlled by the Aragonese Crown were among the most commercially dynamic parts of Spain.

Portuguese Brazil was governed similarly. The Crown imposed royal control under governor-generals in the mid-sixteenth century.[39] Universities and printing presses were banned in the colonies,[40] and metropolitan officials ignored petitions for greater local autonomy. In 1724, two Brazilian municipal councils wrote to the Portuguese Crown with a proposal to reform colonial governance: "the power of overseas governors and justice ministers should be diminished, and that their own children and grandchildren should be given preferential treatment to serve in local positions." The Overseas Council never responded.[41] Creole representation was confined to the local level, with *senados da câmara* (municipal councils) that replicated their counterparts at home.[42] Officers for the *câmaras* were elected via a complicated indirect process, which resulted in small oligarchies dominating the offices.[43] Unlike Spanish colonial *cabildos*, the *câmaras* remained relatively autonomous local institutions throughout Brazil's entire colonial period, although they were not universal throughout Brazil.[44]

French America

In France, Louis XIV's consolidation of personal rule at home in the 1660s yielded authoritarian governance in the colonies.[45] He converted the corporate colony of Canada to a royal colony in 1663 and

---

[38] Haring 1947, 7–8; Elliott 2007, 121.
[39] Fieldhouse 1982, 32; McCann 1997, 15–17.
[40] McCann 1997, 29.
[41] Myrup 2010, 186.
[42] Boxer 1969, 278; Russell-Wood 1974.
[43] Boxer 1965, 3–11; Boxer 1969, 273–286.
[44] For example, the Crown directly governed the diamond district within Minas Gerais and "there was no *câmara* nor any independent judicial authority to limit [the intendant's] power"; see Disney 2009*b*, 268.
[45] Shortt and Chapais 1913, 328–331; McRae 1964, 220.

converted every French West Indian colony to royal control in 1674. Royal agents governed the colonies directly without local assemblies.[46] Starting in 1663, Louis XIV appointed all officials for the Sovereign Council of New France, which replaced the previously elected Council of Quebec (discussed below).[47] The Crown-appointed bishop of New France rebuked the governor's proposal to convene an elected assembly in the 1660s, claiming that his "respect for" and "obedience to" the king prevented him from doing so.[48] In 1672, a later governor of Quebec convened an assembly of unelected notables, but French Minister of Finance Jean-Baptiste Colbert rebuked him upon finding out. He expressed his preference that "everyone speaks for himself and no one speaks for all."[49]

Elections in the French empire prior to the Revolution occurred either before Louis XIV's ascension or at the local level. Private traders and chartered companies initiated exploration and settlement in French Canada.[50] During this early period, an elected representative body existed briefly from 1651 to 1661, which accounts for the temporary positive blip in the French line in the seventeenth century shown in Figure 3.1. In 1651, settlers pressed for representation on the appointed Council of Quebec and complained specifically about the financial burden imposed upon them.[51] Inhabitants of Quebec, Montreal, and Trois-Rivières gained indirect representation in 1651 and direct representation in 1657. However, a new governor in 1661 was dissatisfied with the colony's administration and replaced the Council of Quebec with a wholly appointed council.[52]

After Louis XIV's ascension, a few local institutions had consultative features, as in *ancien régime* France itself. The colonial equivalent to provincial *parlements* in France was *conseils supérieur*, which served primarily as courts.[53] Throughout the seventeenth and eighteenth centuries, local assemblies such as *chambres d'agriculture et de commerce*

---

[46] Fieldhouse 1982, 35–36.
[47] Cahall 1915, 22.
[48] Quoted in Parkman 1875, 150.
[49] Quoted in Maguet 1911, 10, and translated into English by the authors.
[50] Quinn 2000, 41.
[51] Cahall 1915, 14–15.
[52] Lanctot 1934.
[53] Fieldhouse 1982, 38; Pritchard 2004, 247. Although moribund under Louis XIV, in the eighteenth century, *parlements* in metropolitan France functioned

convened occasionally to raise ad hoc taxes. However, these bodies were impermanent and the range of policies they deliberated was highly circumscribed.[54]

Like Spain, France limited colonial settlement by Protestants (Huguenots) and other groups they deemed suspicious, which limited the number of settlers and eventually made the colony vulnerable to British invasion.[55] Taxation was low because, as in metropolitan France, no institutions could levy direct taxes on elites. Aware of this tradeoff, the Crown chose to forgo revenues rather than to dilute its control over policy.[56]

3.2.3 Alternative Explanations

Many scholars contend that institutions varied within the New World not because of differences in colonizer, but instead because of distinct factor endowments, as discussed in Chapter 1.[57] We demonstrate the greater explanatory power of metropolitan institutions by comparing colonies based on whether their primary economic activity entailed substantial labor coercion for production.[58] Labor coercion involving enslaved Africans was high in areas whose climate favored the cultivation of lucrative cash crops such as sugar, tobacco, and cotton. The major centers of such production were the West Indies, Brazil,

---

as courts of law, commanded police powers, and possessed political powers that enabled them to contest the king's decrees; see Cobban 1950, 67–68.

[54] Fieldhouse 1982, 40–41, and Pritchard 2004, 254–260 provide examples from Saint Domingue, Martinique, Guadeloupe, Guiana, and Réunion; see also Maguet 1911, 17. Similarly, in Canada, the governor-general and intendant occasionally convened public meetings in the major towns, but these were infrequent and purely advisory; see Taylor 2002, 374.

[55] Taylor 2002, 369. McRae 1964, 227, speculates about Canada: "[h]ad the colony offered a place of refuge, an escape for dissenters on New England lines, for even a modest fraction of these exiles, the subsequent history of North America might have been vastly different."

[56] Fieldhouse 1982, 41; Pritchard 2004, 248.

[57] Engerman and Sokoloff 2011, 44–46, 218; Acemoglu, Johnson and Robinson 2001, 1388; Hariri 2012, 474.

[58] The Appendix provides regressions (see Tables A.1 and A.2), describes the data used to create these indicator variables, and lists every colony by economic activity (see Table A.3). Our sources are Sokoloff and Engerman 2000; Engerman and Sokoloff 2011; Mahoney 2010; Bruhn and Gallego 2012; Arias and Girod 2014.

and the southern United States. Elsewhere, labor coercion was primarily of indigenous persons. Areas such as New Spain (Mexico) and Peru had precolonial empires, dense populations in the colonial center, and mineral wealth. By contrast, in the northern United States, Canada, and the Southern Cone of South America, family farms predominated.[59]

The degree of labor coercion does not account for the British distinction. Among colonies with low labor coercion, nineteen of twenty-five (76 percent) British colonies held their first election within twenty years of the initial colonial settlement, compared to none of the seven non-British colonies. Early territory-wide elections did not occur in the Spanish Southern Cone, French Canada, or New Netherland (Dutch New York), despite favorable factor endowments. Among colonies with high labor coercion, seventeen of twenty-five (68 percent) British colonies held their first election within twenty years of the initial colonial settlement, compared to one among the twenty-one (5 percent) non-British colonies. Early elections became widespread throughout the British West Indies despite factor endowments that, according to existing arguments, should mitigate against electoral representation.

Other aspects of factor endowments include the density of the indigenous population and the development of state-like institutions above the local level.[60] Territories also differed in precolonial institutions of local direct democracy.[61] None of these factors, nor year-fixed effects, discernibly alter the magnitude of the British coefficient, as shown in Appendix Tables A.1 and A.2.

3.3 Variation within the British Empire

The British advantage in early electoral institutions did not reflect a deliberate design by the Crown, corporations, or proprietors to transplant liberal institutions overseas. Colonies were best positioned to

---

[59] Although many Africans were forcibly migrated to these areas as well (e.g., New York), their population was much smaller than farther south in the United States. Furthermore, enslaved Africans were primarily used for household labor rather than plantation agriculture.

[60] Acemoglu, Johnson and Robinson 2002*b*; Hariri 2012.

[61] Bentzen, Hariri and Robinson 2019.

gain early representative institutions when settled by free, Protestant English citizens. However, voting rights were restricted to property-owning members of the privileged groups and the metropole some-times attempted to limit colonists' autonomy – albeit with fatal consequences in the US case. Later, Britain denied representation en-tirely to colonized territories with smaller white populations comprised of marginal groups such as Catholics or convicts. Electoral represen-tation and autonomy became prevalent in Canada and Australia only after demographic changes that yielded more individuals who would have met voting requirements at home.

3.3.1 Early Elections and Expanding Autonomy

Prior to the American Revolution, the British empire consisted of colonies with sizable white settlements across the East Coast of North America and the West Indies. England's parliamentary tradition cre-ated an opening for settlers to demand representation and autonomy and provided institutional precedents on which to coordinate their demands. Additionally, English settlers had a nonparticipation op-tion to migrate to another colony or to not move overseas at all. Colonial officials took these alternatives seriously because, at least ini-tially, they needed to attract settlers to make their colonies profitable. Consequently, as shown in Tables 3.2 and 3.3, nearly every colony quickly gained elected representation and then substantial policymak-ing autonomy, at least until the Crown began to push back in the 1670s.

White settlements were large in these colonies. European diseases and coercion largely eliminated the native population across the West Indies. On the continent, natives were not considered as part of the colonial population and were not included in the census. Over time, whites became a minority of the population throughout the West Indies (and a smaller majority in the southern United States) because of the forcible relocation of enslaved Africans. However, as of 1650, whites were still numerically preponderant in the West Indies, where they comprised, on average, 53 percent of the population in the colonies listed in Table 3.3.[62]

---

[62] Data from Gerring et al. 2022. This percentage remained high throughout the seventeenth century (average of 42 percent in 1700). The European

Table 3.2 *Pre-1850 electoral institutions: British United States*

Colony	Colonial years	First election	Reversals	Fully elected chamber
Virginia	1607–1776	1619	None	1642
Plymouth (MA)	1620–1691	1639	1686	1639
Massachusetts Bay	1628–1776	1634	1686, 1774	1644
Maryland	1634–1776	1637	None	1650
Connecticut	1636–1776	1637	1686	1698
Rhode Island	1637–1776	1647	1686	1696
New Haven (CT)	1638–1664	1639	None	1639
North Carolina	1663–1776	1665	None	1691
New/East Jersey	1664–1776	1668	1688	1668
New York	1664–1776	1683	1688	1691
South Carolina	1670–1776	1671	None	1691
West Jersey (NJ)	1675–1702	1681	1688	1696
New Hampshire	1679–1776	1680	1686	1692
Pennsylvania	1682–1776	1682	None	1682
Delaware	1704–1776	1704	None	1704
Georgia	1733–1776	1755	None	1755

Notes: This table lists every colony in Squire 2012, 13. The colonial onset year coincides with the first year of English settlement listed in Kammen 1969, 11–12, except for colonies split off from others (New Hampshire, Delaware). The end year coincides either with the US Declaration of Independence or the year a colony was merged into another. In most cases, the first year with a fully elected chamber is the first year that the assembly became the lower chamber in a bicameral legislature, although some colonies had a fully elected unicameral legislature (Plymouth, New Haven, Pennsylvania, and Delaware); see the aforementioned sources for these dates as well as the year of the first assembly and more detail on several disputed dates. The years of autocratic reversals coincide with the creation of the Dominion of New England, which disbanded in 1689, and the Massachusetts Government Act of 1774.

Protest, agitation, and nonparticipation by settlers promoted colonial elections and autonomy. For example, the Jamestown settlement in Virginia was originally an economic failure. As of 1616, the population was tiny (about 350 colonists) because of high mortality

population share plummeted only afterward as the enslaved African population spiked in the eighteenth century, as we discuss in Chapter 4.

Table 3.3 *Pre-1850 electoral institutions: Early British West Indies*

Colony	Colonial years	First election	Reversals	Fully elected chamber
Bermuda	1612–Present	1620	None	1620
St. Kitts	1624–1983	1642	1878	1672
Barbados	1627–1966	1639	None	1639
Nevis	1628–1882	1658	1877	1672
Antigua and B.	1632–1981	1644	1898	1682
Montserrat	1632–Present	1663	1866	1696
Jamaica	1655–1962	1663	1865	1664
Bahamas	1666–1973	1728	None	1728
BVI	1672–Present	1773	1867	1773

Notes: This table lists every colony located in the West Indies or Atlantic Ocean in Wrong 1923, 80–81 that permanently came under British control before 1700 and was not primarily a dependency of other islands. Colonial onset year coincides with the first year of English settlement listed in Kammen 1969, 11–12; plus Sullivan 1989, 521 for the Bahamas and Cichon 1989, 493 for the Virgin Islands. The end year coincides with the year of independence or the year a colony was merged into another; no end year is listed for territories still under colonial occupation. Year of the first election is the earliest of years listed in Kammen 1969, 11–12 for the first assembly or Wrong 1923, 80–81 for the onset of the Old Representative System. The initial year of an autocratic reversal spell coincides with a transition to a wholly nominated legislature, coded from Wrong 1923, 80–81. In the next chapter, we present sources for the later resumption of elections (see Table 4.3). In most cases, the first year with a fully elected legislative chamber is the first year that the assembly became the lower chamber in a bicameral legislature, although Bermuda had a fully elected unicameral legislature. Dates from Kammen 1969, 11–12; plus Wrong 1923, 80–81 for the Bahamas and the Virgin Islands.

rates, which left the Virginia Company deeply in debt.[63] Subsequently, the Virginia Company decentralized economic control by permitting colonists to own and work land as private property. In 1619, the Company created the General Assembly to enable settlers to influence policymaking, which they anticipated would attract more settlers.[64] After the Crown revoked the Virginia Company's corporate charter in 1624, colonists lobbied London to retain their General Assembly,

---

[63] Taylor 2002, 133.
[64] Kammen 1969, 14; Billings 2004, 6–7, 10.

claiming that the assembly was the appropriate means for colonial men to govern themselves. The Crown and royal agents, in turn, agreed that the assembly served well the purposes that had justified its foundation. Over time, the General Assembly expanded its powers (including over taxation) to the point of becoming a "little parliament" by 1660.[65]

In Massachusetts Bay, settlers gained high autonomy from the outset. The original corporate leaders used their knowledge of the English legal system to take advantage of a loophole. The original charter of the Massachusetts Bay Company empowered stockholders to make laws for the colony but (presumably accidentally) omitted the usual clause requiring corporate meetings to be held in London. The stockholders simply moved themselves and the corporation across the Atlantic. By merging corporate management and the colonial elite, they gained legal autonomy from royal intervention. However, the charter did not grant taxation powers to the Company. After two years of rule, ordinary freemen protested that the colonial government lacked the authority to raise taxes without consulting the people.[66] In 1634, freemen in each town began electing two representatives to the General Court.[67]

Most of the original West Indian colonies gained their initial electoral institutions during the English Civil War and Interregnum. Settlers enjoyed an opening to promote their interests because the metropole was weak and royal absolutism was discredited. In 1641, the Civil War cut off the Earl of Carlisle from his colonies.[68] Legislators in Barbados responded by asserting their autonomy, warning that they "had all turned to the way of the parliament and were lik to shake off ... obedience to his Majeste."[69] The remaining colonies followed by establishing their own representative institutions during

---

[65] Billings 2004, xvi–xvii, 11–13, 17. The initial proclamation in 1625 that made Virginia a royal colony did not mention the assembly, although governors continued to convene it regularly. Not until 1639 did Charles I legally recognize the council and issue instructions to the governor that it was to convene at least once per year. As noted by Gailmard 2024, this reflected a practical concession by a monarch who was, at the same time, trying to restrict the powers of his Parliament at home.

[66] Hartwell 1911.

[67] Kammen 1969, 21; Morgan 1989, 43–44.

[68] Rogoziński 2000, 70, 75.

[69] Quoted in Kammen 1969, 30–31.

this period on the model of the English Long Parliament.[70] West Indian assemblies gained high levels of autonomy over time and settlers pressed their prerogative that, as English citizens, they should control their own taxes and other aspects of domestic legislation.[71]

Elected assemblies were established even more quickly in colonies chartered after the Restoration of 1660. In colonies ranging from the Jerseys to the Carolinas to Jamaica, proprietors and royal officials realized English citizens considered political representation in a fiscally powerful elected assembly to be a "most fundamental liberty." This institution was also deemed critical to attract and retain propertied colonists, which in turn was necessary for economic development and bolstering proprietors' revenues.[72] Thus, the combination of agitation, nonparticipation, and earlier institutional precedents yielded colonial assemblies with relatively high levels of policymaking autonomy.[73]

Metropolitan institutions influenced the design of colonial institutions. The institutional components of the Old Representative System that had emerged by the late seventeenth century corresponded, respectively, to the British Crown, Lords, and Commons: a London-appointed governor and a bicameral legislature with a nominated council (upper chamber) and an elected assembly (lower chamber).[74] This contrasted with the arrangement of legislative councils in many later colonies, which had a single chamber in which British-appointed officials outnumbered representatives for settlers. Within the elected assemblies, colonists used the parliamentary rules and procedures from the English House of Commons as a starting point.[75]

---

[70] Kammen 1969, 30.

[71] Wrong 1923, 41–43; Greene 2010*b*, 54–57. Graham 2018 quantifies the high volume of legislation produced in the British North American and West Indies colonies during the eighteenth century.

[72] Whitson 1929, 13–14; Wight 1946*a*, 28; Kammen 1969, 32–51; Taylor 2002, 224, 246–247, 263.

[73] The main exception proves the rule. The Duke of York (later King James II) gained a proprietary charter for New York and refused to call an assembly, but eventually gave in because of turmoil fueled by complaints that settlers were "wholly shut out or deprived of any share, vote, or interest in the government ... contrary to the laws, rights, liberties and privileges, of the subject"; quoted in Elliott 2007, 135.

[74] Labaree 1930, 214; Wight 1946*a*, 27.

[75] Squire 2012, 71.

3.3.2 Franchise Restrictions

Parliamentary metropoles permitted elected assemblies but restricted the franchise to those who could vote at home. In seventeenth- and eighteenth-century Britain, that meant free, adult Protestant males who met property-owning requirements and had an independent legal status.[76] Restrictions to men twenty-one-and-older were universal across the colonies.[77] In practice, this meant *white* men. Native Americans lacked English-recognized property and were not considered royal subjects. Most Blacks were enslaved, and free Black men were explicitly targeted for exclusion in the colonies with the largest Black populations.[78] For example, in 1723, Virginia enacted a law with a provision that "no free negro, mulatto, or Indian whatsoever shall hereafter have any vote at the elections of burgesses, or any other election whatsoever."[79]

Among religious groups, Catholics were frequently targeted for exclusion. In England itself, they typically could not vote, hold office, or inherit property.[80] In Maryland, where Catholics were numerous, they were explicitly barred from voting and holding office at three different times, including permanently after 1718.[81] Six other colonies in the future United States forbade Catholics from voting at various times.[82] In Massachusetts Bay, the suffrage was initially limited to freemen, and only members of the Puritan church could become freemen. These suffrage qualifications excluded many non-Puritan Protestants whose "economic and social position entitled them to be regarded as members of the customary ruling elite," given the metropolitan precedent. Agitation by this group prompted an expansion of voting rights in 1647.[83]

As in England, some form of property-owning restrictions on voting was common but the exact rules varied substantially across colonies

---

[76] Keyssar 2009, 5; Bateman 2018, 46.
[77] McKinley 1905, 473–474. The practice of male suffrage was so well established that formally excluding women was usually considered unnecessary; see McKinley 1905, 35.
[78] Nikolova 2017.
[79] Quoted in McKinley 1905, 36.
[80] Bateman 2018, 209–220.
[81] McKinley 1905, 48–78.
[82] McKinley 1905, 36, 157, 213, 355, 374, 451.
[83] Pole 1966, 35–36.

and localities. Colonists broadly agreed with metropolitan officials that voting and office holding should be restricted to those with "a tangible stake in the community."[84] A dispute in 1676 over Virginia's broad suffrage rights underscored the Crown's desire to restrict voting to those with the suffrage at home. The governor was instructed to "take care that the members of the Assembly be elected only by freeholders as being more agreeable to the custom of England."[85]

Although laws for voting eligibility broadly resembled those in England, the fraction of the population that could vote in the North American colonies was much larger.[86] In contrast to the roughly 3 percent of the adult population that could vote in England in the late eighteenth century, the relative abundance of land in the future United States enabled more white men to own property and hence to meet the suffrage qualifications.[87] Across the thirteen colonies in the eighteenth century, the fraction of the population that could vote was approximately 25 percent of the entire adult population, 50 percent of all adult males, and 67 percent of all free adult males.[88] Thus, the property-owning requirements disenfranchised only about one-third of free adult males who otherwise met qualifications for suffrage. By the eighteenth century, voting restrictions tended to be higher in the South than the North as southern legislators responded to the growing population of enslaved persons (and free Black population) with general increases in voting restrictions.[89]

Greater land inequality in the West Indies yielded a narrower franchise than in the US colonies. In Barbados, approximately 20–25 percent of adult white males could participate in elections in the late seventeenth century.[90] Europeans were roughly a quarter of the population at this time in Barbados,[91] which implies that about 5 to 6 percent of adult males and 2 to 3 percent of all adults had the franchise.

---

[84] Labaree 1930, 188.
[85] Quoted in Chandler 1901, 11.
[86] Brown 1952; Hartz 1955; Pole 1957; Keyssar 2009, 7.
[87] Engerman and Sokoloff 2005.
[88] Bateman 2018, 46. See V-Dem data in 1789 for a similar, albeit postindependence, estimate of 27.5 percent of all adults.
[89] Nikolova 2017.
[90] Dunn 2012, 92–93. The freeholding requirements were even lower in many other West Indies colonies; see Wrong 1923, 40–41.
[91] Data from Gerring et al. 2022.

Thus, the franchise in Barbados was comparable to that in England, but with a larger fraction of white males enfranchised.

3.3.3 Restricted Autonomy and Revolt

A parliamentary tradition at home was a permissive condition for colonial electoral bodies to emerge. However, white colonists succeeded at gaining levels of de facto autonomy, particularly in fiscal matters, that far exceeded what the British Crown deemed acceptable. This reflected a general tension we highlighted in Chapter 2: large white settler populations demanded high levels of autonomy, but the metropole sought to limit their autonomy to protect its rents. These contradictory goals could result in armed conflict if the metropole miscalculated. This tension helps to explain why London failed in its two broad attempts to push back on settler autonomy.

Starting in the 1670s, Charles II made a concerted effort to reduce the autonomy of American legislatures. This began a long-term shift from the Crown's original stance of contractual imperialism to regulatory imperialism, as phrased by Gailmard,[92] given the newfound scope of the economic rents available in the colonies. The first notable attempt, the proposed extension of Poynings' Law in Virginia and Jamaica, would have stripped the legislatures of their powers to initiate legislation and to renew tax laws.[93] However, after both colonial assemblies refused to pass the necessary bills, the Crown relented because direct rule was deemed too costly.[94]

Charles' successor, James II, made even more dramatic attempts to reduce colonial autonomy. James pressured judges to invalidate the colonial charters that provided the legal basis for elected legislatures. In 1686, James united the New England and the mid-Atlantic colonies into the Dominion of New England, which the Crown ruled without an elected assembly. This project reflected metropolitan officials' long-term frustration with assertive colonial legislatures that produced

---

[92] Gailmard 2024.

[93] Poynings' Law (1494) legally subordinated Ireland's Parliament to the English Crown, in part by requiring the Crown to preapprove legislation.

[94] Instead, the Crown conceded to the assemblies the right to legislate in return for gaining medium-term revenue bills that, ultimately, failed to perpetually fund the government; see Whitson 1929, 70–109; Labaree 1930, 219–222; Webb 1979, 432; Gailmard 2024, 217–223.

policies at odds with metropolitan interests.[95] However, the Dominion collapsed immediately after James' overthrow in 1688.[96] Following the news from England of James' deposition, 2,000 militiamen took to the streets in Boston in April 1689 and arrested the governor. The rebels claimed, "it was a Maxim delivered in open Court unto us by one of the Council that we must think the Privileges of English men would follow us to the End of the World."[97] The New York City militia followed suit in May in a bloodless coup. Subsequently, the metropole permitted new or renewed charters that restored rights of representation.

In the subsequent decades, colonists' policymaking autonomy increased across the US and West Indies colonies. The expanded powers of the English Parliament following the Glorious Revolution created a target for settlers' goals.[98] The colonial assemblies constrained the colonial governors and gained legislative supremacy, in particular by establishing prerogatives over raising and distributing public revenue, determining governors' salaries, setting the rules of their chamber, and controlling some aspects of executive affairs.[99] The implicit truce that emerged between the metropole and colonists after the Glorious Revolution left Britain in control of foreign and trade policy and the selection of governors, whereas elected colonists enjoyed substantial de facto autonomy over domestic policy.[100]

However, the Crown never formally accepted these concessions, and the fiscal exigencies created by the Seven Years' War prompted London to again attempt to restrict colonial autonomy. A series of acts between 1763 and 1775 imposed new taxes on the colonists and formally declared the law-making supremacy of the British Parliament over colonial assemblies. Protests by colonists and intensive negotiations with colonial governors yielded the repeal of the Stamp Act in 1766 and of most of the Townshend Duties in 1770. However, spiraling colonial protests and assertions of metropolitan control culminated in the Massachusetts Government Act of 1774, which revoked Massachusetts' charter and introduced direct Crown rule without elected

---

[95] Kammen 1969, 55–57; Greene 1986, 12–17; Taylor 2002, 276.
[96] Kammen 1969, 57.
[97] Mather 1689.
[98] Kammen 1969, 57.
[99] Greene 1963, 3–18.
[100] Greene 1986.

representation. The metropole's broad attempt to reverse the autonomy of large settler populations prompted the American Revolution,
making the ever-looming revolt option a reality.[101]

Settlers in the West Indies also disliked Britain's centralizing policies
but chose not to join the American Revolution. The smaller white population made independence infeasible. The need for British troops to
counter the rising number of enslaved persons reinforced metropolitan ties and made the white minority dependent on the metropole to
maintain their monopoly of power.[102] Legislators in the British West
Indies largely acquiesced in the 1760s to metropolitan tax demands
even though these laws imposed greater costs in the West Indies than
in North America.[103] Dependence on the metropole again affected
outcomes in the next century when direct crown rule replaced most
legislatures in the region, as we discuss in Chapter 4.

3.3.4 Restricted Autonomy in the Second British Empire

Electoral institutions declined in prevalence over time within the
British empire despite reforms to strengthen the metropolitan parliament. The metropole hesitated to grant representative institutions to
the next wave of New-World colonies in the West Indies and modern-
day Canada, as summarized in Table 3.4. The demography of the white
population differed from earlier colonies. In colonies conquered from
France or Spain, the white population was largely Catholic and thus
ineligible to vote in England. With limited command of the English
language or ties to the British political system, they also lacked political connections within the metropole and were suspected of loyalty to
their former colonizers.[104] Furthermore, these colonies were directly
ruled by the British government, as opposed to founded by corporations or proprietors, which better positioned their governors to deny
representative institutions.

Nova Scotia, acquired from France in 1713, was an extreme example of these tensions. The French Catholic settlement in Acadia was
culturally distinct and waged a protracted armed struggle against the

[101] Greene 1986; Simon 2017.
[102] O'Shaughnessy 2000, 47–48.
[103] O'Shaughnessy 2000, 109–111, 130–132.
[104] Wight 1946a, 47.

Table 3.4 *Pre-1850 electoral institutions: British conquered colonies*

Colony	Colonial years	First election	Reversals	Fully elected chamber
North America				
Nova Scotia	1713–1867	1758	None	1758 (1848)
East Florida	1763–1783	1781	None	1781
Quebec	1763–1867	1791	None	1791 (1848)
West Florida	1763–1783	1766	None	1766
Prince Edward Island	1769–1872	1773	None	1773 (1851)
Cape Breton Island	1784–1820	None	n/a	n/a
New Brunswick	1784–1867	1785	None	1784 (1848)
Ontario	1791–1867	1791	None	1791 (1848)
West Indies				
Dominica	1763–1978	1775	1898	1775
Grenada	1763–1974	1766	1877	1766
St. Vincent and G.	1763–1979	1776	1877	1776
Tobago	1803–1889	1803	1877	1803
Br. Guiana (Guyana)	1803–1966	1803	None	Post-1900
Br. Honduras (Belize)	1798–1981	1853	1870	Post-1900
Trinidad	1797–1962	Post-1900	n/a	Post-1900
St. Lucia	1803–1979	Post-1900	n/a	Post-1900

Notes for North America: This table lists every conquered colony (plus territories split off from conquered colonies) in North America that Britain gained during Queen Anne's War (1702–1713), the Seven Years' War (1754–1763), or the French Revolutionary and Napoleonic Wars (1792–1815); excluding parts of North America that lacked notable European settlements. The start date for colonial years is the first year of permanent British control or the year in which the territory became a separate colony. The end date for colonial years is the year of dominion status, merger into another colony, or leaving the British empire. The first year with a fully elected chamber is the first year with a bicameral legislature. For colonies that gained responsible government in the nineteenth century, we additionally put that year in parentheses. For most colonies, the year of first election, fully elected chamber, and responsible government are from Keith 1912, 1–9 and Wight 1946a, 167–169 (for cases with slight discrepancies in years, we consulted additional sources). For Cape Breton, see Girard 2010, 169; for West Florida, see Johnson 1943, 83–84; for East Florida, see Mowat 1943, 127–128.

Notes for West Indies: This table lists every colony located in the West Indies in Wrong 1923, 80–81 that permanently came under British control after 1700; this source also provides most colonial onset years. As an exception, Britain and Spain contested over control of British Honduras until 1798; see Bolland 1992, 163–166.

Table 3.4 *(cont.)*

We use this as the onset year and classify it as a colony conquered from Spain. The end year coincides with the year of independence or the year a colony was merged into another. Years of first election and fully elected chamber (each coincide with the onset of the Old Representative System) and reversals (transition to a wholly nominated legislature) from Wrong 1923, 80–81. In the next chapter, we present sources for the later resumption of elections (see Table 4.3).

British until the 1750s.[105] In a 1727 letter to the Lords of the Privy Council, the Lords of Trade stated their requirement for the English population to increase before permitting an assembly while also acknowledging the problem of nonparticipation – without an assembly, it was difficult to attract English settlers to Nova Scotia.[106] In 1755, during the Seven Years' War, British officials greatly weakened French influence by deporting French Acadians from Nova Scotia.[107] The first elected assembly for the ethnically cleansed colony met in 1758 and, until 1789, only Protestants could vote.[108] Similarly, during the American Revolution, Britain carved out new crown colonies from Nova Scotia, New Brunswick, and Cape Breton. New Brunswick's population of recent English migrants immediately gained electoral institutions.[109] By contrast, Cape Breton's mostly Catholic population was governed without an elected assembly because few of its inhabitants would have been eligible to vote.[110]

Quebec was France's main colony in North America and its population of 55,000 in the 1750s was almost entirely French Catholic.[111] After annexing Quebec following the Seven Years' War, successive British governors refused to create an assembly because imposing the same anti-Catholic franchise rules as in Britain would have disenfranchised almost the entire population.[112] British officials permitted electoral representation in Quebec only after an influx of 45,000 Loyalists during the American Revolution strengthened the English

---

[105] Grenier 2008.
[106] Lords of Trade 1727.
[107] Beck 2009; McCann 2012.
[108] Nova Scotia Legislature 2017.
[109] Forbes 2008.
[110] Girard 2010, 169.
[111] McRae 1964, 227, 234.
[112] Higham 1926, 369, 375.

community in Canada.[113] In the 1780s, English merchants in Quebec City organized a reform movement that pushed for elections whereas the French Party dominated by large French landowners opposed reforms.[114] British officials responded to this pressure with the Canada Constitutional Act of 1791, which mandated legislative elections. The act allowed Catholics to vote but deliberately circumscribed their political power by splitting Quebec into a French-dominant and an English-dominant province (Ontario).[115] The act also limited settlers' autonomy with a fully appointed and powerful executive council, which reflected a shift away from the Old Representative System to a new crown colony system with greater metropolitan control.[116]

The other territories conquered by Britain during the Seven Years' War (Dominica, East/West Florida, Grenada, St. Vincent, and Tobago) gained representation more quickly than did Quebec – on average, eight years after the war. These colonies (similar to Jamaica, conquered a century earlier) had small or no existing settlements of French or Spanish Catholics and, where present, they were not usually allowed to vote in the new legislatures.[117] An explicit goal of introducing assemblies was, as stated in the Royal Proclamation of 1763, to provide "Confidence and Encouragement to such persons as are inclined to become settlers in the new Colonies."[118]

3.3.5 Gaining High Autonomy in Canada and Oceania

Canada, Australia, and New Zealand eventually achieved levels of autonomy commensurate to that of the early US colonies. Their large populations of white settlers used lobbying and the threat of revolt to pressure British officials, despite earlier resistance to permitting representative institutions. These colonies gained self-governance over domestic affairs in the mid-nineteenth century (responsible government) and all had de facto independence (dominion status) by the early

---

[113] McRae 1964, 247; Wilson 2009.
[114] Greenwood 1993, chs. 1–2.
[115] Greenwood 1993, 43.
[116] Wight 1946a, 44–46.
[117] Higham 1926; Wight 1946a, 45; Martin 1989, 265.
[118] Quoted in Wrong 1923, 46.

Table 3.5 *Pre-1850 electoral institutions: Later British-settled colonies*

Colony	Colonial years	First election	Reversals	Fully elected chamber
New South Wales	1788–1901	1842	None	1850 (1850)
Newfoundland	1824–1948	1832	None	1832 (1855)
Tasmania	1825–1901	1850	None	1851 (1855)
Western Australia	1829–1901	1867	None	1890 (1890)
South Australia	1836–1901	1850	None	1856 (1856)
New Zealand	1840–1907	1854	None	1853 (1855)
Vancouver Island/BC	1849–1870	1856	None	1856 (1871)
Victoria	1851–1901	1851	None	1855 (1855)
Queensland	1859–1901	1859	None	1859 (1859)

Notes: This table lists every settled colony in Canada, Australia, and New Zealand in Wight 1946*a*, 167–169. This is the same list as in Keith 1912, 1–9 except we exclude crown colonies in modern-day Canada that formed after 1867, when the country gained dominion status. For the remaining columns, see the notes for Table 3.4.

twentieth century. Table 3.5 summarizes information for each colony (see Table 3.4 for the earlier Canadian colonies).

Lower Canadians (Ontario) petitioned the Colonial Office for greater autonomy in 1836, requesting that the unelected executive council become elected.[119] Revolts in 1837–1838 in both Lower Canada and Upper Canada (Quebec) against the nominated legislative councils and "the irresponsible provincial executive" pushed these demands to the top of the political agenda,[120] in part because Britain feared a repeat of the American Revolution. The need to stimulate new settlement also influenced the ensuing reforms. Lord Durham's report in 1839 concluded, "While the present state of things is allowed to last, the actual inhabitants of these Provinces have no security for person or property, no enjoyment of what they possess, no stimulus to industry. The development of the vast resources of these extensive territories is arrested; and the population, which should be attracted to fill and fertilize them, is directed into foreign states."[121] Reforms to make the executive dependent on voters, the first grant of so-called responsible

---

[119] Bradshaw 1909, 92.
[120] Bradshaw 1909, 277.
[121] Quoted in Lucas 1912, 3.

government within the British empire, were implemented in Lower and Upper Canada over the next decade.

Settler colonies in Oceania gained responsible government in the ensuing decades. The first Australian colony, New South Wales, lacked electoral representation for more than five decades because of its origins as a penal colony. Despite the large white population, denying representation reflected metropolitan practice because felons could not vote in England. Changed demographics among the white population fueled demands for elections; the free population grew over time and felon transportation to New South Wales ceased entirely in 1840. Colonists gained representative government in 1842 when the council became two-thirds elected.[122] In 1854, gold miners in the new colony of Victoria revolted against the colonial government in the Eureka Rebellion, decrying the need to purchase expensive miners' licenses – effectively, a tax – despite lacking any representation. Britain responded by granting responsible government for every colony in Australia in the 1850s except for sparsely populated Western Australia, the last colony with penal transportation.[123] These reforms also encouraged British officials to permit self government in New Zealand less than two decades after its founding.[124]

3.4 Parliamentary Metropoles beyond the British Empire

Britain was the main, but not only, imperial metropole with parliamentary institutions at home during the early colonial period. The Dutch had a competitive political system based on an even narrower oligarchy than in London, which facilitated limited electoral bodies in some Dutch colonies. After the French Revolution, France, Spain, and Portugal each experienced temporary transitions to parliamentary rule

---

[122] Keith 1912, 7; Greene 2010*a*, 19; Waterhouse 2010. This case has similarities to Georgia, where the Crown sought to promote settlement to shore up the southern frontier against attacks by Spain and Native Americans by chartering a "charitable" colony that resettled the English poor. Paupers were ineligible to vote in England, and in Georgia, they were subjected to strict rules about land management to serve this military purpose. Georgia did not hold its first elections until twenty-two years after the initial settlement; see McKinley 1905, 163–168.

[123] Keith 1912, 25–41.

[124] Morrell 1930, chs. v and xiii; Belich 2010.

in the metropole, and changes at home led to colonial reforms. However, failed attempts to reassert central control prompted rebellions and the loss of most of the Spanish and Portuguese American empires.

3.4.1 Oligarchy in the Dutch Empire

Like Britain, the Netherlands had a nonabsolutist form of government. However, the political system in the Netherlands was an even narrower oligarchy than in Britain and lacked a tradition of direct national elections. Consequently, a higher fraction of Dutch colonies had electoral institutions than ones with authoritarian metropoles, but much lower than British colonies.

The *ancien régime* Netherlands had a highly decentralized political system.[125] The de facto head of state was the stadtholder, a role filled by the prince of the House of Orange. The importance of the stadtholder varied over time, and most provinces lacked one in two different periods (1650–1672 and 1702–1747). The main governing body was the States-General, an indirectly elected assembly of delegates from the seven provinces; a "permanent congress of ambassadors" rather than a sovereign legislative and executive body.[126] Municipal councils within each province, dominated by the leading families, provided the delegates (either by election or appointment) to the provincial estates and the States-General. Overall, a small oligarchy of approximately 10,000 individuals controlled the allocation of almost every important provincial and municipal office.[127] Dutch colonies were ruled by proprietary corporations whose shareholders and directors were drawn from the richest sections of the oligarchy. This oligarchy was roughly two orders of magnitude smaller than that of Britain: approximately 0.1 percent of adults in Holland were regents of towns represented in the provincial estates in 1700,[128] compared to the 4.5 percent of the British population that could vote in 1715.[129]

As Table 3.6 shows, two Dutch colonies (both in present-day Guyana) governed by the Dutch West India Company had elected

---

[125] Clementi 1937, 3–7; Boxer 1977, 11–13.
[126] Clementi 1937, 6.
[127] Boxer 1977, 11.
[128] Price 1994, 19–31; Paping 2014.
[129] Estimate based on numbers presented in O'Gorman 1986, 31.

Table 3.6 *Pre-1850 electoral institutions: Dutch empire*

Colony	Colonial years	First election	Reversals
Essequibo (Guyana)	1621–1796	1739	None
New Netherland (NY/NJ)	1625–1664	None	n/a
Berbice (Guyana)	1627–1796	None	n/a
Netherlands Antilles	1634–Present	Post-1900	None
Suriname	1667–1975	1866	None
Demerara (Guyana)	1767–1796	1767	None

Notes: This table lists every Dutch colony compiled from various sources (in addition to the references in the text, see also Oostindie and Klinkers 2012, 57). We include territories with permanent Dutch settlements and exclude trading posts. These sources provide the start dates for Dutch colonial rule and the end year corresponds with the last year in the Dutch empire or the year of independence. No colony had a fully elected chamber of an assembly before 1850, which we list in the British tables, and therefore we omit this column from the table.

assemblies before the French Revolution, albeit over a century after their initial settlement. The first case was Essequibo in 1739, when free white planters gained two representatives on the Council of Policy and Justice. Later, the growing Dutch plantation population in neighboring Demerara gained the same rights.[130] The States-General, which lacked a stadholder at the time, did not intervene.[131] Political rights extended only to propertied whites and power of the assemblies was limited by appointed governors.

However, most Dutch colonies lacked electoral institutions. In New Netherland (present-day New York and New Jersey), settlers directly lobbied in The Hague for rights of self-governance during a period without a stadtholder in Holland. The governor, under pressure, summoned delegates from the colony's towns in 1653. However, the governor disagreed with settler claims that "our consent or that of our representatives is necessarily required in the enactment of such laws and orders," and he avoided calling regular assemblies for the remainder of Dutch rule in New Netherland.[132]

---

[130] Clementi 1937, 24, 25; Fieldhouse 1982, 53–54. Demerara was settled in the seventeenth century but not separated from Essequibo until 1767.
[131] Clementi 1937, 43–47.
[132] Kammen 1969, 47; Taylor 2002, 255.

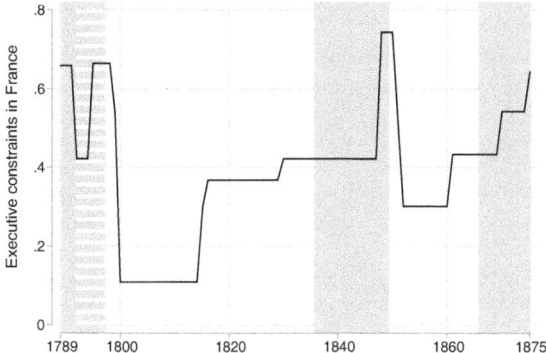

Figure 3.2 French metropolitan and colonial institutions: 1789–1875
Notes: The outcome variable represented by the black line is France's score on
V-Dem's variable for legislative constraints on the executive. The text describes
the gray regions, which denote periods of colonial representation; the period
from 1792 to 1798 is dashed because of the ambiguous status of colonial
representatives.

3.4.2 *French Empire after the Revolution*

The French Revolution unleashed nearly a century of fluctuations
between more parliamentary and more authoritarian regimes in
France. Parliamentary regimes existed during the early French Revolution (1789–1795), Second Republic (1848–1852), and Third Republic (post-1870); constitutional monarchies or other types of hybrid
regimes during the intermediate phases of the French Revolution
(1795–1799), the July Monarchy (1831–1848), and the later years
of the Second Empire (1861–1870); and closed authoritarian regimes
ruled France under Napoleon (1799–1815), the Bourbon Restoration
(1815–1831), and the early years of the Second Empire (1852–1861).
Figure 3.2 summarizes the main changes in metropolitan institutions,
with higher values indicating greater constraints on the executive in
France. Institutional changes in France's major plantation colonies
closely tracked changes in metropolitan institutions. The gray regions
in the figure indicate periods in which any of the major plantation
colonies (Saint Domingue/Haiti, Martinique, Guadeloupe, and French
Guiana) elected representatives to a colonial assembly and/or the
French Parliament.

The first permanent electoral bodies in French colonies were created on the eve of the French Revolution. Desperate for tax revenue,

Louis XVI convened a Council of Notables in 1787. The notables did not solve France's fiscal problems but were receptive to lobbying by West Indian planters. They created local assemblies throughout France and in the main colonies, which replaced older *chambres d'agriculture et de commerce*.[133] In 1789, after the king called the Estates-General into session for the first time since 1614, the settlers resumed their lobbying. Saint Domingue (Haiti) sent a delegation of white planters to Paris that demanded inclusion, and the French metropolitan delegates agreed to admit six representatives to the newly formed Constituent Assembly.[134] Within the next two years, Guadeloupe, Martinique, and several colonies located outside the New World (Bourbon/Réunion, French India, and Île de France/Mauritius) also gained representatives in the French Parliament.[135] In 1790, France granted some legislative autonomy to the colonial assemblies over domestic affairs.[136]

Later changes in colonial policy reflected the decline of revolutionary parliamentarism at home. Colonial assemblies lost their legislative autonomy in 1792.[137] The Constitution of 1795 established the Directory, a more authoritarian regime. By decreeing that the colonies were integral components of the metropole, it banned elections for colonial assemblies.[138] The legal status of colonial representatives in French Parliament was left ambiguous, although colonial delegates were seated throughout the decade.[139]

Napoleon Bonaparte and his Bourbon successors ushered in unambiguously authoritarian regimes that eliminated colonial and metropolitan elections. Napoleon decreed that the colonies were subject to "special laws" that precluded representation, and he also reintroduced slavery.[140] The Bourbon monarchs, restored in 1814, reverted the colonies to the pre-Revolutionary status quo of rule by governors and unelected advisory councils, *conseils générales*, which resembled those of metropolitan France.[141]

---

[133] Maguet 1911, 17–18; Tarrade 1963; Fieldhouse 1982, 39–40.
[134] Fradera 2018, 61.
[135] Maguet 1911, 20–21. Others, such as Guyana, St. Lucia, Saint-Pierre and Miquelon, and Tobago, were deemed too small.
[136] Spieler 2009, 365, 380.
[137] Maguet 1911, 28; Spieler 2009, 365, 385–386.
[138] Maguet 1911, 30–31; Spieler 2009, 366, 399–404.
[139] Spieler 2009, 366, 392–393, 404–407; Fradera 2018, 62–64.
[140] Maguet 1911, 31–32; Spieler 2009, 366, 408; Fradera 2018, ch. 3.
[141] Maguet 1911, 33–34.

The June Revolution of 1830 yielded a more liberal, constitutional monarchical regime governed by the Orleans branch of the Bourbon dynasty.[142] In 1833, metropolitan officials created elected *conseils colonial* to replace the unelected *conseils générales* in Martinique, Guadeloupe, Guiana, and Réunion.[143] During the brief Second Republic that followed the Revolution of 1848 in France, the local assemblies were reduced to advisory status without legislative powers, but the major colonies regained representation in the French Parliament.[144]

The final major fluctuations in French regimes continued into the time period studied in Chapter 4. After overthrowing the Republic in 1852, Louis Napoleon founded the Second Empire and eliminated representation for colonies. When *conseils générales* re-emerged in Martinique, Guadeloupe, and Réunion in 1854, these local assemblies were entirely appointed.[145] At home, the Second Empire liberalized in 1861 by increasing the powers of French Parliament.[146] Under pressure from colonists, Louis Napoleon reformed the *conseils générales* in 1866 along the metropolitan model by allowing for elected officials and granting more financial responsibilities to the assemblies.[147] Finally, upon the establishment of the Third Republic in 1870, metropolitan officials restored colonial representation in French Parliament during the ensuing decade while leaving the elected *conseils générales* in place.[148]

3.4.3 Abortive Reforms in the Iberian Empires

In Chapter 2, we highlighted a general source of tension: large white settler populations demanded high levels of autonomy, but the metropole sought to limit their autonomy to protect its sources

---

[142] Beik 1965, 9, discusses the stronger executive constraints during the June Monarchy. V-Dem legislative constraints on the executive records an uptick, albeit small in magnitude, during this period (see Figure 3.2).

[143] Maguet 1911, 37; Schloss 2009, 152.

[144] Maguet 1911, 42.

[145] Maguet 1911, 44–45.

[146] Homans 1870, 412. V-Dem legislative constraints on the executive records a notable uptick during this period (see Figure 3.2).

[147] Maguet 1911, 47, 49.

[148] Dislère 1906, 366–369; Maguet 1911, 44–61; Winnacker 1938, 261; Idowu 1968, 265, 268.

of rents. Unlike in the British empire, the Spanish Crown had the upper hand in this struggle; settlers lacked electoral representation and were denied access to the upper bureaucracy. However, like their British counterparts, creoles in Spanish America sought greater autonomy and had favorable prospects for successfully revolting. This tension ultimately yielded revolutions throughout Spanish and Portuguese America. Also resembling patterns within the British empire, mainland colonies were more likely to launch anticolonial revolts than were plantation islands.

In the decades preceding the French Revolution, the unwillingness of Spanish and Portuguese officials to relinquish direct authoritarian control clashed with the demands of American-born creoles for greater autonomy and representation. Removing creoles from *audiencia* posts, discussed earlier, created widespread grievances. Unilateral tax increases and centralizing administrative reforms sparked an anti-tax revolt by creoles in Quito in 1765, the large-scale rebellion of the Comuneros in New Granada in 1781, and the multi-ethnic rebellion led by Túpac Amaru in Peru in 1781.[149] One specific demand during the 1781 revolt was for the Crown to choose creoles for *audencia* posts in New Granada.[150] The situation was even more precarious in Brazil, which was larger and wealthier than Portugal. In 1732, a member of the Overseas Council "warned the Crown that the heavy colonial taxes would one day lead the colonists to cast off their loyalty ... the 'larger and richer' would not accept forever being ruled by the 'smaller and poorer.'"[151]

In 1808, a shock to Spanish metropolitan institutions created an opportunity for colonial reform. Napoleon's invasion of Spain displaced the monarchy, which led to the creation of central, regional, and local juntas that organized popular resistance against French occupation. The Junta Central held elections in 1809, called a *cortes* in 1810, and wrote Spain's first constitution in 1812 (which imposed substantial limits on the monarchy). The Junta Central invited some American

---

[149] Elliott 2007, 310–312, 353–368.
[150] Burkholder and Chandler 1977, 118. In another case, in 1771, the City Council of Mexico responded to a government letter that creoles should not hold high positions by contending that "Americans" should occupy most civil and ecclesiastical positions; see pp. 97–98.
[151] McCann 1997, 28.

territories to send deputies (see Table 3.1) and sought to combine Spain and its colonies into a single nation-state.[152]

These reforms, however, failed to resolve creole grievances.[153] A major complaint with the structure of both the Junta Central and the subsequent *cortes* was that, because of malapportionment that favored the metropole, the reforms gave colonists less influence than they deserved.[154] Metropolitan officials also refused creole demands to hold half the seats in the overseas *audiencias* and, more generally, for greater local autonomy.[155] Following the royal restoration of 1814, Ferdinand VII abolished the Constitution of 1812, hence eliminating electoral representation entirely.[156]

Refusals to increase autonomy for creoles, combined with metropolitan weakness, provoked mass settler revolts. Many were led by the local *juntas* that had become increasingly important as imperial control collapsed.[157] Venezuela was the first territory to proclaim independence, in 1811; and Venezuela, Buenos Aires (Argentina), Chile, and New Granada (Colombia) each declined to participate in the elections in 1813. Anticolonial rebellions persisted for the remainder of the decade and resulted in independence for most of Spanish America.

Similarly, in Portuguese Brazil, foreign invasion and liberalization in the metropole prompted formal representation for colonists, which failed to satisfy grievances. However, Brazil's path to independence differed because of a unique event: when Napoleon invaded Portugal, King João VI fled to and lived in Brazil from 1808 to 1821. As residents of the de facto center of the Empire, Brazilian whites won many concessions that an autonomous legislature would have demanded, such

---

[152] Elliott 2007, 375–378.

[153] Demélas-Bohy and Guerra 1996, 46; Elliott 2007, 374–391.

[154] Despite a larger combined population in the colonies than in the metropole, the colonies collectively received only nine deputies (one for each viceroyalty and captaincy-general) compared to metropolitan Spain's thirty-six in the Junta Central. The Constitution of 1812 expanded representation to twenty provinces in the Americas, but disagreements remained over the number of American seats and on key policies such as trade restrictions.

[155] Fisher 1969, 452; Burkholder and Chandler 1977, 140.

[156] Anna 1983, 137. Ferdinand did, belatedly, raise the number of creoles in *audiencia* seats to roughly half, but few were native sons; see Burkholder and Chandler 1977, 142.

[157] Fieldhouse 1982, 21.

as relaxed trade controls.[158] In 1816, the Crown recognized Brazil's equality with the metropole by decreeing the United Kingdom of Portugal, Brazil, and the Algarves.[159] Portugal's Liberal Revolution of 1820 ended this arrangement, as João VI returned to Portugal and accepted new constitutional constraints, including an empowered *cortes* elected by a broad franchise.[160] However, after metropolitan representatives in the *cortes* reimposed trade restrictions on Brazil and replaced Brazilian officeholders with Portuguese ones,[161] Brazilians successfully revolted to gain independence in 1822.

Despite different contexts and institutional structures, the anticolonial revolts in Iberian America had similar causes as those in British North America. Attempts by metropolitan officials to discriminate against large settler populations and to reduce their autonomy (or to simply keep autonomy low) prompted anticolonial revolts.[162] The loyalty of Spain's West Indian plantation colonies (Cuba and Puerto Rico) also echoed the patterns in the British empire, as smaller settler populations could not risk losing the metropolitan connection.[163] Ultimately, the only plantation colony to gain independence was Saint Dominigue (Haiti), where the enslaved majority took advantage of metropolitan weakness to organize a viable revolt.[164] In Appendix Table A.8, we demonstrate a statistically significant negative correlation between plantation colonies and the occurrence of a major anticolonial revolt.

---

[158] Burns 1993, 112; Schultz 2000, 8–9.

[159] Maxwell 1984, 542.

[160] The decision to grant the franchise to free Blacks departed from Spain's earlier refusal to allow this group to vote, which created a more favorable distribution of seats for Brazil. Portuguese officials offered the justification that "this population was socially and economically integrated"; see Nogueira da Silva 2011, 93, 99–101.

[161] Burns 1993, 118–123.

[162] Simon 2017.

[163] Elliott 2007, 391. European settlers in Cuba fought a series of wars to gain independence from Spain later in the nineteenth century, but only after a sizable increase in the European percentage of the population during the nineteenth century (68 percent by the 1870s) as forced-labor production declined in value; see Rogoziński 2000, 201.

[164] The Haitian Revolution also influenced the move toward independence in the neighboring Dominican Republic, which Haiti occupied for two decades.

3.5 Conclusion

Differences in metropolitan political institutions explain if and when the early New-World colonies gained representative institutions. In the mid-eighteenth century, electoral institutions were (nearly) exclusive to the British empire. English citizens with voting rights at home pressured metropolitan officials through lobbying and nonparticipation. By contrast, the authoritarian powers practiced a more centralized style of rule and denied requests for elected legislatures even when doing so undermined colonial tax collection and limited the colonial population.

Yet by the nineteenth century, British colonies were less distinctive than their formerly authoritarian counterparts. Newer British colonies were primarily conquered from other empires. Their non-English settler populations were delegated lower levels of institutional autonomy or denied representation outright, at least until the free English white population grew in size. Conversely, the French Revolution spurred reforms in the formerly authoritarian metropoles, although colonies within the Iberian empires gained independence shortly afterward and the French reforms were periodically reversed in response to regime changes in Paris.

Variance in early electoral institutions affected subsequent outcomes. Many colonies analyzed in this chapter gained independence. Their experiences under colonialism shaped patterns of postcolonial democracy, as we discuss in Chapter 6. As the early settler colonies gained independence, European empires became less centered on the New World. Increasingly, Western empires encompassed colonies with small or nonexistent populations of white settlers, or declining white populations in the long-standing West Indies colonies. In Chapter 4, we examine how these changes altered trends in electoral institutions.

4 | *Imperial Expansion and Restrictive Elections: 1850–1945*

During the nineteenth and early twentieth centuries, the European powers replaced their lost American colonies with new ones in Africa, Asia, and the Pacific. Unlike the cases discussed in Chapter 3, white settlers were never a majority in these colonies, and in most were only a tiny minority. In some cases, a non-white middle class arose that was educated in the colonizer's language and political system. These developments began the shift in power within the colonies from settlers toward non-whites.

Drawing from the theoretical framework in Chapter 2, wherever whites settled in sizable numbers, we expect early representative institutions with small franchises and a level of autonomy commensurate to the size of the white population. Nonsettler cases with a middle class educated in the colonizer's language should also gain early electoral representation, although with a restricted franchise and low autonomy. A final factor that should keep franchise size low throughout the earlier parts of this period was limited franchises within Europe. However, whenever mass franchise expansion occurred in the metropole, this should create a permissive condition for mass franchises overseas.

Three empirical patterns during this period support these theoretical expectations. First, white settlers became a sizable minority in certain parts of Africa, which yielded electoral representation. Even some very small white communities gained political representation, albeit with more limited autonomy. Settler-minority regimes strongly opposed political rights for non-whites.

Second, settlers reversed their support for electoral institutions when their dominance was threatened. This occurred in the British West Indies in the mid-nineteenth century when a rising class of emancipated Blacks confronted a numerically and economically weakened planter class. Settlers responded to the prospect of political control by Black politicians by disbanding their elected legislatures and accepting direct

British Crown rule. Electoral representation re-emerged in the 1920s, following pressure from the Black middle classes. Distinct metropolitan institutions in France yielded a divergent trajectory for their West Indian colonies.

Third, in some colonies with few settlers, a non-white middle class educated in the colonizer's language emerged. These elites were especially strong in the major port cities in South Asia and West Africa. Non-white elites in these areas gained representation by the 1920s, although with limited autonomy and a narrow franchise. In the Middle East, previously Ottoman territories gained broad suffrage because of a credible threat of revolt, which previews the conditions discussed at length in Chapter 5.

Overall, nearly half the colonies in the sample considered in this chapter gained some form of national elections before 1945. This is striking given the absence of the main pressures discussed for earlier periods (very large settler populations; see Chapter 3) or later periods (the ability of non-Europeans to organize a mass revolt; see Chapter 5), which are among the most prominent causal factors discussed in existing research. Instead, small – but politically influential – white settlements and the rise of non-white middle classes propelled electoral development in the century before World War II.

4.1 Main Patterns

Existence of Electoral Institutions

By 1945, all *settler-minority* colonies and almost all *non-white middle-class* colonies had electoral institutions, as Figure 4.1 shows.[1] Most of these gains occurred in the twentieth century as white settlers throughout Africa gained representation and elections were introduced in South Asia and select port cities in West Africa.[2] In the British West Indies (Figure 4.2), representative assemblies for settlers were widespread in the mid-nineteenth century. They collapsed over the next

---

[1] We discuss the operationalization of each colonial category in Appendix A.2.
[2] Dips in the settler line in early years occurred when new colonies entered the sample and did not immediately gain representative institutions, when colonies switched categories (we code the West Indies cases as switching from settler minorities to non-white middle classes in 1883, fifty years after emancipation in the British empire), or (as in Jamaica in 1865) when elections were eliminated.

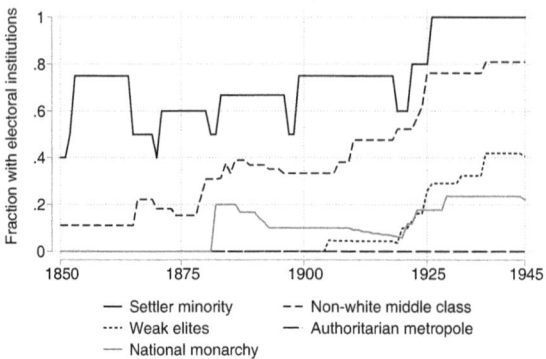

Figure 4.1 Electoral institutions: 1850–1945
Notes: The outcome variable indicates the existence of an electoral body (either a territory-wide colonial body or colonial seats in the metropolitan parliament), averaged across categories of colonies over time. Appendix Table A.9 lists the sample of colonies and the category for each.

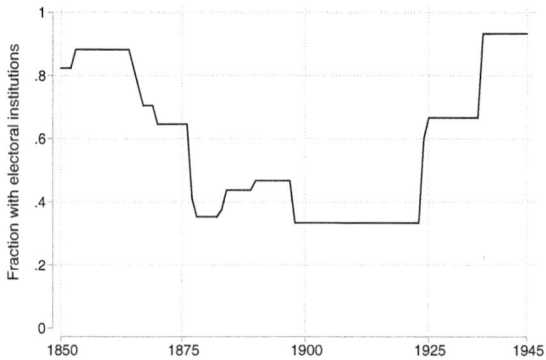

Figure 4.2 Electoral institutions: British West Indies
Notes: The outcome variable indicates the existence of an elected, territory-wide colonial body, averaged across all British West Indies colonies over time. The sample is listed in Tables 3.3 and 3.4 and contains many colonies not in V-Dem (Barbados, Jamaica, and Trinidad and Tobago are the only colonies also in Figure 4.1). This is nearly identical to the list in Table 4.3, after St. Kitts/Nevis and Trinidad/Tobago were each merged in 1882 and 1889, respectively (we change the units in the present figure after each merger).

half century, as captured by the large dip in the line during this period, before pressure from Black middle classes yielded revivals in the twentieth century.

Electoral institutions were rarer elsewhere. *Authoritarian metropole* colonies lacked electoral institutions,[3] the upward trend in *national monarchies* was driven solely by the Middle Eastern Mandate cases of Iraq and Jordan, and less than half of *weak elite* colonies had gained electoral institutions by 1945. Settler minorities and non-white middle classes are each statistically distinguishable from every other category in 1945, even when accounting for alternative explanations such as historical population density, precolonial state institutions, precolonial institutions of local direct democracy, and Protestant missionaries.[4]

Policymaking Autonomy
Colonial assemblies, where present, usually had relatively low policy-making autonomy. For all forty-seven colonies with an elected colonial assembly in 1945, we compiled information about three common limitations on institutional autonomy.[5] In total, 62 percent of colonies had at least one of the following three restrictions on autonomy: colonists elected a minority of members for the assembly (40 percent of cases), the assembly lacked powers over finances (26 percent), or elections were indirect (17 percent). Nor was autonomy necessarily high for local assemblies not inhibited by any of these three restrictions. In the French West Indies and Senegal, local *conseils général* had relatively limited legislative powers.

The largest settler colonies were the main exceptions with high autonomy. Pressure from settlers in Cape, Natal, and Southern Rhodesia yielded internal self-governance, similar to earlier British settler colonies in North America and the West Indies. The Middle Eastern Mandates also had high internal autonomy, which reflected their credible threat to revolt. However, except in Israel and Lebanon, the electoral assembly itself lacked powers over finances (which were controlled by a monarch) or was indirectly elected.

---

[3] The only exceptions occurred during the later years of the French Second Empire, as discussed in Chapter 3 (see Figure 3.2). None of these colonies are in the V-Dem sample, however.

[4] See Appendix Table A.10.

[5] This count is based on the colonies listed in the tables throughout the chapter, not all of which are in V-Dem.

Suffrage

The franchise also tended to be restrictive. For all forty-seven colonies with an elected colonial assembly in 1945, we compiled information about three common franchise restrictions. In total, 85 percent of cases had at least one of the following restrictions. Economic criteria (property-owning, income, or tax-paying requirements) or educational requirements (literacy in a European language) for voting were present in 62 percent of cases. Communal rolls, which consisted of different seats and electoral lists for whites and non-white groups, existed in 36 percent of cases. Geographic restrictions, where only privileged port cities elected representatives to a local or metropolitan council, were less common (11 percent of cases) and almost exclusively confined to West Africa.[6]

In Figure 4.3, we plot the percentage of adults with the legal right to vote, differentiated by colonial category. We restrict the sample to colony-years in which electoral institutions existed to summarize franchise size in cases that had elections. Suffrage was extremely limited in settler minority colonies: in 1945, an average of 7 percent of adults had the right to vote. Some non-white middle-class colonies gained universal suffrage by 1945, including Jamaica, Sri Lanka, and the French West Indies. Yet suffrage tended to be low in other colonies with non-white middle classes. The average in this category was 22 percent of adults with the right to vote, which is statistically discernible from the other categories.[7] Several Middle Eastern cases (not shown in the figure) nominally had universal male suffrage, albeit to indirectly representative bodies that lacked legislative powers.

Democracy Levels

Limitations on both policymaking autonomy and the franchise yielded low aggregate democracy scores. Colonies with a non-white middle-class or settler minorities were more democratic than the other

---

[6] Restricting the franchise to men was also standard, albeit with some exceptions. For example, women gained the right to vote in Jamaica in 1919 and in both Trinidad and Tobago (over 30 years old) and the Gold Coast (Ghana) upon the introduction of elections in the 1920s; see Keltie 1925, 332, 338, and Wight 1946*b*, 44.

[7] See Appendix Table A.11. The French West Indies are not counted in this average because they lack data in V-Dem.

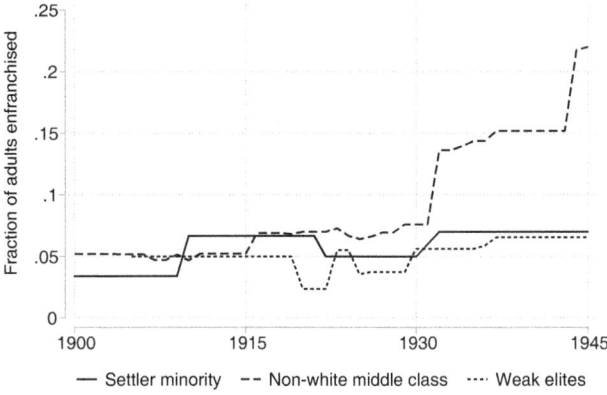

Figure 4.3 Franchise size: 1900–1945
Notes: The outcome variable is the V-Dem variable for the fraction of the adult population with the legal right to vote, averaged across categories of colonies over time. Appendix Table A.9 lists the sample of colonies and the category for each; in the present figure, we include only colony-years in which an electoral institution existed. We exclude the former Ottoman territories from the present figure because they are outliers with early male suffrage. Only one other national monarchy had electoral institutions at this time, and hence we omit a line for this category (in Swaziland, 3 percent of the population was enfranchised). There is no line for authoritarian metropole colonies because no such cases had electoral institutions between 1900 and 1945.

categories, as shown in Figure 4.4.[8] However, as of 1945, the two privileged categories nonetheless had very low average democracy levels in absolute terms, 0.13. This is slightly lower than the average score among global regimes classified as closed authoritarian in 2022. For colonies in any other category, the average democracy score in 1945 was lower than the score for every country in the world in 2022, except Saudi Arabia. Restrictions on autonomy contributed to low democracy scores. The average score in 1945 was 0.06 among colonies in which the elected assembly had only advisory powers and 0.10 where elections were confined to select port cities. Democracy scores were higher,

---

[8] As shown in Appendix Table A.12, non-white middle class is statistically distinct from every category except settler minorities, whereas settler minorities are not distinct from the other categories. The null result stems mainly from the higher variance among settler-minority colonies (only South Africa and Zimbabwe had high scores).

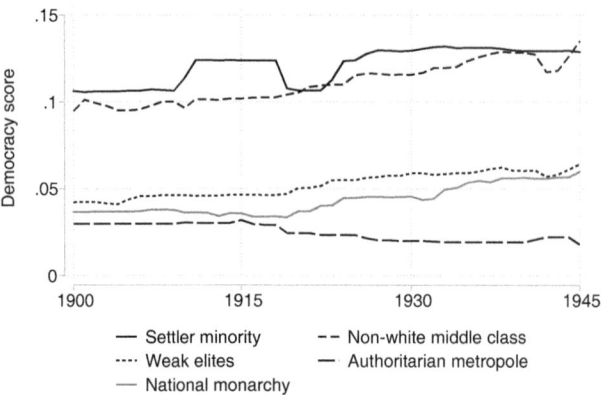

Figure 4.4 Democracy scores: 1900–1945
Notes: The outcome variable is the V-Dem electoral democracy index, averaged across categories of colonies over time. Appendix Table A.9 lists the sample of colonies and the category for each.

albeit still low in absolute terms, in colonies lacking either restriction (0.18).

4.2 Settler Minorities in Africa

White settlements were much smaller in territories colonized during the nineteenth and twentieth centuries. Precolonial population density tended to be higher, many areas had larger states, and the indigenous population was not decimated by European diseases. Nonetheless, certain areas of Africa offered favorable prospects for whites to replicate European-style farming practices.[9] The most important of these were three colonies where settlers were a somewhat large minority (Cape/South Africa, Southern Rhodesia/Zimbabwe, and Algeria) and two cases in which Europeans did not exceed 2 percent of the population but were nonetheless influential (Kenya and Northern Rhodesia/Zambia).[10] White settlers used their political leverage for both pro- and antidemocratic purposes. They gained electoral representation but kept the franchise entirely or almost exclusively for

---

[9] Paine 2019*b*.
[10] For comparative discussions, see Good 1976; Mosley 1983, 1; Lutzelschwab 2013. The importance of Europeans in Northern Rhodesia stemmed in large part from their connection with whites in Southern Rhodesia.

themselves. Buttressing these privileges, bifurcated citizenship regimes distinguished whites from Africans and Arabs. Table 4.1 lists these and every other colony in which white settlers in Africa gained electoral representation before 1945.

South Africa
The first elections in Cape Colony occurred in 1853, roughly five decades after the British conquest. As in Canada, the initial absence and the eventual adoption of elections can both be explained by changes in the ethnic composition of the white population. In the 1820s and 1830s, British officials believed that Dutch speakers would be the dominant element among the white population and that Africans were "unfit" to exercise the franchise.[11] However, the English settlement grew in the following decades.[12] Repeated petitions, large settler protests, and lobbying against a proposal to send convicts to the Cape finally induced British officials in 1853 to create a fully elected bicameral legislature.[13] The high property-owning requirements for holding office favored the British settlers and enabled them to dominate the legislature until the 1880s, despite comprising a minority of the white population.[14] In 1856, the neighboring British colony of Natal followed the Cape's path by transitioning from a nominated legislative council to one with an elected majority.[15] Both colonies gained full autonomy over internal affairs later in the nineteenth century.[16] These two colonies gained dominion status in 1910 as part of the Union of South Africa.

The Cape Qualified Franchise was formally nonracial, as mandated by the Colonial Office, but settlers effectively eliminated African voting rights over time.[17] Following a spike in registration by African voters starting in 1884, Cape legislators passed new education, income,

---

[11] Trapido 1964, 37, 40–41; Watson 1990, 70–71.
[12] The entire European population was one third of the total in 1865, the year of the first census; see Census 1865, viii. This percentage declined over time as Cape grew in territorial size and incorporated more Africans, which is why we code this case as a settler-minority colony rather than settler dominant.
[13] Martin 1865, 614; Saunders 2010, 281–282; Trapido 1964, 40.
[14] Trapido 1964, 46–54.
[15] Wight 1946a, 167; Martin 1865, 618.
[16] Keith 1912, 41–55; Kiewiet 1936, 441.
[17] Hailey 1957, 159–161, 190.

Table 4.1 *Pre-1945 electoral institutions: White settlers in Africa*

		Restrictions on autonomy			Franchise restrictions		
Colony	First election	Indirect elections	Minority of seats elected	No powers over finances	Geographic restrictions	Communal rolls	Economic/education restrictions
Cape (South Africa)*	1853						✓
Natal (South Africa)*	1856						✓
Algeria							
French Parliament	1871		✓			✓	
Local assembly	1898					✓	
S. Rhodesia (Zimbabwe)*	1899		Until 1914				✓
N. Rhodesia (Zambia)	1918		✓			✓	
Kenya	1920		✓			✓	
Bechuanaland (Botswana)	1920			✓		✓	
Swaziland	1921			✓		✓	
Tunisia	1922			✓		✓	
SW Africa (Namibia)	1926			✓		✓	

Notes: This table lists every colony in Africa with electoral institutions prior to 1945 in which the predominant electoral element was Europeans. Some, but not all, of these cases meet our threshold for *settler minority* (Europeans at least 5 percent of the population). In the statistical analysis, South Africa is a single unit. Appendix A.2.5 summarizes cases not analyzed in the text.
* Three cases gained responsible government, or full autonomy over internal affairs, prior to 1945: Cape (1872), Natal (1893), and Southern Rhodesia (1923). Cape and Natal gained dominion status in 1910 as part of the Union of South Africa.

and property-holding requirements for voting in the 1890s that explicitly sought to keep Africans from voting. White politicians in Natal, threatened by high levels of Indian immigration, decreed in 1896 that "persons not of European origin were disqualified from voting if they were descended from persons who had come from a country which had not hitherto possessed parliamentary institutions." As of 1909, in Cape Colony, whites comprised 23 percent of the population and 85 percent of the electorate; and in Natal, whites comprised 8 percent of the population and 99 percent of the electorate. The Boer-led South African Republic and Orange Free State legally restricted the franchise to Europeans, which the Colonial Office left unchanged under crown rule following the Second Boer War.[18]

Southern Rhodesia

Southern Rhodesia (Zimbabwe) also gained high internal autonomy under white rule. As in earlier North American cases, settlers petitioned for elections and the colony's corporate officers sought to attract more European settlers to the colony. From the outset, Southern Rhodesia was perceived to be a "white man's country" along the lines of South Africa.[19] Whites began electing a minority of the legislative council in 1899 and a majority in 1914.[20] Settlers continued to push for greater autonomy with a concerted campaign for white self-government, including the foundation of a Responsible Government Association in 1917.[21] Although the settler population grew less rapidly than originally envisioned,[22] Southern Rhodesia nonetheless followed the maxim understood by metropolitan officials: "We can never govern from Downing Street any part of [Southern] Africa in which the whites are strong enough to defend themselves."[23] White settlers gained responsible government in 1923 upon the transition

---

[18] Thompson 1971, 337–339.
[19] Chanock 1977, 10–37.
[20] Hailey 1957, 282–283.
[21] Lee 1975, 34, 39, 52; Blake 1978, 179.
[22] In 1901, the 11,000 whites were 2.2 percent of the population. This figure reached 34,000 in 1921 (3.7 percent of the population) and continued to grow over time, reaching 178,000 (8.3 percent) in 1956. Data from Gann and Duignan 1962, 159–160 and Easterly and Levine 2016.
[23] Quoted in Blake 1978, 176.

from corporate to crown rule.[24] As in the Cape and Natal, the franchise in Southern Rhodesia upon gaining responsible government was nominally nonracial, but white leaders in practice discriminated heavily against Africans.[25]

Kenya and Northern Rhodesia

The white settler communities were even smaller in Kenya and Northern Rhodesia (Zambia).[26] Their legislative councils became partially elected in the 1920s, although policymaking autonomy was minimal because Europeans elected only a minority of seats in each.[27] British officials repeatedly rejected claims by settlers to greater autonomy, given their minuscule populations. In 1925, an elected member of the Northern Rhodesian Legislative Council asserted that their body was "to all intents and purposes a Parliament and likely to become a Parliament." However, the governor countered this assertion of high autonomy by expounding the retention of official control.[28] Similar declarations by white settlers in Kenya prompted an official British response that "Primarily Kenya is an African territory."[29]

Africans, despite overwhelming population majorities, could not participate in legislative council elections until after 1945. Each colony had a bifurcated legal system in which Africans were governed by a Native Administration Ordinance, a system of indirect rule that empowered unelected African elites by creating local Native Authorities, Native Treasuries, and Native Courts.[30] The large Indian population

---

[24] Blake 1978, 191–193.

[25] Hailey 1957, 282–283.

[26] Whites never exceeded 2 percent of the population in either colony; see data from Gerring et al. 2022. Therefore, in the quantitative figures and tables, these are coded as weak elite colonies.

[27] Settlers elected eight of twenty-two seats (36 percent) for the Northern Rhodesian legislative council. These followed earlier elections, beginning in 1918, to an advisory council while still under corporate rule; see Hailey 1957, 290. An ordinance of 1919 for the Kenyan legislative council decreed that settlers were to elect eleven seats, Indians and Arabs would have three nominated members, and official members would comprise a majority of the council; see Keltie 1921, 179.

[28] Davidson 1948, 33–34.

[29] Devonshire White Paper of 1923; quoted in Hailey 1957, 190.

[30] Hailey 1950a,b. The precise legal basis for denying Africans the vote differed in each. Northern Rhodesia was legally a protectorate, which made its residents "British protected persons" as opposed to British subjects and

in Kenya was able to gain some elected seats, but lobbying by settlers undermined their request for parity.[31] In 1921, settlers in Kenya
published a pamphlet *Memorandum on the Case Against the Claims
of Indians in Kenya*. The governor impressed upon Colonial Secretary Winston Churchill "the very serious position which I am satisfied
will occur if the demands of the Indians are acceded in toto. Europeans
have organization complete for resistance as a last resort." Before making a final decision on the policy, Churchill met with Lord Delamere,
the leader of Kenya's white community who had previously entertained
Churchill as a guest at his Kenyan estate. Churchill was receptive
to the settlers' demands and forwarded a copy of their proposals
to the India Office, claiming that the document represented his own
views.[32]

Algeria
Whites were also a sizable minority in French Algeria.[33] The *pied-noirs*
gained representation in the French Parliament during democratic periods in France (1848–1851 and from 1871 onward). Although settlers
elected only six seats, small groups committed to a narrow set of
issues enjoyed disproportionate bargaining power because of the unstable parliamentary politics of the Third and Fourth Republics. The
pied-noirs influenced policy through their relationship with the *Parti
Colonial*, an informal caucus that tenaciously promoted colonialism
and defended settler privileges.[34] The *pied-noirs* also used extraparlia-
mentary tactics to gain domestic representation. In 1898, anti-Semitic
riots by urban whites prompted the creation of a new elective assembly, the *Délégations Financières*, which made decisions about financial
and economic measures.[35]

---

therefore ineligible to vote; see Davidson 1948, 18–24 and Wight 1952, 7. All
but the coastal strip of Kenya was a Colony, which legally made its residents
British citizens; see Wight 1952, 5. However, the franchise was initially
restricted only to British subjects of European descent, hence reversing earlier
Colonial Office commitments to nominally nonracial franchises; see Hailey
1957, 296.

[31] Hailey 1957, 296–297.
[32] Maxon 1993, 219–230.
[33] They were 7.4 percent of the population in 1860 and 13.7 percent in 1911;
data from Easterly and Levine 2016.
[34] Naylor 2006, 421; Abrams and Miller 1976.
[35] Roberts 1963, 185; Priestley 1938, 137; Liebesny 1943, 80–81.

Whereas all male French citizens could vote, Muslim Arabs could gain citizenship only after renouncing Islamic Law. Following World War I, to reward the service of Algerian Muslims during the war, Paris passed a series of laws that were collectively known as the Clemenceau reforms. These reforms boosted the number of Muslims who could vote for local councils, but not for the French Parliament or the *Délégations Financières*.[36] Settler resistance in Parliament prevented broader citizenship and voting rights for Muslims. In 1936, *pied-noir* Members of Parliament (MPs) convinced the French Parliament to reject the Blum-Violette bill, which would have enfranchised 25,000 French-educated Muslims without requiring them to repudiate Islam.[37]

4.3 Electoral Reversals and Revivals in the West Indies

European settlers supported electoral institutions for themselves but opposed incorporating the non-white majority. As discussed in Chapter 3, white settlers in the British West Indies had gained electoral representation at various points dating back to the seventeenth century, excluding and dominating the Black majority. However, the political and social position of the white population weakened after Britain abolished slavery in the 1830s. White planters feared that English-speaking Black freedmen would begin to meet the property-owning requirements for voting. White planters reacted later in the nineteenth century by cooperating with London to replace elected assemblies from the Old Representative System with authoritarian crown rule. Of the fourteen colonies with electoral institutions in 1860, all but three had eliminated these institutions by the turn of the century.[38] Electoral representation revived across the region during the 1920s, after a Black middle class had emerged. By contrast, the French West Indies followed a divergent trajectory in which Blacks were enfranchised earlier. A

---

[36] The local assembly had three delegations, or chambers: *colons* (French colonial farmers), other French citizens who paid personal taxes, and native Algerian Muslims. The first two were elected, and Muslim representatives were chosen either by a small electorate (5,000 voters) or appointed. The first two chambers elected over two-thirds of the seats.

[37] Naylor 2006, 139–140, 181–182, 327–328.

[38] See Figure 4.2, located at the beginning of the chapter. Note that throughout this section, we refer to small colonies excluded from the V-Dem data set.

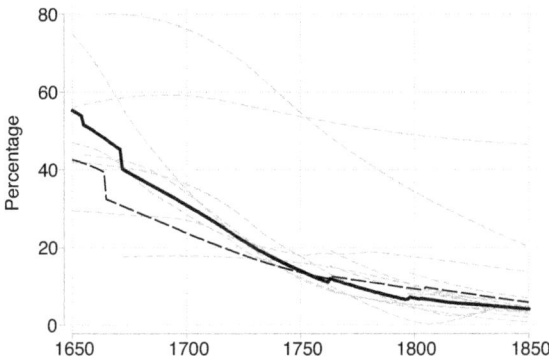

Figure 4.5 European population share in the West Indies
Notes: European population share data from Gerring et al. 2022. The dashed gray lines are seventeen individual British colonies, the solid black line is the average of the fourteen typical colonies (excluding Barbados, Bahamas, and Bermuda), and the dashed black line is the average of three French colonies. British colonies are listed in Tables 3.3 and 3.4 as well as in Table 4.3 (with Trinidad/Tobago and St. Kitts/Nevis each merged by this time).

broader franchise in France than in the United Kingdom made universal male suffrage in the colonies politically possible, especially because the white planter class had always been weaker.

4.3.1 White Minorities and Autocratic Reversals

The rise of slavery in the British West Indies strengthened the economic position of white settlers while weakening their demographic position, as shown in Figure 4.5. By 1850, whites comprised a small minority of the population in almost every British West Indian colony, with an average of 4 percent in fourteen typical colonies (none of which exceeded 7 percent). The three outliers with larger European populations all retained their legislatures: Barbados (14 percent), Bahamas (20 percent), and Bermuda (46 percent). Whites experienced a similar demographic decline across the French West Indian colonies, where the white population did not exceed 6 percent in any colony in 1850.

White slaveowners dominated the colonies until the 1830s despite inferior numbers, although a constant fear of revolts by enslaved

Table 4.2 *Voting population in mid-nineteenth-century British West Indies*

Colony	Year	Voters	Population	% of pop. that voted
Jamaica	1863	1,457	441,300	0.33%
Grenada	1854	191	28,732	0.66%
Barbados	1857	1,350	135,939	0.99%
St. Vincent	1850s	273	22,239	1.23%
Tobago	1850s	135	9,026	1.50%

Notes: Number of voters from Rogoziński 2000, 194. Barbados population measured in 1851 and Jamaica in 1861 from Rogoziński 2000, 188, Grenada in 1829 and Saint Vincent in 1825 from Rogoziński 2000, 120, and Tobago in 1775 from Wells 1975, 253. See also Engerman and Sokoloff 2005, 910.

persons encouraged loyalty to the metropole.[39] Even after slavery ended, restrictive voting rules ensured that the Black majority did not immediately gain political empowerment. Across the colonies, white planters were generally able to keep the franchise small by increasing property-rights restrictions on voting and officeholding.[40] The Jamaican Assembly passed several acts in the 1840s that restricted the franchise, reducing the number of voters from 1,819 to 753.[41] Table 4.2 summarizes available voter data in several colonies. Less than 2 percent of the population could vote in the 1850s, which ensured a white electorate despite no explicitly racial voting restrictions.[42]

Over the longer term, European settlers feared that economic restrictions on the franchise would not prevent Blacks from becoming politically influential. In Dominica, Black representatives gained a majority in the elected lower chamber in 1838, which they maintained

[39] Between 1700 and 1840, thirty-five major slave revolts (involving hundreds or thousands of enslaved persons) occurred across twenty-four colonies in the West Indies; computed by authors from Rogoziński 2000, 161–163.

[40] Rogoziński 2000, 194.

[41] Curtin 1955, 180, 186.

[42] As in Cape Colony, the Colonial Office prohibited explicitly racial franchise rules and some thinly disguised variants. This narrowed the range of possible options for settlers to maintain their political monopoly. In 1834 and 1836, the Jamaican Assembly passed several measures to increase the property-owning requirements "with the specific intention that it would disenfranchise the Negroes." However, the Colonial Office vetoed these measures; see Curtin 1955, 179.

for two-and-a-half decades.[43] An even more immediate threat in most colonies was the rising mixed-race elite, who comprised close to a majority of all representatives in the legislative assemblies across the region in the mid-nineteenth century.[44] In 1852, Britain's Secretary of State for the Colonies warned that Jamaica's white planters would have to reform political institutions to avoid being "overwhelmed in the Assembly by representatives of the colored and black population."[45]

White elites responded to the electoral success (or prospects thereof) of the Black and mixed-race population by eliminating representative institutions. Dominica moved first. White representatives regained a majority in the lower chamber in 1863 and voted to replace the bi-cameral legislature with a single-chamber assembly that included some nominated members. Further changes in 1865 made the number of nominated officials equal to the elected officials, which substantially reduced colonists' policymaking autonomy.[46]

In Jamaica, the most important colony in the region, an autocratic reversal followed soon after whites brutally suppressed a small Black uprising at Morant Bay in 1865. The besieged planter class interpreted the rebellion in starkly racial terms, proclaiming a fear that Jamaica would become a "second Haiti." White planters voted to disband their assembly and to become a British crown colony with a fully nominated legislative council. The main source of opposition to disbanding the legislature came from the mixed-race members of the assembly, who sought to benefit from the same long-term voting trends that frightened whites.[47]

Over the next two decades, most of the region followed these early movers by eliminating electoral representation and moving to British crown rule. Reflecting similar social conditions across the colonies, when St. Kitts followed in 1878, British officials and white settlers stated their belief that the non-white majority would soon vote in large-enough numbers to "threaten the monopoly long enjoyed by the proprietary classes."[48] Electoral institutions persisted only in Bermuda,

---

[43] Martin 1989, 264–266.
[44] Carvalho and Dippel 2020.
[45] Quoted in Green 1976, 363.
[46] Martin 1989, 264–266.
[47] Green 1976, 390–396.
[48] Rogers 1970, 236–237.

the Bahamas, and Barbados, which had the largest white populations in the region (each exceeding 10 percent of the population).[49]

4.3.2 Black Middle Classes and Electoral Revivals

In the decades following electoral reversals, emancipated Blacks gained increasing levels of education in English and more became trained as professional lawyers and doctors.[50] By contrast, the white planter class continued to weaken over time.[51] Although colonial officials had previously sided with white settlers against emancipated Blacks, they increasingly viewed Blacks as more similar to the (expanding) franchise at home. Most of these colonies had regained electoral representation by the 1920s, albeit with circumscribed franchises and autonomy (see Table 4.3).

A generation after the mid-century reversals, half the seats on Jamaica's legislative assembly became elected.[52] The Secretary of State, Lord Derby, "considered that the economic and social advance of the Negro population [in Jamaica] made it less difficult to admit them to a share in the government." The tax-paying requirements in Jamaica post-1884 were lower than in the pre-1865 regime, down from £10 to £1.[53] However, participation nonetheless remained highly circumscribed. Blacks comprised a majority of the electorate, yet less than 1 percent of the Black population was registered to vote in 1886; and, in the 1884 general election, every elected member was white.[54] Voter turnout rose slightly, to 7 percent, in 1894.[55]

After World War I, English-educated Black professionals, ex-soldiers, and trade union leaders throughout the region pressured for the right to elect members to their legislative and local government

---

[49] Gerring et al. 2022, 252–255; Green 1976, 65, 353–354.
[50] Owolabi 2023.
[51] Craig 1952, 32; Rueschemeyer, Stephens and Stephens 1992, 244.
[52] Similar reforms occurred in Mauritius in 1886; see Appendix A.2.5.
[53] Wight 1946a, 75; Will 1970, 59–60. In the 1884 general election, 3,731 voted in elections for the five contested seats, which exceeded the 1,031 who voted in elections for the ten contested seats in the 1863 general election. See also Table 4.2.
[54] Sires 1955, 150.
[55] Percentages calculated by the authors using registration, voting, and population figures from Will 1966, 705–706 and Will 1970, 60–61; plus additional population data from Rogoziński 2000, 188.

Table 4.3 Pre-1945 electoral institutions: Plantation colonies

Colony	First election	Restrictions on autonomy			Franchise restrictions		
		Indirect elections	Minority of seats elected	No powers over finances	Geographic restrictions	Communal rolls	Economic/education restrictions
British empire							
Bermuda	1620						✓
Barbados	1639						✓
Bahamas	1729						✓
Guyana	1739	✓					✓
Jamaica	1884		Until 1944				Until 1944
Mauritius	1886		✓				✓
Fiji	1905		✓			✓	✓
Dominica	1924		✓				✓
Grenada	1924		✓				✓
St. Lucia	1924		✓				✓
St. Vincent & G.	1924		✓				✓
Trinidad & Tobago	1925		✓				✓
Antigua & Barbuda	1936		✓				✓
Belize	1936		✓				✓
Montserrat	1936		✓				✓
St. Kitts & Nevis	1936		✓				✓
British Virgin Islands	1950		✓				✓

Table 4.3 (cont.)

Colony	First election	Restrictions on autonomy			Franchise restrictions		
		Indirect elections	Minority of seats elected	No powers over finances	Geographic restrictions	Communal rolls	Economic/education restrictions
French empire							
Martinique	1866 (1871)						
Guadeloupe	1866 (1871)						
French Guiana	1878 (1878)						
Réunion	1866 (1871)						
Dutch empire							
Suriname	1866			✓			✓
Netherlands Antilles	1936			✓			✓

Notes: This table lists every plantation colony with electoral institutions prior to 1945 that was in the sample for Chapter 3, plus several additional islands located outside the New World that gained early representation (Fiji, Mauritius, and Réunion). Note that St. Kitts & Nevis and Trinidad & Tobago, each formed in the late nineteenth century, merged together two previously distinct colonies. The Bahamas, Barbados, and Bermuda retained the Old Representative System into the twentieth century; see Wight 1946*a*, 171, and Wrong 1923, 80–81. Guyana replaced its Dutch colonial-era constitution in 1928 with a legislative council; see Wight 1946*a*, 164 and Narain 2007, 37. For all other cases, the column for first election lists the first year of representation following any prior reversals (listed in the tables in Chapter 3). For the French colonies, we list the first year with an election to a local *conseil général*, with the first year for elections to French Parliament in parentheses. Although the French West Indian local assemblies lacked any of the explicit restrictions presented in this table, historians routinely stress their mostly advisory role prior to 1945; see Savary 1952, 258; Aldrich 1996, 215. Appendix A.2.5 provides additional details on colonies outside the British or French West Indies.

councils.[56] Colonial officials responded to the ensuing Wood commission report by granting some legislative representation to most islands in 1924.[57] However, the elected seats were minority of the total and the franchise was small.[58] In many cases, the number of appointed officials equaled the number of unofficials (some appointed and some elected), and the governor had an effective veto.[59] Relatively high property-owning requirements deliberately favored the professional classes over the working classes, resulting in electorates between 2 and 10 percent of the adult population.[60] Labor agitation during the Great Depression in the form of strikes and riots prompted another commission, led by Lord Moyne, but the onset of World War II delayed most further reforms until after the war.[61] By 1945, only Jamaica had gained representative government and a large franchise, as we discuss in Chapter 6.

4.3.3 Contrast with French Colonies

Similar demographic changes occurred in the French West Indies: by the nineteenth century, white planters had become a small minority amid an enslaved Black majority. Yet their institutional trajectory differed from British colonies. Long governed without representation under *ancien régime* France, Martinique, Guadeloupe, and French Guinea (plus the Indian Ocean colony of Réunion) gained representative institutions during the periods in which France was democratic at home.[62] Thus, whereas British West Indies colonies lost their elected assemblies in the 1860s and 1870s, the French *vieilles colonies*

---

[56] Rogoziński 2000, 311–312; Harris 1960, 165–166.

[57] Antigua and Barbuda and St. Kitts and Nevis were exceptions in which strong opposition by large plantation owners delayed reforms until 1936; see Forbes 1970, 60. The British Virgin Islands were considered to be a "backwater" and did not regain elections until 1950; see House of Assembly of the Virgin Islands n.d.

[58] Craig 1952, 29.

[59] In 1936, the constitutions of some islands were revised to make the number of elected officials equal the number of nominated officials (both official and unofficial); see Harris 1960, 166; Keltie 1925, 329–341, provides information on the composition of the early legislative councils in each case.

[60] Harris 1960, 166; Marshall 1972, 11.

[61] Rueschemeyer, Stephens and Stephens 1992, 244; Rogoziński 2000, 313–314.

[62] See Table 3.1 and Figure 3.2 in Chapter 3.

gained them and empowered non-whites. Differences in metropolitan institutions and in the power of white settlers yielded this divergence.

Suffrage was broader in France than in the United Kingdom. Male suffrage was universal in the French Second and Third Republics, which was extended to France's major plantation colonies in 1848 and then again in the 1870s.[63] The reforms in 1848 coincided with the end of slavery, and thus formerly enslaved persons immediately gained the right to vote in the West Indies.[64] Victor Schoelcher, French Undersecretary of State for the Colonies and lead author of the 1848 emancipation legislation, argued that emancipated slaves needed immediate civil equality and political representation to become integrated into French society.[65] By contrast, the franchise was much smaller in the United Kingdom, and the paternalistic and racist views that justified the restrictive franchise at home influenced decisions about the West Indies.[66] A typical view in the Colonial Office was to oppose franchise expansion in the West Indies because "democracy in the hands of the uneducated blacks would result."[67] Amid the declining security environment in the 1860s, British officials instead opted to restrict the franchise, which reflected a long-awaited response to strip representation from declining oligarchies who routinely frustrated metropolitan objectives.[68]

Second, although French planters resisted attempts to incorporate non-whites into the political arena, they were less politically influential than their British counterparts.[69] Planters supported the government during the Second Empire but were displaced upon the founding of the Third Republic. Leaders of the governing Republican party retaliated

---

[63] Savary 1952, 258; Aldrich 1996, 212.

[64] Aldrich 2000.

[65] Owolabi 2023, 216–217.

[66] Smith 1994, 142.

[67] Quoted in Curtin 1955, 181.

[68] Rogers 1970; Green 1976, 395–396. Imposing authoritarian institutions throughout the West Indies perpetuated the new standards that Britain had set in Trinidad and St. Lucia, captured from Spain during the Napoleonic Wars, where they refused to grant elected assemblies; see Wrong 1923, 137–138. As far back as 1839, Henry Taylor (the second-ranking official in the Colonial Office) proposed legislation to shift the older colonies to crown colony rule amid a heated dispute between the Jamaican Assembly and British officials; see Curtin 1955, 179.

[69] Schloss 2009, 152–153.

by pushing the planters aside and replacing them with mixed-race elites they saw as progressive allies.[70]

4.4 Port Cities and Non-European Middle Classes

Some colonies developed early electoral institutions without influence from or interference by white settlers. Non-white elites educated in the colonizer's language and familiar with the metropolitan political system emerged in select port cities. This yielded a middle class that agitated and lobbied for institutional concessions. Early elections in South/Southeast Asia and West Africa were held under small franchises and to bodies with little power. By contrast, the Middle Eastern Mandates foreshadowed the types of reforms that became prevalent after World War II in which revolts spurred early elections and independence.

4.4.1 India

In India, peaceful agitation by a small, Western-educated elite resulted in electoral institutions with limited franchises and autonomy. Like settlers in Africa, these elites proclaimed their loyalty to the empire while simultaneously petitioning for autonomy. Table 4.4 summarizes these and other cases in South and Southeast Asia with early elections. We discuss the other colonies, most of which entailed even more highly circumscribed electoral concessions, in Appendix A.2.5.

A middle class emerged in India because the colonial state and European export firms needed to train clerks literate in English, and Indians perceived advantages to interacting with the colonial state in its own language.[71] Beginning in the nineteenth century, the colonial state encouraged Western education for Indians. Thomas Babington

---

[70] The Republicans calculated (correctly) that their party would gain additional seats in the French Parliament if they fostered non-white majorities in the colonies; see Owolabi 2023, 219–221. This reflects the different calculus that metropolitan officials faced depending on whether the representative institutions in question were located in the colonies or in the metropole.

[71] The European population in India was small and predominantly employed by the government. In 1921, 67 percent of Europeans worked in the army or public administration, compared to only 12 percent in trade, agriculture, mining, or industry; see Census of India 1922, I: 2, 245.

Table 4.4 *Pre-1945 electoral institutions: South and Southeast Asia*

Colony	First election	Restrictions on autonomy			Franchise restrictions		
		Indirect elections	Minority of seats elected	No powers over finances	Geographic restrictions	Communal rolls	Economic/education restrictions
Cochinchina (Vietnam)	1880	✓	✓		✓		✓
Philippines	1907		Until 1916			✓	✓
India	1910	Until 1920	Until 1920			✓	✓
Ceylon (Sri Lanka)	1910		Until 1923			Until 1931	Until 1931
Dutch East Indies (Indonesia)	1917	✓	✓	✓		✓	✓
Burma (Myanmar)	1923					✓	✓

Notes: This table lists every colony in South and Southeast Asia with electoral institutions prior to 1945. The text discusses India, and Appendix A.2.5 discusses every other case.

Macaulay, who served on the Supreme Council of India between 1834 and 1838, declared in his influential *Minute on Indian Education* that "we must at present do our best to form a class who may be interpreters between us and the millions whom we govern, a class of persons Indian in blood and colour, but English in tastes, in opinions, in morals and in intellect."[72] The first government colleges were established in 1835 as were the first three universities in 1857. By 1931, 3.8 million Indian men were literate in English. Secondary schools enrolled 2.2 million students and universities enrolled 92,000 students.[73]

Expanded access to education created a class of wealthy, English-taught Indians. This middle class was especially large in the three presidency cities of Calcutta (Kolkata), Madras (Chennai), and Bombay (Mumbai). These port cities, over which the British East India Company had gained control in the seventeenth century, served as the launching point for British expansion in India. A disproportionate share of the comprador class, the indigenous civil service, and anticolonial activists were recruited from certain high-status caste groups and religious communities that had embraced English-medium education, such as the Bengali *bhadralok* in Calcutta, Tamil Brahmins in Madras, and Parsis in Bombay.[74] The presidency cities were the home of India's first three universities, hosted the first three sessions of the Indian National Congress, and had the highest fraction of English literates in 1931 (roughly 10 percent of the population).[75]

The earliest electoral reforms were concentrated in the presidency cities. The Indian Councils Act of 1861 created a territory-wide Imperial Legislative Council and granted limited legislative powers to the legislative councils in all three cities. Each created municipal governments that, as of the 1870s, contained elected majorities.[76] As a British official stated in 1876, these reforms responded to dissatisfaction by the "educated middle class ... [which] desired to have a voice and share in the urban administration."[77] However, in addition to franchises circumscribed by tax-paying restrictions, the autonomy of these local

---

[72] Macaulay 1835.
[73] Government of India 1936.
[74] Lee 2017.
[75] Census of India 1931; see Hutton 1933.
[76] Cross 1922, 170–181.
[77] Cross 1922, 172.

assemblies was limited, especially over policies that affected European exporters. When Indian National Congress leaders within the Calcutta municipal corporation refused a permit for a British merchant's warehouse, the government responded by reducing the number of elected members and creating a veto-holding "permanent committee" with a majority of Europeans, which triggered the elected members to resign in 1899.[78]

The same class of Indian elites led the push for national-level representation. Leaders among the English-educated elite were highly effective at navigating the British political system, such as the "Unofficial Ambassador of India," Dadabhai Naoroji. While teaching at University College London, he founded the London Indian Society and its successor, the East India Association. These pressure and discussion groups aimed to promote Indian interests through lobbying and petitioning to government committees.[79] Naoroji's "The Poverty of India," originally delivered as testimony to the Select Parliamentary Committee on East India Finance, developed the theory that the "drain" of external rule was impoverishing India. His fundamental grievance concerned the absence of political representation, complaining that Indians "are not allowed any vote in the Imperial Parliament or a vote in the Indian Legislative Councils on their own financial expenditure." These facts made it "a mockery and an insult to call the Indians 'fellow subjects and citizens of the Empire.'"[80] Naoroji's highly effective rhetorical strategy was to repeatedly proclaim his loyalty to the British crown and his gratitude for the "many blessings of law and order" that Indians gained while simultaneously highlighting that many specific colonial practices were "un-British" and likely to diminish support for British rule in the long run.

The Indian National Congress, of which Naoroji was a founding member, engaged in a similar program of elite-driven loyalist activism. The Congress was firmly committed to "constitutional agitation for our rights," in particular representation in the legislative councils and the civil service.[81] The early Congress was firmly rooted in the English-speaking bourgeoisie and its initial members were generally wealthy

---

[78] Ray 1979, 1207.
[79] Patel 2020.
[80] Naoroji 1901, 361.
[81] Quoted in Argov 1964.

and worked in professions such as law and journalism.[82] As late as 1919, 64 percent of Congress attendees were lawyers, 7 percent were journalists, and 4 percent were doctors.[83] These men professed a "deep and unswerving loyalty to the British Crown" and averred that "the principle on which the Indian National Congress is based is that British Rule should be permanent and abiding in India."[84] Their nonconfrontational approach sought to "demonstrate by our conduct, by our moderation, by the justness of our criticisms, that we fully deserve [freedom of association]."[85]

British officials responded to pressure from English-educated Indian groups by granting electoral representation, while acknowledging the rising education levels among Indians and expressing a desire to not alienate moderates.[86] However, these reforms were gradual and limited. The Indian Councils Act of 1892 introduced indirect elections for provincial legislative councils, with constituencies defined by religion. Following the election of a Liberal government, the Morley–Minto reforms of 1909 introduced indirect elections for the Imperial Legislative Council. The Montagu–Chelmsford reforms of 1919 created direct elections for a minority of seats on the Imperial Legislative Council and elected majorities for the provincial councils. However, even at the provincial level, autonomy was restricted by "dyarchy," in which the governor retained full discretion over the policy areas deemed most important, such as finances and police. Economic restrictions on voting limited the electorate to less than 3 percent of the total population

---

[82] Sisson and Wolpert 1988, 21.

[83] Krishna 1966, 424.

[84] Quoted in Argov 1964.

[85] Gokhale 1895, 36.

[86] Lord Minto, the governor of India who sponsored electoral reforms in 1909, wrote (condescendingly) in 1906 that "The growth of education, which British rule has done so much to encourage, is bearing fruit. Important classes of the population are learning to realize their own position, to estimate for themselves their own intellectual capacities and to compare their claims for an equality of citizenship with those of a ruling race, whilst the directing influences of political life at home are simultaneously in full accord with the advance of political thought in India"; quoted in Cross 1922, 189. MP Henry Harrison remarked, "Repress the educated natives, their ambitions and then aspirations and you turn them into a solid phalanx of opposition against the Government; gratify their ambitions, and you make them the allies of the Government"; quoted in Banerjea 1925, 91.

of British India,[87] and certain seats were reserved for groups perceived as loyal, such as landlords and merchants.[88] The next major reform occurred in 1935, which we discuss in Chapter 6.

Disaggregated evidence at the level of district boards further showcases the importance of education for promoting electoral reforms. In Appendix A.2.3, we summarize the positive and statistically significant relationship between the percentage of Indians literate in English and the percentage of seats of district boards that were elected, both measured in 1931.

4.4.2 West Africa

The earliest sites of formal European colonial penetration in West Africa were coastal port cities such as Saint-Louis (Senegal), Freetown (Sierra Leone), and Lagos (Nigeria). An African middle class educated in English or French emerged in these port cities and lobbied for representation. These were the only parts of Africa in which Africans gained the right to vote for a territory-wide legislative body prior to 1945, with the exception of the small Black electorate in southern Africa.[89] Reflecting the small fraction of the colonial population that made political demands, early elections occurred under small franchises and conveyed minimal policymaking autonomy to Africans. Furthermore, only citizens in the major port cities elected officials for the national assembly. Table 4.5 provides summary information for each West African colony with early elections.

Overview

Within West Africa, electoral representation was common among port cities but not elsewhere. Table 4.6 lists fifteen major port cities founded before the 1880s. Of the thirteen in British or French colonies, ten began electing representatives to a territory-wide body before 1945. These included elections to French Parliament and to local *conseils*

---

[87] Misra 1970, 46–77; Mansingh 2006, 197, 400–402.

[88] The 1919 Government of India Act also reserved nine seats for Europeans (out of 104), even though Europeans constituted only 0.06 percent of the population and 0.8 percent of literates; see Census of India 1922, 72; Schwartzberg 1992, 67.

[89] Many of these voters resided in Cape Town and Durban, both port cities.

Table 4.5 *Pre-1945 electoral institutions: West Africa*

Colony	First election	Restrictions on autonomy			Franchise restrictions		
		Indirect elections	Minority of seats elected	No powers over finances	Geographic restrictions	Communal rolls	Economic/education restrictions
Senegal							
French Parliament	1879		✓		✓		
Local assembly	1879				✓		
Nigeria	1923		✓		✓		✓
Sierra Leone	1924		✓		✓		✓
French West Africa	1925	✓	✓	✓		✓	✓
Gold Coast (Ghana)	1925		✓		✓		✓
French Equatorial Africa	1937	✓	✓	✓		✓	✓

Notes: This table lists every colony in West and Equatorial Africa with electoral institutions prior to 1945; in all cases, the predominant electoral element was non-white. The text provides details and sources for all cases.

Table 4.6 *West African port cities and early elections*

Port city	Colonizer	Colony	Early elections
Bathurst	Britain	Gambia	✗
Accra	Britain	Gold Coast	✓
Cape Coast	Britain	Gold Coast	✓
Keta	Britain	Gold Coast	✗
Bonny	Britain	Nigeria	✗
Calabar	Britain	Nigeria	✓
Lagos	Britain	Nigeria	✓
Freetown	Britain	Sierra Leone	✓
Sherbro Island	Britain	Sierra Leone	✗
Cotonou	France	Dahomey	✗
Ouidah	France	Dahomey	✓
Porto-Novo	France	Dahomey	✓
Dakar	France	Senegal	✓
Gorée	France	Senegal	✓
Saint-Louis	France	Senegal	✓
Bissau	Portugal	Guinea-Bissau	✗
Cacheu	Portugal	Guinea-Bissau	✗

Notes: This table lists every town located on the coast shown as colonized in the "West Africa c. 1884" map in Ajayi and Crowder 1985. Crowder 1968 provides background on many of these places.

général in Saint-Louis, Gorée, and Dakar of the Senegalese Four Communes; elections to a local *conseil d'Administration* in Dahomey/Benin (Porto-Novo and Ouidah); and elections to a British legislative council in Nigeria (Lagos and Calabar), Sierra Leone (Freetown), and Gold Coast/Ghana (Accra and Cape Coast). Furthermore, elections were almost exclusive to the towns listed in Table 4.6. Only three other locations held elections prior to 1945: Rufisque (the fourth Senegalese Commune), Sekondi (minor port city in the Gold Coast), and Abomey (Dahomey).[90] Neither of the two port cities in Portuguese Guinea gained early representation, which supports our theoretical expectations about authoritarian metropoles.

To create a proper control group, we use colonial districts within British and French colonies in West and East Africa as the unit of

---

[90] Other than Dahomey, we lack information about the other localities that participated in elections for the French *conseils d'Administration*.

analysis and compare the prevalence of electoral representation based on early European penetration. Two strong proxies of early European penetration are (1) sites of early European trade, much of which stemmed from slaving, and (2) areas with natural harbors or capes.[91] These geographical features enabled Europeans to land their ships, whereas coastal areas lacking these features were largely impenetrable to Europeans, and control over the interior was exclusive to Africans. Ten of the twenty-four districts with precolonial European trading posts experienced early elections (41.7 percent), compared to two among the 288 districts without precolonial posts (0.7 percent); and port cities with early elections were predominantly based in areas with a natural harbor.[92]

British Colonies

All of Britain's major port cities that gained early representation had developed an African middle class educated in English. Freetown (Sierra Leone) was originally founded in 1787 to resettle emancipated Africans.[93] Crown rule began in 1808, during which time Freetown became a commercial center with a sizable middle class of Black Creoles who identified with Britain's "civilizing mission" in Africa.[94] Early colonial governors supported efforts by Protestant missionaries to educate Black Creoles in English, and nearly the entire population of the Colony was enrolled in primary school in the mid-nineteenth century. This rate declined over time but was still roughly half of the population at the turn of the twentieth century, which compared favorably to an enrollment rate of less than 1 percent in the mostly rural Protectorate

[91] Data from Ricart-Huguet 2022. See Appendix Table A.13 for accompanying regressions.

[92] To avoid sampling on the dependent variable, we include colonies in East Africa in the regressions. The aforementioned geographical fundamentals help to account for why early elections for Africans did not occur in East Africa. Of the 134 districts in East Africa, only six had precolonial European trading posts and only five had natural harbors or capes. As of 1885, all the port cities in East Africa were under the nominal control of the Sultan of Zanzibar rather than a European power (see the "East Africa 1885" map in Ajayi and Crowder 1985).

[93] The roughly 400 Black settlers initially elected their own representatives under corporate rule, although this practice ended in 1800; see Wight 1946*a*, 41–43.

[94] Owolabi 2023, 136–137.

area of Sierra Leone.[95] Lagos and Calabar (Nigeria) each had a large number of lawyers and were distinguished by their cosmopolitan nature.[96] These cities produced the majority of Nigeria's newspapers in the 1920s and had the highest rates of schooling, with one-third of all children in Lagos attending compared to 1 percent in the Northern provinces and 5 percent in the other Southern provinces.[97] Accra, Cape Coast, and Sekondi (Gold Coast) also developed sizable populations of Western-educated elites during the nineteenth century.[98]

Starting in the 1890s, these port cities gained elected representation in municipal or town councils.[99] Yet English-educated Africans continued to push for representation in the legislative councils of their respective colonies, given the limited nature of the local institutional concessions and their inability to remedy disliked policies such as colonial favoritism for traditional chiefs over English-educated urban elites. The first coordinated movement formed in 1920, the National Congress of British West Africa. Its initial leading members were T. Hutton-Mills (lawyer from Accra), Casely Hayford (lawyer from Cape Coast), H. C. Bankole Bright (physician and surgeon from Freetown), and H. Van Hien (merchant from Cape Coast). Their institutional goals were limited reforms for legislative councils that would entail some elected seats for urban Africans. They considered this to be a moderate goal, in contrast to complete self-government, reforming the executive council, or demanding universal suffrage.[100] The Congress pressured British officials with lobbying and agitation, such as writing memoranda, visiting the Colonial Office in London, and interviewing with colonial officials.[101]

---

[95] Owolabi 2023, 145.

[96] Tamuno 1966, 2.

[97] Wheare 1949, 56–57.

[98] In the Gold Coast Census of 1921, colonial administrators distinguish these three towns in their commentary throughout the document: Accra (p. 66), Cape Coast (p. 83), and Sekondi (p. 112).

[99] Freetown gained a Municipal Council in 1893 with an elected majority. In Cape Coast and Accra, town councils became half elected and half appointed starting in 1894, following an abortive experiment with municipal elections from 1858 to 1861. The first elections to the Lagos Town Council occurred in 1919. These were the only sites with early municipal elections in British West Africa; see Hailey 1951, 26, 216–217, 287.

[100] Wight 1946*b*, 26–27; Tamuno 1966, 3–4, 19–24; Eluwa 1971.

[101] Wyse 2003, 47.

British officials responded by adding African-elected seats to the legislative councils in each of Nigeria, Sierra Leone, and the Gold Coast, although the institutional concessions were limited in three ways. First, African-elected representatives were a small minority on each legislative council until the 1940s: four of forty-six seats in Nigeria,[102] three of twenty-two seats in Sierra Leone,[103] and three of thirty in the Gold Coast.[104] Second, only a small elite could vote. In Lagos, property and income requirements meant that approximately 3,000 of 40,000 adult African males were eligible to vote, of whom only 1,381 individuals were registered in 1925.[105] Similar rules in the Gold Coast meant that in 1939, 6.2 percent of the population in three port cities and only 0.4 percent in the Gold Coast Colony as a whole were registered to vote.[106] In Sierra Leone's first election, the vote total for each of the three candidates who won seats ranged from 173 to 607.[107] For these reasons, elected officials were exclusively members of the professional, English-speaking intelligentsia, such as lawyers, doctors, clergymen, schoolmasters, ex-civil servants, and newspaper directors.[108]

The third limitation was perhaps the most important impediment to subsequent democratic development. Although each legislative council made laws applicable for a broader territory, only these port cities elected their representative.[109] Other parts of these colonies were represented by British-appointed unofficials or not at all. In Sierra Leone, all government-appointed officials from the rural Protectorate areas were paramount chiefs who were loyalists to the administration.[110] As we discuss in Chapter 6, early elections in West Africa did not coincide with the development of nationally oriented political parties, unlike in cases such as India and Jamaica where elections were more nationally representative at an earlier date.

---

[102] Wheare 1949, 38.
[103] Hailey 1951, 327–328.
[104] Wight 1946*b*, 41–45.
[105] Wheare 1949, 55–56, 65.
[106] Wight 1946*b*, 44.
[107] Wyse 2003, 57.
[108] Wheare 1949, 63; Wight 1946*b*, 41–44, 71; Hailey 1951, 327–328.
[109] See Wheare 1949, 38, for Nigeria, Hailey 1951, 327–328, for Sierra Leone, and Wight 1946*b*, 41–45, for the Gold Coast.
[110] Wyse 2003, 53.

French Colonies

In French West Africa, the privileged port cities were the Four Communes in Senegal: Saint-Louis, Gorée, Rufisque, and Dakar. France's presence along the Senegalese coast dated back to the seventeenth century, and the French government and Catholic missionaries began to establish schools following the Napoleonic Wars.[111] Saint-Louis and Gorée gained a distinctive legal status in 1848 when the Second Republic granted Senegal (which, at the time, consisted only of these two port cities) an elected seat in the French National Assembly. Mirroring voting rights in the metropole, this seat was elected by universal male suffrage.[112] Although the Second Empire ended these elections, the distinct citizenship regime persisted in the major port cities.[113] During the 1870s, following the foundation of the Third Republic, Senegal regained its seat in the French Parliament and its local *conseil général*, with the electorate restricted to the Four Communes.[114]

Africans began to dominate these elections in the 1910s, displacing the numerically minuscule French business community that had pressured for the original concessions.[115] French-educated Africans organized to promote Black political participation.[116] In 1914, Blaise Diagne became the first Black African elected to the French Parliament. His victory signified the first time that Black Senegalese had unified politically to elect a candidate viewed as critical of the colonial regime.[117] Starting in 1919, the newfound ability of Black Senegalese to organize politically enabled them to hold a perpetual majority on the *conseil*

---

[111] Johnson 1971, 25, 139–144.
[112] Crowder 1967, 13–14; Johnson 1971, 26. Although 1848 marked the onset of universal male suffrage in Senegal, these were not the first elections. In 1840, Saint-Louis and Gorée each gained a *conseil général* that was elected on a more restricted franchise; see Idowu 1968, 265.
[113] By the later nineteenth century, Dakar and Rufisque (both located close to Gorée) had each became important trading centers, resulting in four port cities distinguished as autonomous communes by the end of the 1880s. These were the only areas of direct administration in Senegal; see Crowder 1967, 18, Johnson 1971, 25–37, and Nelson 1974, 23.
[114] Crowder 1967, 18; Idowu 1968, 265. In Table 4.5, we list 1879 as the first year with an election to French Parliament, although Senegal temporarily had a seat from 1871 to 1875.
[115] Idowu 1968, 271; Johnson 1971, 93–105; Cruise O'Brien 1972, 48–54.
[116] Johnson 1971, 144; Crowder 1967, 23.
[117] Johnson 1971, 86, 173–174.

général. However, French administrators circumscribed their autonomy by stripping some of the council's powers,[118] and suffrage was not in fact universal even for men because of substantial rural-to-urban migration.[119]

Prior to World War II, the political situation in the Four Communes of Senegal was unique in French Africa. The citizenship concessions granted by the Second Republic were not repeated elsewhere by the Third Republic, which rejected assimilation despite its democratic nature. Consequently, non-Europeans gained early French citizenship rights only in areas with substantial colonial penetration by 1848 (Senegalese Four Communes, French West Indies).[120] The only other electoral bodies in French Africa prior to World War II were largely inconsequential. Local *conseils d'Administration*, established in parts of French West Africa in the 1920s and in French Equatorial Africa in the 1930s, were purely consolatory for the French Lieutenant-Governor and contained only two or three African-elected seats (elected indirectly by tiny franchises) alongside three official members and two elected by French citizens.[121] Even these bodies, though, privileged port cities. A majority of primary schools in Dahomey (Benin) were located in its three major port cities,[122] and Porto-Novo and Ouidah gained two of the three elected seats on the *conseil d'Administration* in the 1920s.[123]

4.4.3 Middle Eastern Mandates

During World War I, Britain allied with Arab groups in the Middle East to fight against the Ottomans. Britain and France then partitioned the newly conquered territories between themselves as League of Nations

---

[118] Johnson 1971, 203, 213–216; Hailey 1957, 340.

[119] Only those born within the Four Communes or who could prove a long residence enjoyed voting rights. Given rural-to-urban migration, this meant that only 5,000 of the 30,000 Africans living in the Four Communes were *originaires* who were qualified to vote as of 1879; see Johnson 1971, 88.

[120] Crowder 1967, 14; Crowder 1968, 167–168. Thus, Muslims in Algeria (which was lightly colonized by 1848) did not gain citizenship rights, which prompted their struggle described earlier in the chapter.

[121] Hailey 1957, 340–341; Nelson 1975, 24–25; Collier 1982, 35; Conklin 1997, 70; Bradshaw and Fandos-Rius 2016, 247.

[122] Staniland 1973, 291–292.

[123] Manning 1982, 266. Electoral concessions were a response to antitax riots in Porto-Novo.

Mandates. The threat of revolt encouraged reluctant colonizers to hold early elections under universal suffrage and to grant early indepen- dence, foreshadowing the conditions that became widespread across the colonial world after World War II (the subject of Chapter 5). In ad- dition, Jews in Palestine and Maronite Christians in Lebanon enjoyed some of the advantages of metropolitan-descendant white settlers. Generally, these electoral reforms were hasty and did not establish stable postcolonial democracy. Table 4.7 summarizes the cases.

The populations of the Middle Eastern Mandate territories had mil- itary capabilities independent of the colonial state because of their participation in World War I and the general instability of the region following the defeat of the Ottoman empire. In terms of government casualties, the revolts in this region were by far the most costly colonial wars between the two world wars. In Iraq and Syria, the constitu- tional reforms that introduced elections responded directly to revolts. In 1920, Iraqis rebelled en masse against British rule with the aim of establishing an Iraqi state. After repressing the revolt, British officials acknowledged the mobilization potential of Iraqi tribes and installed a king and a constitution.[124] However, the monarch was not responsi- ble to parliament, elections were indirect, and the government selected the list of candidates permitted to run.[125] In Syria, French officials repressed the Great Revolt of 1925–1926, which sought to establish an independent Arab state.[126] French popular outrage after the bom- bardment of Damascus prompted elections to a constituent assembly in 1928 to write a new constitution, and the first elections to the Chamber of Deputies were held in 1931–1932.[127] Suffrage was uni- versal for men, although the elections were indirect.[128] In both cases, metropolitan officials explicitly treated these reforms as initial steps toward Arab self-government.[129]

---

[124] Vinogradov 1972, 138–139.

[125] Axtmann 2002, 85–86. In Transjordan, the parliament was similarly weak relative to the ruling monarch; see Dieterich 2002.

[126] This followed earlier French repression of the indigenous Syrian Congress of 1920, which proclaimed democratic aims; see Thompson 2020.

[127] Antonius 1934, 528–531.

[128] Zisser 2002, 216–217. Similar to the communal rolls in Lebanon, there were reserved seats for Christians and Bedouins.

[129] The legal stipulations associated with their Mandate status also encouraged political reform. These Middle Eastern territories were Class A Mandates

Table 4.7 Pre-1945 electoral institutions: Former Ottoman territories

Colony	First election	Indirect elections	Restrictions on autonomy		Geographic restrictions	Franchise restrictions	
			Minority of seats elected	No powers over finances		Communal rolls	Economic/education restrictions
Egypt	1882	✓	✓	✓			✓
Palestine (Israel)	1920					✓	
Lebanon	1922	Until 1934				✓	
Iraq	1923	✓		✓			
Transjordan (Jordan)	1929	✓		✓			
Syria	1931	✓				✓	✓

Notes: This table lists all former Ottoman territories conquered in the late nineteenth or early twentieth centuries with electoral institutions prior to 1945; in all cases, the predominant electoral element was non-white. See Appendix A.2.5 for Egypt, which is not discussed in the text.

Palestine (Israel) and Lebanon held direct elections prior to gaining independence because of metropolitan sympathy toward their non-Muslim populations and the vocal lobbying and agitation of these groups. As of 1945, Palestine had the largest European-descendant population of any colony considered in this chapter (30 percent).[130] Jewish settlers drew on European precedents and created a local Assembly of Representatives in 1920. Elections were direct and universal for Jewish males, but Arabs were excluded. The settlers, although non-British, benefited from metropolitan responsiveness to creating a self-governed Jewish homeland, as espoused in the Balfour Declaration issued during World War I. The Assembly of Representatives served as a quasi-government that held five elections under Mandate rule and was officially recognized by Britain in 1928. Jewish colonists staffed the departments of the quasi-government and considered the elected assembly as the sovereign authority of the territory whose decisions were binding on the Jewish community.[131] Thus, the Jewish community achieved an institutional structure that resembled the white settler colonies of Africa.

In Lebanon, the French favored the Maronite Christian community of Mount Lebanon, many of whose leaders were educated in French.[132] A Representative Council created in 1922 was elected under universal male suffrage. The council contained a mix of elected and nominated members, and elections became direct in 1934. The most important feature of the electoral system was its consociational structure, specifically, quotas of seats for members of different religious groups, which intended to protect the Christian community.[133]

---

decreed by the League of Nations, which the Treaty of Versailles 1920 decreed were ready for some form of autonomy: "Certain communities formerly belonging to the Turkish Empire have reached a stage of development where their existence as independent nations can be provisionally recognized .... The wishes of these communities must be a principal consideration in the selection of the Mandatory."

[130] Data from Gerring et al. 2022.
[131] Kraines 1953, 518–520; Ries 2002, 109–113.
[132] Hartwig and Ghali 1979.
[133] Landau 1961, 120–124; Scheffler 2002, 169–176.

4.5 Conclusion

Non-Europeans became influential actors in some colonies between the mid-nineteenth and mid-twentieth centuries. Individuals who gained education in the colonizer's language often formed a middle class in urban areas who could agitate and lobby the colonial state for electoral representation. Where present, white settlers continued to be important actors, either by creating racially exclusive elections or by abandoning electoral institutions entirely to prevent former slaves from participating.

Even as colonial rule reached its apogee, there was thus a modest move toward electoral representation. Among colonies that gained independence after World War II, nearly half experienced their first election before 1945. Early electoral concessions were typically limited by small franchises, numerous appointed members, or geographical restrictions on where elections were held. In some cases, the representative institution itself was purely advisory and did not control finances.

Nonetheless, early electoral institutions mattered. In the settler-minority colonies, whites often leveraged the institutional position they gained in this period to block decolonization reforms (Chapter 5). In colonies with influential non-white middle classes, early national electoral institutions broadened over time to incorporate the entire population and foster the development of institutionalized parties. In Chapter 6, we link these experiences to postcolonial regime trajectories.

5 | *Mass Franchise Expansion after 1945*

Prospects for successful mass revolts increased dramatically after 1945. Previously unimaginable forms of resistance became viable because of changes in the international system following World War II, accompanied by the spread of nationalist ideas and Western military technology across the colonial world. But the pace of reform and approaches to decolonization varied. Some colonizers moved to mass-franchise elections and high autonomy, ending with formal independence – whereas others sought to cling to power.

Drawing on the theoretical framework developed in Chapter 2, we anticipate that the colonial response to demands for mass franchise expansion depended on the structure of metropolitan political institutions and the influence of the white settler population. Strong threats of revolt prompted metropolitan democracies to expand the franchise because rebellions were costly to combat. By contrast, the domestic political costs of reform were higher in authoritarian metropoles and in colonies with large white settler populations.

Three empirical patterns support these expectations. First, franchise size and legislative autonomy expanded rapidly in most colonies ruled by democratic powers. These processes tended to occur earlier when left-wing governments were in power, who were less tied to the colonial project. Second, white settler elites and the governing class in authoritarian metropoles opposed empowerment for non-whites, who they perceived as an existential threat to their social status and economic rents. This prompted anticolonial revolts by disenfranchised Africans and Arabs. Third, colonial officials sometimes granted autonomy to nonelectoral institutions if doing so would avoid revolt and be acceptable to metropolitan opinion. This desire led to a distinct type of authoritarian decolonization, prevalent among British colonies, in which the colonizer handed off power to a national monarch.

5.1 Main Patterns

Existence of Electoral Institutions

Elections were already common in *settler-minority* colonies and colonies with *non-white middle classes* by 1945, as shown in Figure 4.1 in Chapter 4. In the subsequent two decades, as democratic colonizers responded to the rising threat of revolt, elections became nearly universal among *weak elite* colonies as well, as shown in Figure 5.1. Nearly half of *national monarchs* had an electoral body by 1965, although most of these assemblies were weak vis-à-vis the monarch. Few colonies of *authoritarian metropoles* gained any form of electoral representation, and in Appendix Table A.14, we show that this difference is statistically significant.[1]

Franchise Restrictions

The franchise became large in colonies without vested interests for a minority to cling to power, as shown in Figure 5.2.[2] Among cases

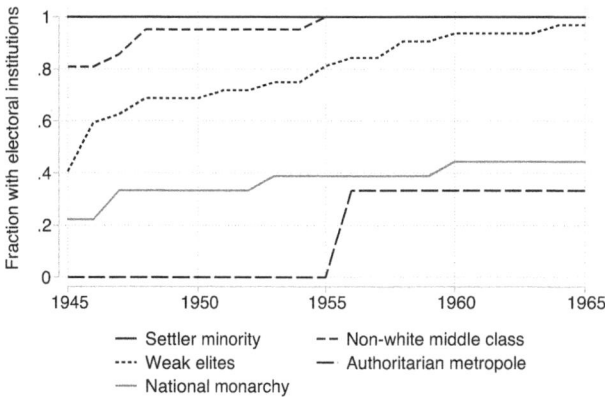

Figure 5.1 Electoral institutions: 1945–1965
Notes: The outcome variable indicates the existence of an electoral body (either a territory-wide colonial body or colonial seats in the metropolitan parliament), averaged across categories of colonies over time. Appendix Table A.9 lists the sample of colonies and the category for each.

---

[1] This and most other regressions for this chapter incorporate the same covariates as Chapter 4: state antiquity in 1500, population density in 1500, precolonial democracy, and Protestant missionaries in 1923.
[2] Appendix Table A.15 provides regressions.

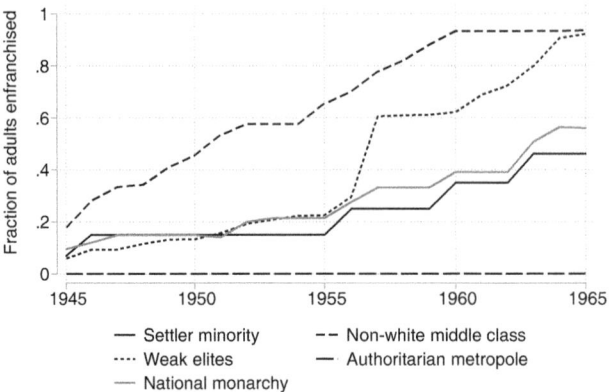

Figure 5.2 Franchise size: 1945–1965
Notes: The outcome variable is the V-Dem variable for the fraction of the adult
population with the legal right to vote, averaged across categories of colonies
over time. Appendix Table A.9 lists the sample of colonies and the category
for each. Unlike the corresponding pre-1945 figure (Figure 4.3), the present
figure contains the full sample, not only colony-years in which an electoral
body existed.

with *non-white middle classes* or *weak elites*, the average franchise size
rose from 11 percent of the adult population in 1945 to 41 percent in
1955 to 93 percent in 1965. By contrast, *settler-minority* colonies and
authoritarian metropole colonies each experienced significant delays
to gaining majority rule, which typically occurred only after lengthy
anticolonial rebellions. The line for *national monarchies* runs largely
parallel to the settler-minority line, albeit with a distinct combination of institutions. All settler-minority cases had elections, but usually
with small franchises. By contrast, fewer national monarchies had any
elections, but those that did often had nominally universal suffrage.
Appendix Table A.15 confirms these differences across categories.

Policymaking Autonomy

Mass franchise expansion usually went hand-in-hand with increased
policymaking autonomy. In the two decades after 1945, *non-white
middle-class* and *weak elite* colonies routinely moved from some
form of representative government (usually with universal suffrage)
to self-governing status to full independence. The main exceptions
were microstates (mostly islands), where revolts were unlikely to succeed. To demonstrate this discrepancy, we expand the sample beyond

the V-Dem colonies to include many colonies with small populations and/or that never gained independence.[3] Among colonial categories that tended to have a negotiated decolonization process,[4] 91 percent with a population exceeding one million in 1960 (N = 45) had gained independence by 1965 in contrast to only 13 percent of colonies with a smaller population (N = 56).

Authoritarian colonizers and powerful settler minorities usually sought to retain a monopoly of political control, regardless of population size. White colonists and metropolitan officials remained preponderant in local assemblies, which exerted minimal autonomy in the authoritarian colonies, and independence was either delayed or declared unilaterally by the settlers.[5] In Appendix Table A.17, we confirm that the discrepancies in the propensity for early independence are statistically significant after accounting for microstates.

Democracy Scores

Non-white middle-class and *weak elite* colonies had converged in many ways by the 1960s: existence of electoral institutions, mass franchises, and high autonomy. But they diverged in overall democracy scores, as shown in Figure 5.3. As of 1965, the average V-Dem democracy score for *non-white middle-class* colonies was 0.36. This slightly exceeds the average score among global regimes classified as electoral authoritarian in 2022. By contrast, the average score for *weak elite* colonies was 0.22, which is closer to the level of a closed authoritarian regime in 2022.[6] Democracy scores in *settler-minority* colonies were lower than those in *weak elite* colonies in 1965, hence reversing the earlier advantage for settler minorities.[7] Democracy scores among *au-*

---

[3] Data from Owolabi 2015.

[4] This includes *non-white middle-class*, *weak elite*, and *national monarchy* cases.

[5] For these purposes, it is useful to think of Zimbabwe as gaining independence in 1980 and South Africa in 1994, given the inextricable connection with majority rule; see Reno 2011.

[6] In Chapter 6, we discuss why the earlier onset of elections in colonies with a large non-white middle class created favorable conditions for promoting higher democracy levels during colonial rule and afterwards.

[7] The settler-minority advantage in 1945 is not statistically significant (see Table A.12), but the weak elite advantage in 1965 is.

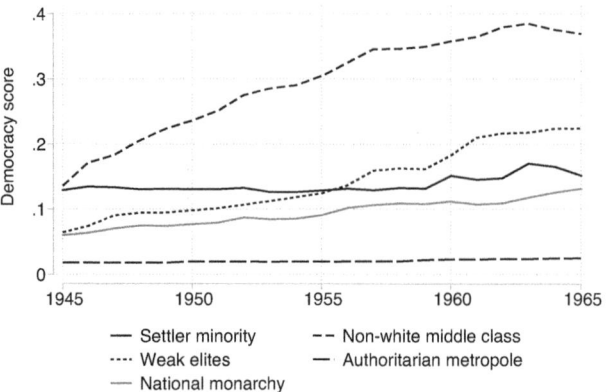

Figure 5.3 Democracy scores: 1945–1965
Notes: The outcome variable is the V-Dem electoral democracy index, averaged across categories of colonies over time. Appendix Table A.9 lists the sample of colonies and the category for each.

thoritarian metropoles and *national monarchies* were notably lower. Appendix Table A.16 confirms these differences across categories.

5.2 Democratic Metropoles and Mass Franchise Expansion

5.2.1 The Rising Threat of Revolt

Starting in the 1940s, several changes made mass anticolonial revolts more viable. World War II weakened the Western European colonial powers economically and militarily, and led to the global hegemony of two anticolonial superpowers (the United States and Soviet Union). The rise of the Soviet Union provided an ideological alternative to contest Western imperialism, which preoccupied Western leaders. A report entitled "Africa in the next ten years" written in 1959 by the British Colonial Office summarized the dilemma: "If Western governments appear to be reluctant to concede independence to their dependent territories, they may alienate African opinion and turn it towards the Soviet Union; if on the other hand they move too fast they run the risk of leaving large areas of Africa ripe for Communist exploitation."[8] Earlier in the 1950s, the Governor-General of Nigeria contended that "we are not strong enough now as a result of two world wars to insist on having longer to build up democratic forms of government

---

[8] Quoted in Hyam 2007, 256.

... partly because of dangers from our enemies, the Communists, we have had to move faster than we should have wished."[9]

The Soviet Union offered aid and arms to communist-aligned anticolonial groups. The Soviet Union and Cuba provided the African Party for the Independence of Guinea and Cape Verde (PAIGC) with military training over a fourteen-year period, large quantities of small arms, and surface-to-air missiles, which enabled them to end Portuguese air superiority.[10] The Soviets also provided aid to the People's Movement for the Liberation of Angola (MPLA), the Mozambique Liberation Front (FRELIMO), the National Liberation Front (FLN) in Algeria, the Vietnamese Communist Party, and the Malayan Communist Party. Chinese-donated heavy artillery further assisted the Vietnamese defeat of the French at Dien Bien Phu.[11]

The anticolonial stance of the United States and United Nations was also influential because American military and economic aid was extremely important in Cold War Europe. The best-known American intervention occurred during the Suez crisis in 1956, when President Dwight Eisenhower used the threat of refusing loans from the International Monetary Fund to compel Britain and France to withdraw from Egypt.[12] American intervention was important at other points as well. For example, Dutch Prime Minister Willem Drees remarked that the Dutch entered into negotiations with the Indonesian rebels to not "antagonize America."[13] The United States also adopted an arms embargo against Portugal, which impeded Portugal from using NATO arms in its anticolonial wars. The consequent distancing of Portugal from NATO amid its wars was a major cause of the discontent among the officers who overthrew the Salazar regime in 1974 and promptly granted independence to the colonies.

Finally, World War II directly destabilized some colonial regimes. Colonies in Southeast Asia were especially vulnerable to revolts because Japanese occupation temporarily severed Western control. Major anticolonial revolts opposed attempts to reimpose European colonial regimes in French Indochina (Vietnam, Cambodia, and Laos), the Dutch East Indies (Indonesia), and British Malaya (Malaysia). These

[9] Quoted in Hyam 2007, 266.
[10] Gleijeses 1997.
[11] Fall 1967.
[12] Boughton 2001, 432–445.
[13] Sulaiman 2008, 158.

conflicts pitted colonial armies against armed local groups who had arisen during World War II either as allies or opponents of the Japanese occupation.[14] Despite reflecting deep-seated hostility to Western regimes, a consolidated colonial state likely would have defeated these rebel groups more easily, as they had in Indochina and Burma (Myanmar) in the early 1930s. Colonial rule in French North Africa was similarly disrupted during World War II by German and Allied invasions, which contributed to the eventual guerrilla war in Algeria.[15]

As the rising threat of revolt raised the costs of maintaining colonial control, the economic benefits of colonialism declined. The drop in international commodity prices in the early 1950s made the colonies a net liability in fiscal terms. In the French empire by the 1950s, public investments in the colonies outstripped the returns from private transfers, which convinced many French officials that autarkic assumptions about benefits of trading within the empire were flawed.[16] Upon becoming the UK Prime Minister in 1957, Harold MacMillan asked the Colonial Office to conduct a cost/benefit analysis for each colony in the empire. They concluded that "the economic considerations tend to be evenly matched and the economic interests of the United Kingdom are unlikely in themselves to be decisive in determining whether or not a territory should become independent."[17] Multinational corporations usually realized the need for reforms as well.[18] Larger firms operating in more modern industries relied less on preserving closed colonial markets because they were more competitive internationally. Many recognized the benefits of establishing a moderate nationalist elite with whom to work after independence rather than potentially letting a guerrilla group take power.

5.2.2 Political Reforms

The newfound threat of mass revolts prompted the major democratic powers to initiate political reforms. As summarized in Tables 5.1 and 5.2, these reforms entailed not only *introducing* elections where they

---

[14] Goodwin 2001; Tarling 2001.
[15] Lawrence 2013.
[16] Fieldhouse 1986, 6–9, 12–17.
[17] Quoted in Brook 1957, 34.
[18] Kahler 1981; Fieldhouse 1986, 9–12, 17–21; Spruyt 2005, 101–104, 124–127.

Table 5.1 *Post-1945 electoral institutions: Non-white middle class*

Colony	First election	Universal suffrage		Year of independence
		Male	Female	
Barbados	1639	1951	1951	1966
Guyana	1739	1957	1957	1966
Suriname	1866	1949	1949	1975
Senegal	1879	1957	1957	1960
Vietnam	1880	1954	1954	1954
Jamaica	1884	1944	1944	1962
Mauritius	1886	1959	1959	1968
Philippines	1907	Post-indep.	Post-indep.	1946
India	1910	Post-indep.	Post-indep.	1947
Sri Lanka	1910	1931	1931	1948
Indonesia	1919	Post-indep.	Post-indep.	1949
Nigeria	1923	1951	Post-indep.	1960
Sierra Leone	1924	1957	Post-indep.	1961
Cote d'Ivoire	1925	1957	1957	1960
Ghana	1925	1951	1951	1957
Trinidad and Tobago	1925	1946	1946	1962
Gabon	1937	1957	1957	1960
Gambia	1947	1960	1960	1965
Seychelles	1948	1968	1968	1976
Singapore	1948	1955	1955	1965
Malaysia	1955	1955	1955	1957

Notes: For colonies whose first election occurred before 1945, see the sources presented in the tables and notes in the Chapters 3 and 4. For colonies whose first election occurred after 1945, see the codebook for Paine 2019*a*. Most data points for male and female suffrage onset are from V-Dem (using variables *v2x_suffr*, *v2msuffrage*, and *v2fsuffrage*), although we used additional sources cited throughout to adjust some years. Year of independence from Hensel 2014.

had not previously been held, but allowing mass franchises, non-white legislative majorities, and moves toward self-governance and independence.

In French Africa, only the *originaire* elites of the Four Communes of Senegal had participated in parliamentary elections prior to 1946.[19]

---

[19] As noted in Chapter 4, the *conseils d'Administration* established in several other colonies were extremely limited in their powers and franchise.

Table 5.2 *Post-1945 electoral institutions: Weak elites*

Colony	First election	Universal suffrage		Year of independence
		Male	Female	
Fiji	1905	1966	1966	1970
Zambia	1918	1964	1964	1964
Botswana	1920	1965	1965	1966
Kenya	1920	1961	1961	1963
Lebanon	1922	1922	Post-indep.	1943
Myanmar	1922	1947	1947	1948
Benin	1925	1957	1957	1960
Guinea	1925	1957	1957	1958
Mali	1925	1957	1957	1960
Syria	1932	1932	1932	1946
Central African Republic	1937	1957	1957	1960
Chad	1937	1957	1957	1960
Congo (Rep.)	1937	1957	1957	1960
Cameroon	1946	1957	1957	1960
Djibouti	1946	1957	1957	1977
Madagascar	1946	1957	1957	1960
Mauritania	1946	1957	1957	1960
Niger	1946	1957	1957	1960
Togo	1946	1957	1957	1960
Comoros	1947	1957	1957	1975
Burkina Faso	1948	1957	1957	1960
Sudan	1948	1948	Post-indep.	1956
Papua New Guinea	1951	1964	1964	1975
Rwanda	1953	1961	1961	1962
Malawi	1955	1964	1964	1964
South Yemen	1955	Post-indep.	Post-indep.	1967
Somalia	1956	1956	1956	1960
Tanzania	1958	Post-indep.	Post-indep.	1961
Uganda	1958	1961	1961	1962
Congo (DR)	1960	1960	Post-indep.	1960
Solomon Islands	1964	1964	1964	1978
Vanuatu	1975	1975	1975	1980

Notes: See the notes for Table 5.1.

Two modest reform laws were enacted immediately after the war, one that allowed Africans to elect several seats in the French National Assembly and another that created local territorial assemblies with low autonomy. However, France's bifurcated citizenship laws initially disenfranchised most Africans, creating "a franchise so restricted that Senegal, with a hundred years of representative institutions, had only 2.9 percent of its population eligible to vote."[20]

By the 1950s, France was acutely aware of the costs of revolt. When withdrawing from Indochina, French Premier Pierre Mendès-France conceded that "as long as we go on losing all these officers and men in Indo-China, as long as we go on spending 500 billion francs a year, we shall have no army in Europe, and only 500 billion francs worth of inflation, poverty, and fuel for Communist propaganda."[21] The Algerian struggle similarly made French officials more willing to implement reforms elsewhere in Africa to avoid new rebellions.[22] Reforms in 1951 broadened the franchise somewhat across French Africa, but the major reform occurred in 1956 – two years after the revolt in Algeria began. The *loi cadre* granted universal suffrage, eliminated the double electoral rolls that overweighted European votes, and transformed local assemblies from consultative bodies to ones with high policy autonomy and responsible budgets.[23] Almost all of France's African territories gained internal self-government within the French Union in 1958 and full independence in 1960.[24]

British officials also feared mass revolts. One contemporaneous historian contended, "When a country is granted independence by the British government is determined largely by the time the nationalists were able to mobilise and display sufficient power and national unity to compel a commitment."[25] Gold Coast (Ghana) was an early example. In 1946, the colony became the first in British Africa to have a legislature with an elected African majority. However, property-holding voting restrictions remained in place and the reserve powers retained by the Governor limited the extent to which legislators could

[20] Crowder and O'Brien 1974, 665–671, 680–681.
[21] Logevall 2014, 313.
[22] Delivagnette 1970, 278; Crowder and O'Brien 1974, 685; Cooper 2014, 228.
[23] Delivagnette 1970, 261–263; Cooper 2014, 214.
[24] The exceptions were Guinea, which voted to secede in 1958; and tiny Djibouti, which was considered of strategic importance in the Horn of Africa.
[25] Coleman 1963, 396; quoted in Aluko 1974, 626–627.

effectively oppose government policies.[26] In 1947, the United Gold Coast Convention (UGCC) formed "partly to protest against the 1946 Constitution ... and partly to demand self-government 'in the shortest possible time.'"[27] The nationalist struggles between 1948 and 1951 were marked by violent demonstrations, strikes, and rioting. The government's immediate response was to arrest the leaders of the UGCC, including Kwame Nkrumah.

However, the ongoing threat of mass revolt prompted British officials to pivot from repression to concessions in the Gold Coast. In a new constitution enacted prior to the general elections in 1951, seventy-five of the eighty-four seats were for Africans, including thirty-eight members elected by adult male suffrage and another thirty-seven members chosen by territorial councils.[28] Although the new constitution was designed to "win the collaboration of 'moderate opinion,'" Nkrumah's newly formed Convention People's Party (CPP) won thirty-four of the thirty-eight elected seats.[29] Britain responded by releasing Nkrumah from prison in return for a promise to "follow the Colonial Office to the end of the 'constitutional road' [rather than] revolutionary struggle."[30] Therefore, despite the aggressive stance of the CPP on gaining self-government, the electoral reforms achieved their goal. Nationalist pressure subsequently took the form of "speeches in the Legislative Assembly and articles in the newspapers" as opposed to "boycotts and mass demonstrations."[31] Full internal self-government (1954) and independence (1957) followed shortly thereafter.

In India, British officials granted independence shortly after World War II in response to the threat of mass revolt. By the interwar period,

---

[26] Wight 1946b describes franchise restrictions dating back to 1925 (pp. 43–44) and the new constitution (pp. 203–207). Upon the constitutional reform in 1946, there were eighteen elected African members, six officials, and six nominated unofficials (who could be either Africans or Europeans). V-Dem estimates that the fraction of the population with suffrage increased from 3 to 20 percent following the constitutional reform, which reflects the extension of elected representatives to Ashanti.

[27] Aluko 1974, 627.

[28] Of the thirty-eight elected seats, only five (all in the major urban areas) were directly elected, whereas elsewhere the adult male electorate chose electors; see Hargreaves 1996, 125. See also Steinberg 1952, 317.

[29] Hargreaves 1996, 128.

[30] Hargreaves 1996, 129.

[31] Aluko 1974, 632.

the Indian National Congress had outgrown its origins as an elite pressure group to become a mass movement that conducted nonviolent campaigns, which destabilized British rule. Officials also questioned the reliability of the colonial military. Many Indian soldiers had served in the Japanese-sponsored Indian National Army, and Indian Navy and British troops in India had each mutinied after World War II. The religious riots after the war further convinced British politicians that "[t]he Indian situation is rapidly passing beyond our grasp and nothing but widespread and bloody murder will be the result."[32] Although Conservatives such as Winston Churchill strongly opposed Indian independence, the new Labour government was sympathetic. Prime Minister Clement Atlee, in a speech to the House of Commons in 1946, stressed that earlier concessions were insufficient. "The tide of nationalism that at one time seemed to be canalised among a comparatively small proportion of the people of India – mainly a few of the educated classes – has tended to spread wider and wider ... Today I think that national idea has spread right through and not least, perhaps, among some of those soldiers who have given such wonderful service in the war."[33] The Labour government held a general election in 1945 but failed to broker an agreement for a unified government, which prompted them to agree to separate independence for India and Pakistan. The large-scale sectarian violence that marked the partition process confirmed the views of many that retaining India by force would have been impossible.

Colonizers with weaker militaries were even more intimidated by the prospect of revolt. In the Belgian Congo, Africans did not participate in elections at any level of government until 1957, and the limited initial reforms were confined to municipal elections in three cities, including the capital of Leopoldville. However, the status quo changed suddenly following the Leopoldville riots in January 1959, which Belgian officials repressed harshly.[34] The riots signaled to Belgian officials that holding onto the Congo might require fighting an "Algerian-type war."[35] Even if successful, combating a rebellion would be fruitless because it would undermine Belgium's goal of fostering a harmonious

---

[32] Former Foreign Secretary Sir John Simon; quoted in Owen 2003, 418.
[33] House of Commons 1946.
[34] Bustin 1963, 51–55; Anstey 1970, 217; Lemarchand 1964, 561–566.
[35] Hargreaves 1996, 193–194.

relationship with postindependence leaders. Belgian public opinion, an important factor in a democratic metropole, also played a "massive role" because most Belgians opposed sending troops to fight in the Congo. This enabled the Minister of the Congo, Maurice van Hemelrijk, to push for independence in 1960 despite his assessment that "[m]y subordinates are almost unanimously against me."[36] The first national elections occurred in May 1960 and the Congo gained independence the next month.

5.2.3 Female Franchise Expansion

The spread of electoral reforms also enfranchised women. Female suffrage reforms moved in the same direction as for men, as we show in Figure 5.4. In 1945, women usually could not vote, as they had suffrage in only twelve of thirty-nine (31 percent) colonies with electoral institutions. By contrast, women were seldom disenfranchised in 1965, as they had suffrage in fifty-four of sixty-seven (81 percent) colonies or recent ex-colonies with electoral institutions. Elections also became nearly synonymous with full suffrage for both men and women after World War II. Figure 5.5 shows these patterns more directly by

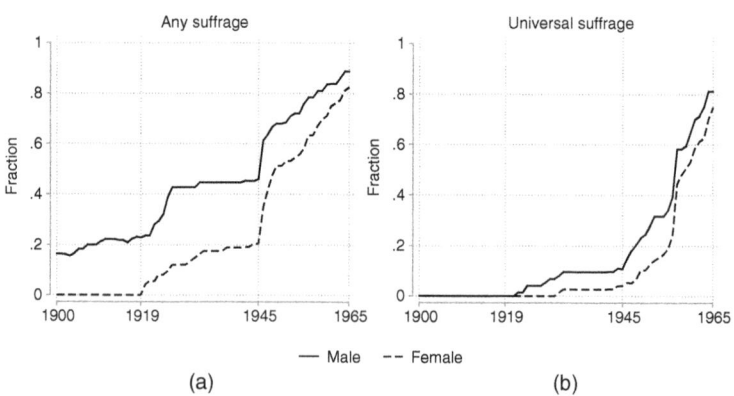

Figure 5.4 Suffrage for men and women
Notes: The outcome variables indicate whether any individuals had voting rights (a) and whether suffrage was universal (b), disaggregated by gender, over time. Appendix Table A.9 lists the sample of colonies. Data from V-Dem using their separate variables for male and female suffrage.

[36] Stengers 1982, 329–333.

Figure 5.5 Differential suffrage for men and women

Notes: The outcome variables are the difference between the lines in the Figure 5.4.

depicting differences in the fraction of colonies with male but not female suffrage. These patterns echo Teele's observation that in many countries, women initially gained the right to vote under external rule.[37]

Our theory highlights two reasons that help to explain the spread of female suffrage: reforms to European metropolitan franchises and agitation and lobbying by suffragette organizations in the colonies. In India, women gained limited representation starting in the 1920s, following the introduction of female suffrage in the UK in 1919. The Indian and British suffragettes who founded the Women's Indian Association (WIA) pressured the Montague-Chelmsford reform commission by touring the UK and publishing newspaper articles. The Joint Parliamentary Committee responded by removing a proposed gender qualification from the new voting laws, and instead allowed provincial legislatures to decide their own eligibility rules. However, although women's suffrage spread throughout much of India during the decade, property, education, and wifehood restrictions made women a minuscule fraction of the local electorates.[38]

Women in French Africa initially gained the right to vote in 1946, and the *loi cadre* of 1956 introduced universal suffrage. The enfranchisement of French women in 1944 created a precedent, and the subsequent colonial reforms reflected the desire for the French to

[37] Teele 2018, 2.
[38] Sinha 1999; Basu 2008.

showcase the long-proclaimed "civilizing mission" to justify their imperial project.[39] Protests by non-white elites also played a role. In Senegal's Four Communes, the Governor-General attempted to prevent African women from voting in 1944 even though the introduction of voting rights in France should have automatically applied to all women in the Communes, who were legal French citizens. In response, African women threatened to violently prevent European women from voting, which caused the Governor-General to reverse his position. He cabled to Paris that "[a]gitation on subject of vote for Senegalese women continues at Dakar and Saint-Louis and reaches a certain degree of violence .... Given these considerations, I am led to propose to extend the vote to Senegalese women."[40]

5.3 Variation among Metropolitan Democracies

Politicians in metropolitan democracies usually obliged the "wind of change" and implemented decolonization reforms before mass revolts broke out, but the exact timing of reforms varied. Drawing from the theory in Chapter 2, we highlight two aspects of metropolitan institutions: left-wing governing coalitions and the susceptibility of metropolitan governments to special interests.

5.3.1 Left-wing Metropolitan Governments

The costs and benefits of empire varied across social classes within the metropole. Elites tended to gain a disproportionate share of the benefits, whereas the costs were spread more widely. Consequently, left-wing parties were more willing to grant electoral reforms in the colonies. Among *non-white middle-class* and *weak elite* cases between 1945 and 1965, a colony without universal male suffrage in a particular year had a 10.3 percent chance of gaining this concession the next year when a left-wing party governed in the metropole, compared to 4.8 percent under right-wing governments and 1.5 percent under center governments.[41]

---

[39] Fransee 2018, 3.
[40] Cooper 2014, 47.
[41] Appendix Table A.18 provides regressions, where we confirm that these differences are statistically significant when controlling for substantive covariates and colony and year fixed effects.

The left influenced decolonization across the major empires. The French *loi cadre*, the single largest grant of universal suffrage within a colonial empire, was passed by the center-left Republican Front government, headed by Socialist Prime Minister Guy Mollet and Socialist Colonial Minister Gaston Defferre. After taking office early in 1956, they immediately granted independence to Morocco and Tunisia, and then pivoted to ward off rebellions in the remaining African colonies by granting "a true decentralization and a true deconcentration."[42] In the UK, the Labour Party opposed acquiring or retaining Britain's colonies abroad, although for pragmatic reasons, they did not seek to imminently liquidate the empire. In 1948, Labour Colonial Secretary Arthur Creech Jones proclaimed that "the central purpose of British colonial policy is simple. It is to guide the colonial territories to responsible government within the Commonwealth in conditions that ensure to the people concerned both a fair standard of living and freedom from oppression from any quarter."[43] The 1945–1951 Labour government oversaw the introduction of universal suffrage in the Gold Coast, granted independence to India, and supported critical democratic reforms and moves toward decolonization in the West Indies.[44] In Belgium, the out-of-power Socialist Party pressured a centrist coalition government to offer reforms rather than to continue repression in the Congo in 1959.[45] In Portugal, the left-wing government that succeeded the *Estado Novo* immediately granted independence to the colonies.[46]

Right-wing parties sometimes embraced colonial reforms because they believed the alternative to be worse. Following the establishment of the Fifth Republic in 1958, Charles de Gaulle deepened the reforms implemented by the preceding left-wing government by allowing most

---

[42] Cooper 2014, 228–229. By contrast, pressure from *pied-noirs* influenced the Mollet government's hardline stance on Algeria.

[43] Quoted in Aluko 1974, 626.

[44] Rueschemeyer, Stephens and Stephens 1992, 240.

[45] Stengers 1982, 332.

[46] Conversely, left-wing politicians rejected franchise expansion when their coalition benefited from colonialism. For example, the French Communist Party favored the repression of Muslim "terrorists" in Algeria to avoid losing its strong electoral base among European settlers; see Bowen 2007. Similarly, British Labour party members who represented Lancashire mill workers often expressed skepticism of Indian nationalism because they feared losing market access; see Owen 2007, 186–189.

French African colonies to gain full domestic autonomy. De Gaulle implemented this major reform despite the conservative and national-ist reputation of his government and the violent opposition of much of the military. De Gaulle saw the reforms as a regrettable necessity in the face of international pressure: "I know that decolonization is disastrous. That most of the Africans are hardly at the stage of our Middle Ages .... But what can I do about it? The Americans and Rus-sians think they have a vocation to free the colonized populations and are outbidding each other to do so."[47] Similarly, the British Conserva-tive government headed by Prime Minister Harold MacMillan took crucial steps toward decolonization in Africa.[48] Absent compelling economic interests to retain the empire, the fear of revolts and of bur-geoning communist influence ultimately pushed MacMillan to follow the self-proclaimed "wind of change."

5.3.2 Comparing British Colonialism: Contestation and Participation

Colonies of metropolitan democracies differed not only in the timing of franchise expansion, but also in contestation elements of democracy. In Figure 5.6, we compare British colonies to all others with democratic metropoles in 1965. Aggregate democracy levels were slightly higher in British colonies, although the difference is not statistically significant. This is largely because the franchise was, on average, slightly smaller in British colonies. However, British colonies are positively distinguished on various measures of political contestation: freedom of association, freedom of expression, clean elections, and executive constraints.[49]

British metropolitan institutions were less influenced by special in-terest groups, which enabled British politicians to implement reforms with less resistance from European settlers and large businesses.[50] In Rhodesia, the British government ignored settler lobbying and pres-sured European settlers to grant broader rights to Africans. In 1968, reformists overcame prosettler forces in the House of Lords to im-pose economic sanctions on the rogue settler regime.[51] In East and

---

[47] Quoted in Jackson 2018, 53.
[48] Stockwell and Butler 2013, 5; Aluko 1974, 626.
[49] Table A.19 provides regression analysis. See also Lee and Paine 2019.
[50] Spruyt 2005.
[51] Coggins 2006.

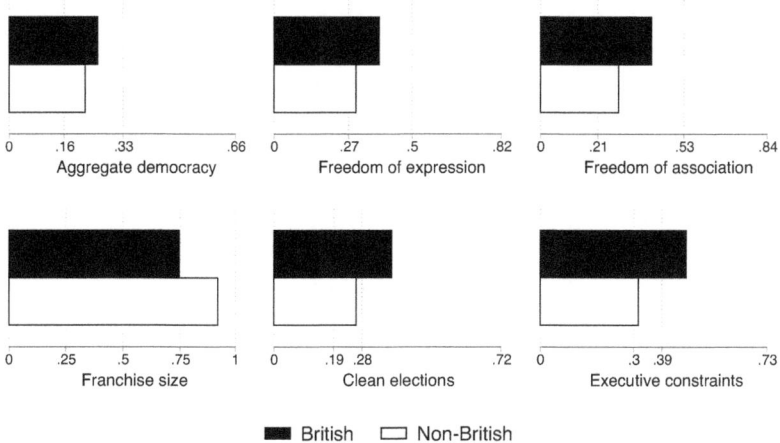

Figure 5.6 Comparing British colonialism: Contestation and participation

Notes: The outcome variables are various measures of contestation and participation from V-Dem, with averages among British colonies presented in black and averages for non-British colonies presented in white. For each part of the figure except franchise size, the three nonzero ticks correspond with the average values of the specified index in 2022 among closed authoritarian, electoral authoritarian, and electoral democratic regimes. Franchise size is the percentage of the adult population with the legal right to participate in elections. The sample is all colonies with democratic metropoles in 1965.

Central Africa, British officials overrode the demands of settlers and allowed for African-majority rule, as we discuss later for Kenya. British colonies tended to gain independence in a more gradual process that lasted decades, which typically led to relatively competitive elections.

By contrast, stronger special interests in France and Belgium helped to delay action until the threat of revolt became very pressing. French citizens in Algeria could vote in French elections. The settler lobby often held the balance of power in unstable Fourth Republic governments, and obstruction by settlers prevented Algerian Muslims from gaining voting rights. Coalition governments in France were notoriously unstable during the Fourth Republic, with twenty-four governments formed in its twelve years. In 1959, the constitution of the new Fifth Republic delegated more powers to its first president, Charles de Gaulle, which inspired some independence leaders to adopt constitutions with a strong presidential executive.[52] The constant shuffling of governments and constitutional change made it difficult to engage in longer-term planning about decolonization reforms and enabled special interest groups to exert undue influence. Investors with colonial interests also favored limiting devolution. The *Société Générale de Belgique* controlled one-third of the economy of Belgium and 60 percent of the economy of the Belgian Congo, including the colony's largest bank and part ownership in the mining giant *Union Minière du Haut-Katanga*.[53] These interests could not delay decolonization forever, but their lobbying kept decolonization off the table in French and Belgian colonies until crises intervened to necessitate reforms.

These sources of instability influenced the hasty nature of decolonization from the French and Belgian empires. France's general approach to colonial reform was insensitive to local conditions, which undermined electoral competitiveness. France militarily lost control of its North African and Southeast Asian empires in the 1950s, and almost all its Sub-Saharan African colonies followed the same timeline: introduction of electoral representation in 1946, universal suffrage in 1956, full internal autonomy in 1958, and independence in 1960. Competition was rarely free and fair, as French officials sought to cripple parties they deemed radical and used their control over "the chiefs, the agents of local administration, to encourage the growth of pro-Administration parties and in many cases to ensure the election of their representatives to the National, Federal and Territorial assemblies."[54] For example, in elections in Chad, the colonial government routinely "actively and visibly ... lent the weight of its office to the chiefly and traditional parties of the territory."[55] Senegal followed the same rigid timeline as the other colonies despite the long electoral history of the Four Communes. Belgian decolonization of the Congo was similarly hasty. The Leopoldville riots of 1959 prompted an immediate pivot to granting independence, with the first national election held one month prior.

---

[52] At independence, five former French colonies in Africa had presidential constitutions compared to zero British colonies; see Robinson and Torvik 2016, 909.

[53] Peemans 1975, 178.

[54] Crowder and O'Brien 1974, 671.

[55] Decalo 1980, 497.

5.4 Resisting the Wind of Change: Authoritarian Decolonization

Despite the rising threat of revolt, strong vested interests were sometimes able to block electoral reforms and decolonization. The largest white settlements formed politically dominant classes that strongly opposed majority rule. In authoritarian Portugal (as well as Spain and Italy), narrow governing oligarchies dominated by business interests and the military sought to hold on to preserve material and psychological benefits. Even as revolts became more threatening, white settlers and autocratic officials tolerated conflict in attempts to perpetuate their control.

Major decolonization wars occurred in Algeria, Angola, Guinea-Bissau, Mozambique, South West Africa (Namibia), South Africa, and Southern Rhodesia (Zimbabwe). The wars were costly for the governments that fought them and, of course, for the Africans and Arabs who suffered. In all seven cases, a victorious rebel group gained control of the state at independence or upon majority rule. Across the entire Africa sample, settler-minority colonies and Portuguese colonies had significantly smaller franchises in 1965 and were significantly more likely to experience a major decolonization war.[56] Similar to the earlier anticolonial wars in British North America and Spanish America (see Chapter 3), sizable white settler populations fought decolonization wars to secure autonomy for themselves. However, in the earlier colonies, white settlers fought the *metropole*, whereas in the later colonies, white settlements combated *non-Europeans*.

Authoritarian decolonization was not synonymous with revolts, however. In some cases (often British), the colonizer handed off power to a national monarch without introducing meaningful electoral reforms.

5.4.1 African Settler Colonies

White settlers in Africa enjoyed a privileged economic position and used repression to prevent decolonization and majority rule. Where they controlled the state (South Africa and its dependency of South West Africa, Southern Rhodesia) or wielded outsized influence in

---

[56] See Appendix Table A.20.

Table 5.3 *Post-1945 electoral institutions: Settler minority*

Colony	First election	Universal suffrage		Year of independence
		Male	Female	
South Africa	1853	1994	1994	1910/1994*
Algeria	1871	1962	1962	1962
Zimbabwe	1899	1980	1980	1965/1980*
Israel[†]	1920	Post-indep.	Post-indep.	1948
Tunisia	1922	1956	1956	1956
Namibia	1926	1980	1980	1990

Notes: See the notes for Table 5.1.
* South Africa gained dominion status in 1910 but white-minority rule persisted until 1994, and hence we analyze South Africa as a de facto colony in this chapter. Whites in Rhodesia unilaterally declared independence in 1965, although the country did not gain international recognition until 1980 amid a transition to African-majority rule.
[†] Israel is a settler-dominant regime, not settler minority; see the note for Appendix Table A.9.

metropolitan politics (Algeria), they held on for long periods, as summarized in Table 5.3. Where they were smaller and less politically influential, the metropole eventually reclaimed control and overrode the desires of settlers (Kenya and Northern Rhodesia).

Whites feared they would lose control over valuable land under African-majority rule. Land inequality between Europeans and Africans was very high in settler colonies, a product of forced redistribution during the colonization process.[57] The percentage of total land alienated to Europeans was extreme in the major settler colonies: 89 percent in South Africa, 60 percent in South West Africa, 49 percent in Southern Rhodesia, 34 percent in Algeria, and 7 percent in Kenya. By contrast, most other colonies did not disrupt local tenure practices and alienated less than 0.5 percent of their total land.[58] African rebel groups in settler colonies routinely coupled demands for renewed

[57] Herbst 2000, 189–190; Mosley 1983, 13–29; Hailey 1957, 685–815; Boone 2014, 21–25.
[58] The exceptions reflected concessions either for settlers (e.g., Botswana, 6 percent) or corporations (e.g., Belgian Congo, 9 percent). All data points from Hailey 1957, 687, except Lutzelschwab 2013, for Algeria and Oliver and Atmore 2005, 297–298, for South West Africa.

access to land with their overarching goal of majority rule. In Rhodesia, armed African nationalists in the Zimbabwe African National Union (ZANU) and the Zimbabwe African People's Union (ZAPU) sought to regain land that white settlers had expropriated. Land reform negotiations were crucial in the Lancaster House Agreement of 1979, which yielded internationally recognized independence and majority rule in Zimbabwe.[59]

Where European settlers directly controlled the state, they could protect their interests by implementing repressive policies. In South Africa, the franchise in practice became restricted to whites. In the 1930s, suffrage became universal for whites by extending the vote to all adult European women and removing all property qualifications, whereas Africans were removed from the common electoral roll.[60] In 1948, legislative victory by the Nationalist Party led to apartheid policies that legally subordinated non-whites. South Africa also extended these policies to its self-proclaimed "fifth province" of South West Africa (Namibia), which it governed as a League of Nations mandate.[61]

In Southern Rhodesia, whites gained autonomous self-government in 1923. Although the franchise was nominally nonracial, in practice, white colonists strategically used educational and income requirements to restrict the franchise to whites. After white legislators doubled the income requirements in 1951, only 481 Africans were left on the register.[62] African leaders rejected a proposed constitution in 1961, which prompted the white electorate to vote into power the Rhodesian Front. This far-right party campaigned to maintain white rule and to reject modifications to the Land Apportionment Act.[63] Backed by a colonist-controlled military and with economic and military support from South Africa and Portugal, the Rhodesian Front unilaterally declared Rhodesian independence in 1965.

Reactionary policies in South Africa and Southern Rhodesia made them less democratic in relative terms. In 1945, these colonies had the two highest V-Dem democracy scores in Africa and among the highest in the colonial world. However, over the next twenty years, these were

---

[59] Mlambo 2014, 191–193, 220–221; Reno 2011, 96. For other examples, see Paine 2019*b*, 520.

[60] Hailey 1957, 161–162.

[61] Oliver and Atmore 2005, 297.

[62] Hailey 1957, 185.

[63] Oliver and Atmore 2005, 272.

the only two colonies in Africa in which democracy levels fell, yielding scores close to the regional average. On average, 95 percent of the adult population could vote in *non-white middle-class* and *weak elite* cases in Africa in 1965, compared to 20 percent in South Africa and 5 percent in Southern Rhodesia.

Outcomes were mixed in cases in which the metropole exercised greater control. French settlers in Algeria used their influence in the French Parliament to block reforms. They rigged the local elections in 1948 to prevent a majority for Algerian nationalist parties, who subsequently eschewed participation in French electoral bodies and instead turned to armed revolt.[64] By contrast, the settler community was smaller and politically weaker in Kenya. The Mau Mau rebellion in the 1950s required £20 million pounds and British military intervention to suppress. The revolt convinced British officials that white Kenyans could not defend themselves without metropolitan assistance, which prompted decolonization reforms.[65] In 1961, the Secretary of State for the Colonies, Reginald Maudling, summarized official thought by proclaiming that "'arithmetic and African nationalism' had destroyed European political power, and that an attempt to maintain it by force would only lead to 'another outbreak of Mau Mau' and great disorder, 'possibly reaching even Congo proportions.'"[66] After a 1960 agreement that the Legislative Council would contain an African majority, a settler leader commented that "I regard the outcome of this conference as a death blow to the European community in Kenya."[67]

5.4.2 Portugal and Authoritarian Decolonization

The Portuguese *Estado Novo* dictatorship gained economic and psychological rents from colonial control. These benefits prompted the Portuguese government to spend enormous amounts to maintain centralized colonial control. At the height of its decolonization wars, Portugal spent over 6 percent of its national income on defense and tens of thousands of Portuguese youth were conscripted to serve in Africa.[68] Table 5.4 lists the colonial cases.

---

[64] Spruyt 2005, 105.
[65] Oliver and Atmore 2005, 256.
[66] Quoted in Hyam 2007, 280.
[67] Quoted in Wasserman 1976, 44–45.
[68] Ferraz 2022, 248.

Table 5.4 *Post-1945 electoral institutions: Authoritarian metropoles*

Colony	First election	Universal suffrage		Year of independence
		Male	Female	
Angola	1956	Post-indep.	Post-indep.	1975
Mozambique	1956	Post-indep.	Post-indep.	1975
Equatorial Guinea	1968	1968	1968	1968
Cape Verde	1972	1975	1975	1975
São Tomé and Príncipe	1972	1975	1975	1975
Guinea-Bissau	1973	1973	1973	1974

Notes: See the notes for Table 5.1. Libya and Somalia were in this category until 1945; see the note for Appendix Table A.9.

The wealthy core coalition of Portugal's authoritarian regime strongly supported colonial rule. A small number of conglomerates dominated both the metropolitan and colonial economies.[69] They concentrated in low-technology industries with high barriers to entry such as cement, shipbuilding, cork, and banking. These firms were largely uncompetitive within Western Europe and therefore relied on rents extracted from their privileged position within the colonies. White settlers created another vested interest that sought to preserve economic rents, despite minimal formal political power.[70]

The psychological benefits of colonial rule also militated against decolonization. Among the European colonizers, Portugal was by far the smallest in terms of population and national wealth. Possession of a large empire, the only tangible reminder of Portugal's early modern golden age, was vital to the self-esteem of the Portuguese elite. The regime printed postcards proclaiming that "Portugal is not a small country" by superimposing their colonies on the map of Europe, which demonstrated that the landmasses were similarly sized.[71]

Reflecting these interests, Portugal pursued a centralizing policy. Portugal's colonies in Africa and elsewhere were administratively

[69] Pimlott 1977, 337–338.
[70] Duffy 1962, 204; Bender 1974, 144, 152; Spruyt 2005, 187. In Angola, early African nationalist publications in the 1950s focused on European settlement as a primary grievance; see Marcum 1969, 24, 86.
[71] Cairo 2006.

incorporated into the metropole as Overseas Provinces, which prevented officials in the colonies from making autonomous decisions.[72] Reforms in the 1950s permitted some nominal participation for Africans, who began electing a minority of seats on new Legislative Councils in each of Angola and Mozambique. However, these councils offered purely advisory opinions on legislative decrees and other permitted subjects, and were strictly forbidden from discussing measures that would increase expenditures.[73] Following more than a decade of revolts, in 1973, the authoritarian regime introduced Legislative Assemblies with powers over taxes and expenditures in all its colonies. However, even at this very late date, Portuguese literacy requirements limited the African electorate and Europeans gained more seats than Africans.[74]

Portugal was not the only authoritarian colonizer during this period. Italy lost its colonies during World War II, after which Libya and Italian Somaliland (Somalia) became British Trust Territories and Ethiopia incorporated Eritrea. Available evidence suggests (speculatively) that Italy might have followed the Portuguese path had its authoritarian regime and colonial empire survived World War II. Like Portugal, fascist Italy was dominated by procolonial interests: ruling elites who enjoyed psychological rents from possessing a large empire and politically influential crony capitalists who benefitted from colonial control. Prior to World War II, Italy had moved toward integrating its colonies with the metropole culturally and economically, as opposed to increasing autonomy.[75] Spain also resisted decolonization and relinquished control over Spanish (Equatorial) Guinea, Spanish (Western) Sahara, and parts of Morocco only because of UN pressure and military incursions by Morocco.[76] Equatorial Guinea held its first elections one month before independence in 1968.

5.4.3 National Monarchies

In some colonies, the European power handed off power to a national monarch. This was an alternative form of authoritarian decolonization

[72] Pimenta 2016, 19.
[73] Hailey 1957, 355.
[74] Keesing's 1973; Pimenta 2016, 21.
[75] Novati 2008.
[76] Marks 1976.

Table 5.5 *Post-1945 electoral institutions: National monarchies*

Colony	First election	Universal suffrage		Year of independence
		Male	Female	
Egypt	1882	Post-indep.	Post-indep.	1922
Swaziland	1921	1967	1967	1968
Iraq	1923	1923	Post-indep.	1932
Jordan	1929	1929	Post-indep.	1946
Cambodia	1947	1947	Post-indep.	1953
Laos	1947	1947	Post-indep.	1953
Burundi	1953	1961	1961	1962
Lesotho	1960	1960	1965	1966
Bahrain	Post-indep.	Post-indep.	Post-indep.	1971
Bhutan	Post-indep.	Post-indep.	Post-indep.	1947
Kuwait	Post-indep.	Post-indep.	Post-indep.	1961
Libya	Post-indep.	Post-indep.	Post-indep.	1951
Maldives	Post-indep.	Post-indep.	Post-indep.	1965
Morocco	Post-indep.	Post-indep.	Post-indep.	1956
Nepal	Post-indep.	Post-indep.	Post-indep.	1947
Qatar	Post-indep.	Post-indep.	Post-indep.	1971

Notes: See the notes for Table 5.1. Maldives held a presidential election in 1952, but a royalist coup in 1954 reverted to unelected monarchical institutions until after independence. A similar constitutional reversal occurred in Kuwait in 1938–1939. We do not count these failed attempts to introduce parliaments as the onset of elections.

that did not yield mass revolts. Of the European colonizers, Britain most frequently chose this decolonization path. This confirms our expectation from Chapter 2 that metropoles with a monarchy at home should be more willing to delegate control to authoritarian national monarchs as a substitute for mass franchise expansion. Table 5.5 summarizes the cases.

Britain often relied on local dynasties to rule indirectly in subnational Native Authority jurisdictions. Many had limited territorial scope and were not plausible heirs to the colonial state. But in some cases, a monarchy was a truly national institution, or potentially so. This created a possible pathway between elites favored under earlier practices of indirect rule and elites who could inherit the postcolonial state. They drew from traditional institutions to rule in a manner that was often broadly accepted by the population, thus reducing pressure for electoral reforms even amid the changed international environment following World War II.

Many colonies in which Britain handed off power to a ruling monarchy at independence had enjoyed high internal autonomy even before 1945, as in the Persian Gulf.[77] Nepal and Bhutan each had virtually no colonial presence at all, with the British role being confined to control over foreign relations.[78] In Swaziland and Lesotho, British officials relied on the customary authority of national monarchs for governance throughout the colonial period. Each monarch had a traditional council comprised of unelected chiefs, which delayed the introduction of legislative councils until the 1960s.[79]

We test the claim that Britain was more likely than other powers to hand off power to a national monarch by assessing which colonies had a "potential" national monarch. Some cases, such as Kuwait and Swaziland, are obvious because one monarchy encompassed the entire colonial territory. But to address issues related to endogenous state creation, we include any case in which a sizable monarchical state existed – controlled by members of an ethnic or cultural group that constituted a plurality or at least one quarter of the country's population. We thus pick up additional cases in which a monarchy was large enough that the colonizer plausibly *could have* placed them within their own colony or allowed them to govern territory beyond their core area.[80] For example, the Sokoto Caliphate in Nigeria corresponds with ethnic Hausa and Fulani, who constitute roughly a quarter of Nigeria's population. The Sokoto Caliphate encompassed a huge territory and was originally governed as a separate Northern Nigeria Protectorate. Expanding the sample in this manner conditions, at least roughly, on how the existence of ruling dynasties affected decisions regarding which states to create in the first place; as retaining the small colonies of Kuwait and Swaziland while amalgamating Nigeria was undoubtedly an endogenous choice.[81]

---

[77] Crystal 1995.

[78] Dutt 1981.

[79] Hailey 1953; Hailey 1957, 271–272; MacMillan 1985.

[80] The ideal comparison would be based on precolonial population estimates, which generally are not available.

[81] Appendix A.3.5 provides more details on the cases. For evidence that precolonial states affected the colonial borders in Africa, see Paine, Qiu and Ricart-Huguet 2023.

Among British colonies with a potential national monarch, fourteen of eighteen (78 percent) held formal political powers at independence: Bahrain, Bhutan, Egypt, Kuwait, Lesotho, Libya, Malaysia (federal elective monarchy), Maldives, Nepal, Oman, Qatar, Swaziland, Uganda (*Kabaka* of Buganda as president), and the United Arab Emirates (federal elective monarchy).[82] The exceptions are Burma/Myanmar, the Gold Coast/Ghana (Asante), Nigeria (Sokoto), and Sudan (Mahdist). In these cases, the royal dynasty was either deposed during colonial rule or held powers only at the subnational level upon independence. By contrast, only four of ten (40 percent) potential monarchs were intact at independence in French colonies: Cambodia, Laos, Morocco (where the French had temporarily exiled the monarch), and Tunisia (where the monarch was overthrown one month after independence). A potential monarch did not govern at independence in Benin (Dahomey), Burkina Faso (Mossi), Guinea (Futa Jalon), Madagascar (Merina), Mali (Tukulor), or Vietnam. Elsewhere, the metropolitan monarchies of Germany and Belgium preserved monarchies in Rwanda and Burundi, although the Tutsi monarchy in Rwanda was overthrown by a domestic revolution shortly before independence.

5.5 Conclusion

After 1945, non-whites posed a viable threat to rebel against external rule. The European reaction depended upon metropolitan institutions and the size of the white settler population. Most European metropoles had become democratic by the mid-twentieth century, which made them willing to grant concessions, especially when left-wing parties were in power. By contrast, authoritarian powers such as Portugal had a strong colonial lobby of large businessmen and army officers who rejected decolonization. Politically influential white settler communities in Africa took a similarly intransigent stance. Finally, Britain (itself a constitutional monarchy) often tolerated national monarchies.

Experiences with elections and other democratic pieces under colonial rule strongly influenced postindependence regime trajectories. In countries with an early electoral history and without a notable white

---

[82] Brunei and Zanzibar also support the pattern, but neither is in our statistical sample. Brunei does not meet the V-Dem threshold and Zanzibar was merged with Tanganyika (Tanzania) shortly after independence.

settlement, post-1945 reforms usually broadened the franchise and deepened democratic competition. In many cases, postindependence leaders consolidated democratic regimes. By contrast, the late onset of colonial elections usually succeeded at preventing major anticolonial revolts but failed to promote durable democracy after independence. Finally, countries with no democratic experience before independence usually became durable authoritarian regimes. We discuss these patterns in depth in Chapter 6.

6 | *Postcolonial Persistence*

Colonial electoral institutions influenced levels of democracy after independence. Colonies with extensive democratic exposure under colonialism, or what we call *lengthy colonial pluralism*, tended to remain stable democracies afterward. In many such cases, a non-white middle class pushed for and participated in elections for multiple decades prior to independence. Although the initial colonial elections usually involved only a tiny segment of the population, electoral reforms deepened over time and yielded institutionalized parties. After independence, institutionalized parties and democratically socialized elites acted as a buffer against military coups and executive power grabs.

Many other colonies inherited democratic-looking institutions at independence, but these institutions reflected relatively shallow, post-World War II concessions to thwart mass revolts. Parties tended to be weaker in these colonies and elections were not perceived as the exclusive legitimate means of gaining and retaining power. Militaries faced few obstacles to displacing civilian rulers and elected officials could opportunistically consolidate a dictatorship. Few colonies with *short colonial pluralism* were democratic within a decade of independence, although some experienced democratization episodes after the Cold War ended.

Other colonies gained no meaningful electoral experience. *No colonial pluralism* precluded postcolonial democracy. Regimes established by successful anticolonial rebels and precolonial monarchies monopolized military power and constructed durable authoritarian regimes after independence. Low democracy levels in these countries resembled those in countries colonized by non-Western powers or that avoided colonization entirely.

Colonial electoral institutions also affected postcolonial patterns in countries that became independent before 1945. The neo-British settler colonies had lengthy experiences with electoral institutions before independence and consolidated democratic regimes afterward, with the US South providing a rule-proving exception. In Latin America, anticolonial rebellions in countries that lacked exposure to colonial pluralism empowered landed white settler minorities, who used authoritarian means to dominate politics until the late twentieth century or beyond.

6.1 Colonial Pluralism and Self-enforcing Democracy: Theoretical Mechanisms

Democracy is self-enforcing only when electoral winners and losers both cooperate with democratic rules.[1] The faction that loses today's election must peacefully accept their loss and await participation in future elections, and the winner must hold fair elections in the future despite the risk of losing. Each side will comply only when continued democratic competition yields better expected outcomes than subversive actions, such as a coup (if out of power) or weakening electoral competitiveness (if in power).

The degree of exposure to plural colonial institutions should affect both the opportunity cost of and the coordination problems involved with subversion. In general, institutions become path dependent when leading actors sink costs to maximize their competitiveness under the existing set of rules and are otherwise socialized to believe that set of rules is legitimate. Such conditions create vested interests in perpetuating the institution, which raises the opportunity cost of subversion, and make it more difficult to coordinate on an alternative.[2] Lengthy colonial pluralism generally induced actors to sink costs in activities that advantaged them in democratic competition, whereas short colonial pluralism did not. Absent exposure to colonial pluralism, actors sunk costs that advantaged them within authoritarian institutions. Consequently, we expect differences in postcolonial democracy levels around independence to exhibit path dependence.

Opportunity Cost of Subversion
In the context of democratic competition, actors sink costs by gaining skills and connections specific to the electoral and legislative processes.

---

[1] Przeworski 1991, 2018.

[2] David 1985; North 1991; Mahoney 2000; Pierson 2000; Greif and Laitin 2004; Page 2006. For examples of theories applied to colonial institutions based on sunk costs and path dependence, see Acemoglu, Johnson and Robinson 2001 on economic institutions and Herbst 1989 on borders in Africa.

Politicians organize parties that manufacture brands for voters and cultivate networks that build voter support. Within the government, politicians learn the nuances of the legislative and legal processes that draw press coverage and enable them to outmaneuver their opponents while playing by the constitutional rules. Exposure to electoral and legislative competition can also create norms and common expectations consistent with upholding institutions believed to be legitimate. Mainwaring and Scully identify four components of institutionalized party systems, all of which can contribute to democratic persistence.[3] First, the rules and nature of interparty competition are stable, meaning that new parties do not frequently appear and disappear. Second, the major parties have stable roots in society, which enables them to structure mass political preferences over time. Third, influential political actors consider the electoral process and parties to be legitimate. Fourth, party organizations acquire an independent status and value of their own, and are not subordinated to the interests of ambitious leaders.

The magnitude of sunk costs in democratic institutions depends in part on the duration of electoral competition. Colonialism was a critical juncture because politicians could, potentially, build democratic experience without the threat of a coup or rebellion. Early colonial elections were usually contested by factions of elites in the colonial capital presiding over loose networks of rural elites, and with sufficient time, these networks could expand. The Indian National Congress, for instance, grew from 18,339 members in 1925 to 4,511,858 in 1939.[4] Well-developed organizations made leaders confident that they could succeed electorally after independence. By contrast, in newly independent states where elections were initially held shortly before independence, politicians had little time to build institutionalized mass parties. Lesser prospects for sustained electoral success reduced the opportunity cost to governing autocratically.

Coordination Problems to Subversion
All politicians, even ones with exceptional democratic credentials, can benefit from ruling without constraints, and a nondemocratic seizure

---

[3] Mainwaring and Scully 1995, 4–6.
[4] See Tomlinson 1976, 38 and National Archives of India file Home/Political/I/1941/NA/F-4-7/41.

is always tempting for out-of-power parties. But coups or attempts at incumbent consolidation can fail, which generates a cost. The strength of democratic institutions affects this cost by influencing expectations about failure. A common belief that democratic institutions are strong can thwart potential challenges by exacerbating coordination problems – it is difficult to get others to join when they believe that the prospects for failure are high.

Coups and rebellions each entail coordination problems. A successful coup requires that the coup plotters organize secretly. Despite the high rewards to succeeding, picking the wrong side can be deadly. Failed coup plotters are often jailed or executed; but if the coup succeeds, the new junta usually purges elements of the military they believe are disloyal. Given the need for military officers to make life-and-death decisions in a timeframe of minutes and hours, their expectations about whether the coup will succeed are paramount.[5] Similarly, rebellions almost always start small, and decisions by early movers hinge largely on their expectations about others joining.[6]

In countries where democratic institutions are well-established and function effectively, officers can reasonably anticipate that few others will join a plot and that takeover attempts will encounter mass protests. In Finer's formulation, the public's attachment to and involvement in institutions affect the opportunity for military intervention in politics.[7] Countries with "high political culture" exhibit broad public approval of established procedures for transferring power as well as wide recognition of which civilian authorities are sovereign. Consequently, attempts at military intervention would be perceived as "wholly unwarrantable intrusions" that would trigger strong public resistance. Conversely, the belief that a coup will succeed can be self-fulfilling in countries where parties are organizationally weak, legislators are inexperienced, and elections are not accepted as the sole means for gaining power. Finer contends that in such countries, public opinion would not strongly resist military intervention because mass political participants are few and weakly organized.[8]

---

[5] Singh 2014.

[6] Lewis 2020.

[7] Finer 2002, 87–89.

[8] For related arguments on how parties guard against military intervention, albeit in authoritarian contexts, see Levitsky and Way 2010 and Geddes, Wright and Frantz 2018, 131–134.

A similar calculus constrains incumbents from violating democratic norms. In a strong party system, opposition parties are well-positioned to rally their supporters if the incumbent attempts to cancel or otherwise heavily manipulate elections.[9] A strong judicial system can similarly increase the likelihood that subversion attempts will face legal punishment. Moreover, even if successful, subversion makes the ruling coalition more reliant on the military and more vulnerable to future coup attempts.[10]

The incumbent's calculus also depends on the expectation that, upon losing a future election, the new incumbent will perpetuate free and fair competition. A positive expectation is more likely in countries with lengthy colonial pluralism either because elites had already observed electoral turnover or because of the knowledge that other parties had also sunk costs in democratic competition. By contrast, such common knowledge would be lacking in countries with a shallow history of colonial electoral competition.

Authoritarian Path Dependence

Some countries lacked any electoral experience under colonialism. In these colonies, the challenges to self-enforcing democracy were irrelevant because there were no democratic institutions to either uphold or disband. Instead, elites had incentives to sink costs in authoritarian institutions. Monarchies encourage elites to cultivate links with the royal family. Where rebel groups swept away obstinate Europeans, civilian and military elites often banded together with the ruling party. These sunk costs, plus the unique advantages of these regimes for inducing military loyalty, should foster path-dependent authoritarian regimes. However, authoritarian equilibria, whether developed before independence or afterward, do not necessarily last forever, and could be disrupted by external shocks such as the end of the Cold War.

6.2 Main Patterns

6.2.1 Persistent Democratic Differences

Differences in democracy levels under colonialism have persisted since independence. In Figure 6.1, we examine the relationship between

---

[9] Fearon 2011.
[10] Svolik 2013.

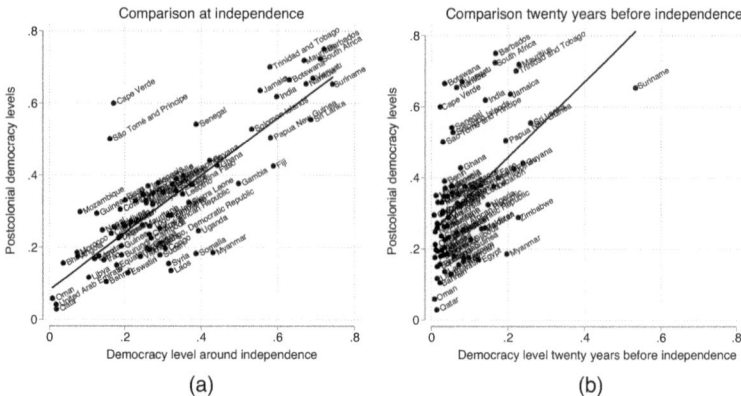

Figure 6.1 Persistent democratic differences
Notes: In both (a) and (b), the y-axis is the country's average value on the
V-Dem electoral democracy index in all postindependence years (with 1945 as
the earliest year). In Figure 6.1(a), the x-axis is the value of the democracy score
around independence, by which we mean the maximum score recorded for
each country within its first five years of independence. This captures reforms
that were planned, but not yet implemented, under colonial rule; although
the findings are qualitatively similar when instead using the democracy score
in the first year of independence. In Figure 6.1(b), the x-axis is the country's
democracy score twenty years before gaining independence. Appendix Table
A.9 lists the sample of countries, and the tables throughout the present chapter
list each country's democracy score around independence.

a country's democracy score around independence and its average
postcolonial democracy score, through 2022. These quantities are
strongly positively correlated, as Figure 6.1(a) shows. Jamaica was
more democratic than Uganda at independence, which in turn was
more democratic than Qatar, and this ordering has remained unchanged over time. Figure 6.1(b) reveals a similar pattern when we
change the initial democracy score to twenty years before independence. The terminal decades of colonial rule tended to perpetuate
earlier advantages, while also bolstering democracy scores across the
board.[11]

---

[11] The average democracy score among all colonies was 0.08 twenty years
before independence and rose to 0.31 at independence, a jump from a
lower-than-average score for a closed authoritarian regime in 2022 to a
typical contemporary electoral authoritarian regime. If the average country

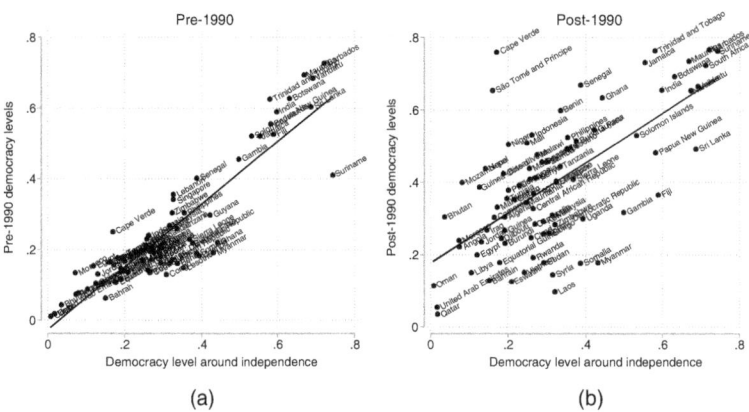

Figure 6.2 Persistent democratic differences: Pre- and post-1990
Notes: The note for Figure 6.1 provides details. The only difference is the time periods over which postindependence democracy scores are measured (either pre- or post-1990, as opposed to all postcolonial years).

Figure 6.2 shows that persistence was strongest in the decades immediately following independence. In Figure 6.2(a), colonies are clustered tightly around the regression line, which itself is close to a 45° line. This means that a country's democracy level around independence is nearly identical to its average democracy score between independence and 1990. Democracy levels around independence are highly predictive of average democracy scores after 1990 as well, but countries are less tightly clustered around the regression line in Figure 6.2(b). These differences are statistically significant, as we confirm in the Appendix.[12] In all the regressions models for this chapter, we control for common covariates from the democracy literature: GDP per capita, population, oil and gas income per capita, Muslim population share, ethnic fractionalization, and year fixed effects. We also evaluate

---

hypothetically gained independence two decades prior to its actual year (hence dropping its initial democracy score from 0.31 to 0.08), the regression model from Column 1 of Table A.21 estimates a predicted drop of 0.18 in the average postindependence democracy score. This is roughly the difference between Jamaica and Guyana, between Guyana and Uganda, and between Uganda and Qatar.

[12] See Tables A.21 and A.22.

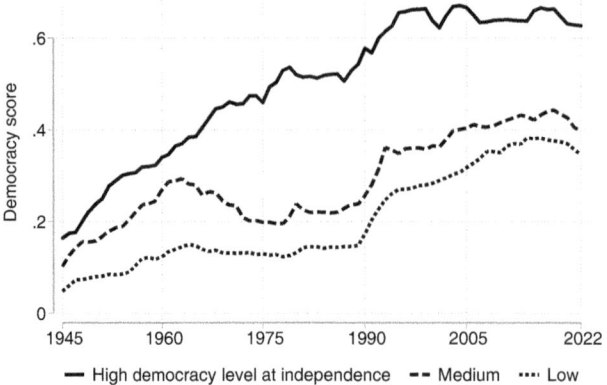

Figure 6.3 Postcolonial democracy by initial democracy level
Notes: The outcome variable is the V-Dem electoral democracy index, averaged across categories of colonies over time. The categories are based on
democracy scores around independence (measured by their highest democracy
score within five years of independence). Low is less than 0.3, medium is between 0.3 and 0.5, and high is at least as high as 0.5. The median years of
independence for each category are 1968, 1960, and 1960, respectively. Appendix Table A.9 lists the sample of countries, and the tables throughout this
chapter list each country's democracy score around independence.

samples with ex-Western colonies only (i.e., the cases discussed
throughout the book) and with all non-European countries.[13]

   Grouping countries into bins based on their democracy levels around
independence and tracking scores over time yields further evidence of
persistence. In Figure 6.3, we disaggregate countries into three groups:
high, medium, and low democracy scores at independence. By con-
struction, these three groups of countries differed in their democracy
scores at independence. Postcolonial democracy levels stayed roughly
constant during the Cold War era before rising in the 1990s, but the
differences across categories remained qualitatively unchanged.

6.2.2 Enduring Effects of Colonial Electoral Institutions

Why did countries differ in their democracy levels at independence?
Why have these differences persisted over time? Countries did not

---

[13] This includes cases such as Thailand that were never colonial dependencies
   and cases such as Taiwan that were colonized by non-Western powers.

inherit, by fiat, particular constellations of political institutions upon gaining jurisdictional sovereignty. Instead, as we have shown in throughout the book, democracy levels at independence were influenced by experiences under colonial rule.

Democracy levels at independence provide only a snapshot of the colonial experience. A more direct way to demonstrate the long-term consequences of colonialism is to categorize countries by their length of exposure to pluralistic electoral competition under Western colonial rule.[14] By contemporary standards, democracy scores were uniformly low throughout the colonial era, at least until the eve of independence, but early experiences with limited elections could nonetheless provide launching points for politicians to sink costs in electoral and legislature procedures and for professional political parties to emerge.

We code colonial institutions as plural in any colony-year with an elected assembly that had at least minimal legislative powers (i.e., not advisory) and nation-wide elections (i.e., elected seats were not restricted to a handful of specific areas). We additionally require that the colony-year meets a minimal V-Dem democracy score to further rule out colony-years with very low electoral autonomy. The threshold is democracy scores within the top quartile of scores among all colony-years within forty years of independence, 0.12.[15] We then tallied for how many years each colony met this standard for pluralism within the forty years prior to independence. In Figure 6.4, we distinguish colonies by *long* (twenty years or more), *short* (between one and nineteen years), and *no colonial pluralism*. Democracy scores around independence are strongly associated with the length of experience with colonial pluralism, and these differences have persisted over time.

In the Appendix, we show that colonies with short or no episodes of colonial pluralism are significantly less democratic than long-pluralism countries in all years, pre-1990, and post-1990; whether

---

[14] This approach resembles Wilkinson and Onorato's 2013 measure of a country's democratic capital accumulated during colonial rule. However, their stock variable equals the difference between a country's year of independence and the first year with a colonial election, and therefore does not distinguish the quality of democratic competition nor account for autocratic reversions in colonies such as the British West Indies.

[15] This is a low standard; for comparison, Swaziland had this democracy score in 2022.

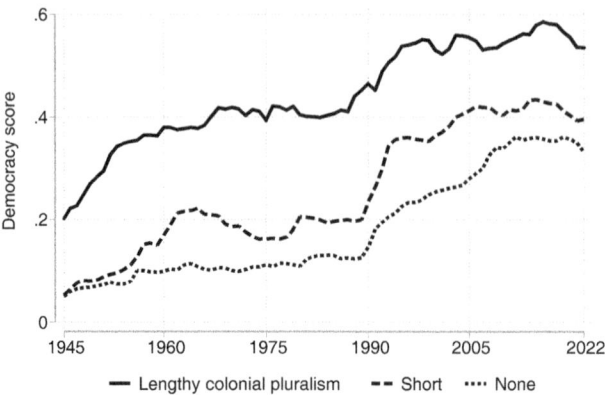

Figure 6.4 Postcolonial democracy by colonial pluralism
Notes: The outcome variable is the V-Dem electoral democracy index, averaged across categories of colonies over time. The categories are based on the number of years of colonial pluralism. Long is at least twenty years and short is between one and nineteen years. Appendix Table A.9 lists the sample of countries, and the tables throughout the present chapter list each country's number of years of colonial pluralism.

or not controlling for covariates; and whether including only former Western colonies or the full sample of non-Western colonies.[16] The findings are also similar when using a continuous, logged version of plural colonial years. Finally, we analyze an alternative version of the pluralism variable that adds another necessary condition (on top of nonadvisory/national elections with a high-enough democracy score) for a colony-year to be coded as plural: a political party must have existed. This more directly isolates our proposed mechanism by distinguishing cases in which parties competed in competitive elections from ones in which all candidates ran as independents or were selected by local elites, and therefore did not contribute to building institutionalized parties.

The distinct categories into which we group colonies throughout the book are also highly correlated with postindependence democracy levels. In Figure 6.5, we distinguish countries by *white settler minorities, non-white middle classes, weak elites, national monarchs,* or

---

[16] See Tables A.26 and A.27.

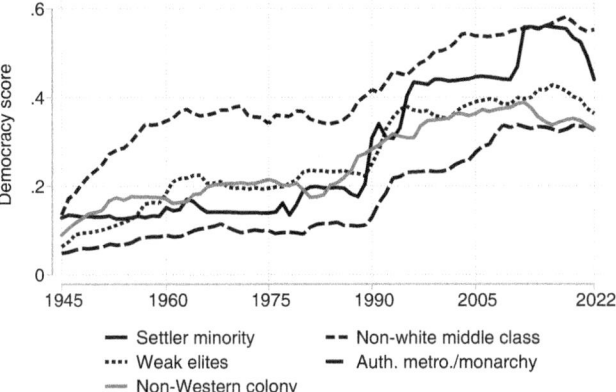

Figure 6.5 Postcolonial democracy by colonial categories
Notes: The outcome variable is the V-Dem electoral democracy index, averaged across categories of colonies over time. Appendix Table A.9 lists the sample of countries and the category for each. The beginning of Appendix A.4 lists every country that was never a Western colony.

authoritarian metropoles (we combine the latter two because of similar theoretical expectations for postcolonial trajectories). We also show the pattern for non-European countries that were *not colonized by a Western power*.

Countries with an early non-white middle class were by far the most democratic at independence. These countries have remained the most democratic in the subsequent decades, even as the absolute levels have changed, in particular because of increases for all categories after the Cold War ended. The Appendix shows that non-white middle class cases are statistically distinct from every other category except settler minorities, for which the difference is significant only before 1990.[17] Compared to weak elite colonies, settler minorities were more democratic in 1945, less democratic starting the 1950s and lasting until the early 1990s, and then more democratic again. However, the differences between these two categories are not statistically significant for either pre-1990, post-1990, or all postcolonial years.

---

[17] See Appendix Tables A.23, A.24, and A.25. Namibia's independence in 1990, the end of apartheid in South Africa in 1994, and the Arab Spring in Tunisia in 2011 each bolstered the average democracy score among ex-settler colonies. By contrast, Tunisia's more recent democratic regression lowered the average.

Conversely, colonies of authoritarian metropoles and national monarchies were the least democratic at independence, and these differences have also persisted. These countries have similar democracy levels to countries not colonized by a Western power, which confirms our expectation that such countries are relatively undemocratic.

6.3 Mechanisms of Persistence

Varied experiences with colonial elections yielded persistent democratic differences after independence. Countries with lengthy experiences of colonial pluralism developed institutionalized political parties that helped to consolidate postcolonial democratic regimes. Conversely, countries with short periods of colonial pluralism had less-developed norms of electoral competition and weaker parties. Consequently, they often experienced coups and incumbent consolidation after independence. Colonies lacking any experience with plural colonial institutions were authoritarian at independence and remained so for decades afterward, often under the same regime that took power at independence. Some noncolonized territories developed early electoral institutions, but they usually endured autocratic reversals before democratic competition was consolidated.

6.3.1 Lengthy Colonial Pluralism

Countries with twenty years or longer of colonial pluralism account for almost all instances of durable postcolonial democracy. These were mostly cases such as India and Jamaica in which non-white middle classes pushed for early elections before World War II and, subsequently, strong parties subjugated the military to civilian rule. Settler cases such as South Africa and Zimbabwe were more heterogeneous because of conflicting pro- and antidemocratic legacies. Table 6.1 summarizes the cases.

Early Non-White Middle Classes
India experienced a relatively long and gradual transition to independence. Following the introduction of elections in the 1910s, continued agitation by Indians led to the Government of India Act in 1935, by which provincial legislatures gained full responsibility over local policies and the education and property requirements for voting were lowered to enfranchise approximately 10 percent of the population.

Table 6.1 *Postcolonial outcomes: Lengthy colonial pluralism*

Country	Independence	Colonial pluralism	Initial level of democracy	Regime change year (event)
South Africa	1910/1994*	40+ years	0.71	none
Mauritius	1968	40+	0.70	none
Fiji	1970	40+	0.59	1987 (coup)
Jamaica	1962	40+	0.55	none
Guyana	1966	40+	0.42	1973 (incumbent)
Zimbabwe	1965/1980*	39	0.32	none
Sri Lanka	1948	38	0.69	1982 (incumbent)
Trin. & Tob.	1962	37	0.58	none
Philippines	1946	36	0.35	1972 (incumbent)
Barbados	1966	28	0.72	none
Israel	1948	27	0.61	none
Seychelles	1976	27	0.29	1977 (coup)
Suriname	1975	26	0.74	1980 (coup)
India	1947	26	0.60	none
Pakistan	1947	26	0.20	1958 (coup)
Papua NG	1975	24	0.58	none
Myanmar	1948	22	0.43	1962 (coup)
Lebanon	1943	21	0.33	1975 (civil war)

Notes: This table lists every country from our core sample (see Appendix Table A.9) with at least 20 years of colonial pluralism. We cap our counting of years of colonial pluralism at forty to avoid left-censoring for any observations. The regime-change event "incumbent" includes various acts of incumbent consolidation in previously pluralistic regimes, such as heavily tilting an election and declaring martial law.
* South Africa gained dominion status in 1910 but white-minority rule persisted until 1994, and hence we analyze South Africa as a de facto colony for most of the twentieth century. Whites in Rhodesia unilaterally declared independence in 1965, although the country did not gain international recognition until 1980 amid a transition to African-majority rule. To count years of colonial pluralism for each of these two cases, we use the year of majority rule as the terminal colonial year.

The leading party, the Indian National Congress, continued to be led by urban, educated, and middle-class Indians who built a broad social coalition that encompassed members from all of India's major religious groups.[18] Although prospects for revolts and violent political

---

[18] Tudor 2013, 4; Wilkinson 2015, 13.

instability influenced the exact timing of independence, these earlier electoral reforms yielded relatively strong democratic foundations at independence. Shortly afterward, the Constituent Assembly designed a more democratic constitution that introduced universal suffrage.

India has sustained high democracy levels throughout most of its postindependence period, holding seventeen general elections at regular intervals. Although the Indian National Congress has usually won (eleven times) and ruled for two years by emergency decree, they have ceded power four different times. Even at the height of their power, they permitted the opposition to "constantly pressure, criticize, censure and influence it by influencing opinion and interests inside the margin and, above all, [to] exert a latent threat that if the ruling group strays away too far from the balance of effective public opinion ... [that] it will be displaced from power by the opposition groups."[19]

Scholars often cite the strength and internal cohesion of the Indian National Congress as crucial to the country's democratic stability, especially in contrast to neighboring Pakistan.[20] The Congress was broadly inclusive in its membership and coupled a nationalist ideology with concrete programmatic content, which created a basic consensus for the direction of policies. Internally, the party was competitive and had clear rules for challenging and replacing incumbents. Wilkinson summarizes the importance of the colonial era: "By 1947, the Indian National Congress was over sixty years old and had been a substantial mass presence across India for three decades .... Congress's leaders also, crucially, had experience in government and the art of political management and compromise, going back to the party's first provincial election victories in the 1920s and especially after the party's clear victories in eight out of eleven provinces in the 1936 provincial elections."[21]

The Congress not only tolerated opposition, but kept the military out of politics. In contrast to many ex-colonies with late electoral reforms, postcolonial India is remarkable for the absence of military intervention in politics. Wilkinson, Tudor, and others contend that the

---

[19] Kothari 1964, 1162. More recently, since 2014, India has experienced democratic backsliding under Prime Minister Narendra Modi and the Bharatiya Janata Party; see Varshney 2022.

[20] Tudor 2013; Wilkinson 2015.

[21] Wilkinson 2015, 13.

organizational strength of Congress helped to deter coup attempts.[22] Indian generals had, on occasion, contemplated military intervention because of concerns about the ideological direction of the country, but ultimately rejected the possibility. As a British diplomat recounts from a 1966 conversation with the Chief of the Army Staff [COAS] General J. N. Chaudhuri:

COAS told me that they had discussed this matter at some length and that he had expressed the categorical view that such a possibility did not exist. He based his belief on (a) His view that there was a deep-seated respect for constitutional government at all levels in the country .... (b) The size of India and the degree of decentralisation of its government machine. From this he argued that it would be administratively and operationally impracticable for the Army to seize power from both the Union and the State governments in a single operation. (c) If the Army were to attempt a coup against the Union government without seizing power in the States simultaneously, the Congress machine would remain operational and the coup would almost certainly be ineffectual.[23]

In Jamaica, elections restarted in 1884 under a very small franchise, but more important reforms occurred after riots and strikes spread throughout the West Indies in the 1930s. Britain commissioned the Moyne Report, which recommended expanding both the franchise and the number of elected members on the legislative councils.[24] Pressure by the People's National Party (PNP) was critical for, as they proclaimed, "prov[ing] that Jamaicans of all classes were now ready to combine in a demand for constitutional change."[25] In 1944, Jamaica became the first colony in the region to hold elections under universal suffrage and also gained a fully elected legislative council. Alongside these developments, another major party emerged, the Jamaica Labour Party (JLP). The first leaders of both parties, Norman Manley and Alexander Bustamante, were mixed-race elites (one educated at Oxford) who started their political careers as lawyers and journalists prior to the emergence of mass politics in Jamaica. Their parties co-opted key societal groups such as labor unions, cemented

---

[22] Tudor 2013; Wilkinson 2015.
[23] Khan 2002, 480–481.
[24] Rogoziński 2000, 313–314.
[25] Quoted in Post 1981, 156.

by patterns of campaign contributions and control over print media.[26] Jamaica gained full domestic autonomy in 1957 with the introduction of cabinet government and became independent in 1962.

Jamaica has been continuously democratic since independence.[27] Within the first three decades, the PNP and JLP rotated in power three times (1972, 1980, and 1989). Alternation in office followed precedents set between 1944 and 1962, when universal-suffrage elections twice changed the majority on the legislative council. Universal suffrage for roughly two decades before independence enabled the core of each party to remain constant: an alliance between the middle class and the working class.[28] Amid continued electoral competition under colonialism, the PNP and JLP came to a basic agreement over the "general lines of policy for promoting Jamaican development and the limits to the arena of politics."[29] The colonial electoral experience "routiniz[ed] party politics,"[30] which created strong foundations for postcolonial democracy despite lingering problems of election violence and corruption.

Many other British plantation colonies, including Barbados, Trinidad and Tobago, and Mauritius, also experienced long periods of colonial pluralism in which voting was initially confined to the non-white middle classes, followed by colonial-era franchise expansion and then democratic consolidation after independence. The list is even longer when including microstates that do not meet the population threshold for inclusion in the V-Dem data set.[31] Guyana and Dutch Suriname had similar colonial histories, but neither has been consistently democratic amid ethnic conflict. However, each re-democratized after a period of authoritarian rule and both have an average postindependence democracy score much higher than the typical non-Western country. These cases contrast with ex-plantation countries such

---

[26] Rueschemeyer, Stephens and Stephens 1992, 242–244, 249–250.

[27] This paragraph draws mostly from Ledgister 1998.

[28] See also Rueschemeyer, Stephens and Stephens 1992, 244.

[29] Ledgister 1998, 61.

[30] Ledgister 1998, 20.

[31] In the West Indies, the microstates that gained independence are Antigua and Barbuda, Bahamas, Dominica, Grenada, St. Kitts and Nevis, St. Lucia, and St. Vincent and the Grenadines (see the tables in Chapters 3 and 4). Boix, Miller and Rosato 2013 code a binary democracy variable for every independent country in the world and consider all but Antigua and Barbuda and Grenada as continuously democratic since independence.

as Cuba and Haiti, in which authoritarian colonial rule yielded postindependence authoritarianism.

The French West Indies colonies likely would have followed a similarly democratic path, but never gained independence. In Chapters 3 and 4, we discussed how Martinique, Guadeloupe, Réunion, and French Guiana experienced elections to local assemblies and to the French Parliament under universal suffrage, dating back to the nineteenth century. These territories became Overseas Departments in 1946 and gained increasingly high levels of autonomy after France lost its African empire.[32] But France never granted independence to its colonies that endured the deepest electoral reforms, biasing downward estimates of the French colonial effect in standard cross-national comparisons.

White Settler Minorities

South Africa and Zimbabwe had lengthy periods of colonial pluralism because white settlers established early electoral institutions. However, settlers jealously guarded their monopoly of political power, which prompted decolonization wars for majority rule. These cases have since diverged in democracy levels. Since 1995, most observers characterize South Africa's regimes as democratic whereas Zimbabwe is unambiguously authoritarian.

The democratic nature of South Africa's majority-rule regime likely stems from the relative military weakness of the African National Congress (ANC). South Africa was the strongest white military power that any rebel group in Africa confronted, which prompted the ANC to build broad nationalist support among Africans and to reach electoral compromises with the white South African government.[33] By contrast, the majority-rule struggle in Zimbabwe relied more heavily on coercion.[34] During the rebellion and afterward, Robert Mugabe had to struggle to become the leader of ZANU and then to sideline the opposition outside of ZANU. Mugabe used his tight control over the security forces to achieve these aims. Whereas many observers point to violent events in 2000 as constituting an authoritarian shift in

---

[32] Aldrich and Connell 1992, 70, 282.

[33] Reno 2011, 98–118. Namibia experienced a similar trajectory under colonial rule and after independence, although its V-Dem democracy score under colonialism falls below our threshold for colonial pluralism; see Table 6.2.

[34] Reno 2011, 85–98; Martin 2021.

Zimbabwe, Compagnon contends instead that "the political system set in place at independence and throughout the 1980s was authoritarian in essence."[35] Although multi-party elections have occurred regularly since independence, the regime's origins in violent struggle – caused by intransigent white rule – have determined the direction of politics in Zimbabwe since independence.

6.3.2 Short Colonial Pluralism

Colonies with fewer years of colonial pluralism (between one and nineteen) rarely became full democracies, at least until several decades after independence.[36] Instead, these colonies were often electoral authoritarian or closed authoritarian regimes at independence and remained so throughout the Cold War era. Parties that formed late in the decolonization era lacked either a national organization or internal checks on the consolidation of power. Coups and incumbent consolidation episodes predominated among these cases, a process only partially reversed after the Cold War ended. Table 6.2 summarizes these colonies.

Colonial Elections without Pluralism

A lengthy period of colonial elections *was not* equivalent to long-term exposure to plural institutions if the elections were geographically circumscribed. Thus, despite introducing elections in the 1920s, Nigeria, the Gold Coast (Ghana), and Sierra Leone each experienced less than twenty years of colonial *pluralism* because only select port cities competed in elections until after 1945. Similarly, the introduction of mass politics in Senegal in the 1950s dramatically transformed its political arena, despite the long electoral history of the Four Communes. Senegal has been somewhat more democratic than the average French African country, but nonetheless became a single-party state for decades after independence.[37]

In Nigeria, the narrow scope of elections prevented parties in the emergent electoral system from achieving a national consensus along the lines of that reached by Congress in India or the two major parties in Jamaica. The country's first parties emerged in Lagos in the 1920s

---

[35] Compagnon 2011, 8.
[36] In the Chapter 7, we discuss two exceptions, Botswana and Vanuatu.
[37] Coulon 1989.

Table 6.2 *Postcolonial outcomes: Short colonial pluralism*

Country	Independence	Colonial pluralism	Initial level of democracy	Regime change event (year)
Gambia	1965	17 years	0.50	1994 (coup)
Singapore	1965	17	0.33	none
Solomon Isl.	1978	14	0.53	2000 (civil war)
Senegal	1960	14	0.39	2000 (demo.)
Chad	1960	13	0.26	1975 (coup)
Mauritania	1960	13	0.25	1978 (coup)
Burkina Faso	1960	11	0.38	1966 (coup)
CAR	1960	10	0.27	1965 (coup)
Comoros	1975	10	0.23	1975 (coup)
South Yemen	1967	10	0.08	1990 (merger)
Syria	1946	8	0.32	1958 (coup)
Ghana	1957	6	0.44	1966 (coup)
Laos	1953	6	0.32	1959 (coup)
Nigeria	1960	6	0.26	1966 (coup)
Vanuatu	1980	5	0.69	none
Botswana	1966	5	0.63	none
Uganda	1962	4	0.39	1966 (coup)
Somalia	1960	4	0.39	1969 (coup)
Sierra Leone	1961	4	0.37	1968 (coup)
Benin	1960	4	0.34	1963 (coup)
Togo	1960	4	0.27	1963 (coup)
Swaziland	1968	4	0.21	none
Cameroon	1960	4	0.16	none
Congo (Rep.)	1960	3	0.31	1963 (coup)
Sudan	1956	3	0.29	1958 (coup)
Madagascar	1960	3	0.26	1972 (coup)
Mali	1960	3	0.25	1968 (coup)
Gabon	1960	3	0.22	none
Ivory Coast	1960	3	0.19	1999 (coup)
Tanzania	1961	2	0.34	none
Malaysia	1957	2	0.32	2018 (demo.)
Zambia	1964	2	0.30	1991 (demo.)
Malawi	1964	2	0.28	1994 (demo.)
Namibia	1990	1	0.67	none
Lesotho	1966	1	0.35	1986 (incumbent)
Kenya	1963	1	0.27	2002 (demo.)
Rwanda	1962	1	0.27	1973 (coup)
Niger	1960	1	0.20	1974 (coup)
Burundi	1962	1	0.19	1966 (coup)
Guinea	1958	1	0.19	1984 (coup)

Notes: This table lists every country from our core sample (see Appendix Table A.9) with between one and nineteen years of colonial pluralism. The regime-change event "demo." is an abbreviation for democratization; and "incumbent" includes various acts of incumbent consolidation in previously pluralistic regimes, such as heavily tilting an election and declaring martial law.

to compete for the handful of urban seats on the legislative council. One of these, the National Council of Nigeria and the Cameroons (NCNC), grew to become a mass party.[38] Despite their stated desire to compete as a truly national party after the expansion of elections in the 1940s, subsequent reforms enacted by British officials perpetuated the regionally circumscribed nature of Nigerian elections. Rather than creating a national prime minister, the federal constitution of 1954 strengthened the three regional governments, each based on a different dominant ethnic group: Igbo in the East, Yoruba in the West, and Hausa-Fulani in the North. Subsequently, "the political center of gravity in the NCNC shifted to the east, while central direction of the party organization as a whole lapsed seriously."[39] Each of the three regions had a quota of seats based on their population, which reinforced tendencies toward regional party formation.[40]

Fears of a costly insurgency and early reforms in the nearby Gold Coast prompted a push for Nigeria to gain independence before deeper constitutional reforms could occur. Officials complained that the pace set by the Gold Coast "lost us a vital fifteen to twenty years in Nigeria. Successive Governments since have taken the line that the risks of going too slow were probably greater than the risks of going too fast; and it remains true that a slow pace would lose us the great goodwill we have at present and cause much friction."[41] Consequently, ethnoregional differences persisted as the primary political cleavage in Nigeria after independence.[42] In 1966, Igbo officers led a successful coup attempt. Although the officers proclaimed the goal of creating a unitary government without ethnic bias, deep-seated regional cleavages caused northern leaders to perceive the coup "not so much as an effort to impose a unitary government as a plot by the Igbo to dominate Nigeria."[43]

---

[38] Tamuno 1966, 41–60.

[39] Sklar and Whitaker 1964, 598–604.

[40] In the general election of 1959, NCNC won 34 percent of total votes compared to 25 percent for the NPC (Northern People's Congress). However, because the North was allocated half the seats in parliament, the NPC gained 43 percent of seats compared to 26 percent for NCNC; see Bendel 1999, 707, 713.

[41] Quoted in Brook 1957, 9.

[42] Lovejoy 1992, 47–61.

[43] Lovejoy 1992, 56. This coup led to a countercoup later that year led by officers from the North, followed by the expulsion of Igbo from federal ministries and an Igbo secession attempt in 1967.

Stable Authoritarianism

In seven cases, the initial ruling faction survived for at least three decades after independence under authoritarian rule. In the Ivory Coast, the consolidation of one-party rule had occurred by independence with the connivance of the colonial government. Only one party, the Democratic Party of the Ivory Coast (PDCI), competed in the final decolonization elections. Its leader, Félix Houphouët-Boigny, served as president until his death in 1993. He became a popular representative in the French Parliament, in particular because of his sponsorship in 1946 of legislation to end forced labor in French Africa.[44] Morgenthau attributes the development of a one-party state here and elsewhere in French West Africa to late electoral reforms. At independence, the parties were less than two decades old and their experience with mass elections was even shorter. Starting in 1956, "formal institutional change took place very quickly and with sharp discontinuities. The franchise grew from practically zero to become universal; the power of elected representatives grew from purely consultative to legislative and eventually executive, while the place where power was exercised shifted from Paris to Africa."[45]

Similarly, in Nyasaland (Malawi), the first elections occurred in 1955 and conveyed minimal autonomy. Africans elected only five of the twenty-three seats on the legislative council and the electorate was tiny (2 percent of the population).[46] Africans in Nyasaland sought to disband the Central African Federation, in which they had been federated with Southern Rhodesia (Zimbabwe) and Northern Rhodesia (Zambia) in 1953. The turning point occurred in 1959 when British troops killed at least twenty Africans protestors, an event that "signaled the moral end of the British empire in Africa."[47] In his memoirs, the Secretary of State for the Colonies Iain Macleod recalled that "this was the decisive moment when it became clear to me that we could no longer continue with the old methods of government in Africa, and that meant inexorably a move toward African independence."[48] Over the protests of its few settlers, Nyasaland's legislative council

---

[44] Houphouët-Boigny fits the general pattern whereby a country's "founding father" is hugely popular and able to survive for long periods with minimal constraints on his rule; see Bienen and Van De Walle 1989; Meng 2020, Ch. 5.
[45] Morgenthau 1964, 330.
[46] Hailey 1957, 291–292.
[47] Hyam 2007, 263.
[48] Quoted in Hyam 2007, 263.

became fully elective in 1961, although the franchise remained small (10 percent of the population) because of income requirements. Nyasaland gained internal self-government in 1963 and the franchise became universal in 1964, with independence occurring later in the year. However, by 1960, Hastings Banda had already become the Life President of the Malawi Congress Party (MCP), and the final preindependence elections in 1964 were cancelled because only the MCP nominated candidates, who all ran unopposed. Thus, Malawi was effectively a one-party state at independence,[49] and remained so throughout the Cold War era.

The initial ruling coalition also survived for a long period in postcolonial Malaysia, albeit with more extensive electoral competition. General elections with multi-party competition have been held regularly throughout Malaysia's postcolonial history, occurring every four or five years. However, only one party (the Alliance party/Barisan Nasional) ever won until 2018.[50] Limitations on electoral competition after independence reflected the shallow roots of electoral competition under colonialism. Only one general election occurred in British Malaya prior to independence in 1957, in which the Alliance party won 82 percent of the votes and all but one of the fifty-two seats. The most important political event in Malaya between 1945 and 1957 was guerrilla warfare by Chinese communists, which British troops suppressed.[51] Ethnic violence by Chinese communists broke out again in 1969, which led to a more authoritarian style of rule as the Alliance repressed the opposition.[52]

Coups and Military Rule
Stability was the exception rather than the rule in colonies with late colonial electoral reforms and short colonial pluralism. In twenty-two cases, an authoritarian regime at independence fell to a military coup within two decades. In Sudan, politics were competitive at

---

[49] Meinhardt 1999, 549–551; Hyam 2007, 285; Steinberg 1962, 509.
[50] Brownlee 2007, 7. The party benefitted from gerrymandering, campaign finance advantages, control over the media, and harassment of the opposition; see p. 94.
[51] Brownlee 2007, 56–64; Slater 2010, 57–60.
[52] Slater 2010, 116–124. Malaysia's democracy score dipped during the early 1970s, when Lührmann, Tannenberg and Lindberg 2018 temporarily code Malaysia as a closed rather than electoral authoritarian regime.

independence and there was no dominant party. In the final preindependence elections in 1953, the leading party (the Democratic Unionist
Party, DUP) gained only fifty-one of ninety-seven seats in the lower
chamber and thirty-one of fifty seats in the upper chamber of parliament.[53] But electoral competition was relatively recent. Sudan had
gained a Legislative Assembly in 1948 that contained a mixture of
directly elected, indirectly elected, and appointed members. Collins
contends that "the assembly could hardly claim to be a representative
body when all of its members were bound by close ties to religious or
tribal notables, merchants, or government officials who were leaders of
small, elite groups masquerading as political parties."[54] The military
intervened shortly after independence in 1958, stating that "[t]he aim
of the revolution is to maintain the independence of the Sudan and to
raise the standard of living. Former politicians failed to do that in view
of the fact that no one party had a clear majority."[55] The weakness
of electoral political organizations resulted in no popular resistance to
the coup.[56]

In Niger, one party dominated upon independence in 1960 but
subsequently fell to a coup in 1974.[57] The Nigerien parties that
emerged to compete in colonial elections lacked permanent organizations and programmatic policy platforms. Instead, they represented
shifting coalitions of French-educated urban elites and chiefs who
could mobilize votes. Urban party leaders lacked the traditional status to create a power base independent of chiefs and chiefs lacked
education in French, which prevented them from becoming party
leaders. The leading party in the final decolonization elections in
1958, the Nigerien Progressive Party – African Democratic Assembly
(PPN-RDA), moved in 1959 to ban the main opposition party. They established a regime that rested upon an alliance of chiefs but lacked the
nationalist appeal of the PDCI in the Ivory Coast. Declining economic
conditions triggered protests and, in 1974, a coup that established a
military regime.

In Uganda, the incumbent ruling faction struck first and purged opposition politicians from the cabinet. Uganda's first election occurred

---

[53] Doebbler and Fleischhacker 1999, 857.
[54] Collins 2008, 57.
[55] Quoted in McGowan, *African Military Coups d'Etat Code Sheet.*
[56] Finer 2002, 118.
[57] This paragraph draws from Decalo 1990, 250–267.

in 1958, only four years before gaining independence. The country's final colonial elections in 1962 were closely contested. The Uganda People's Congress (UPC) received 52 percent of votes and thirty-seven seats, and the Democratic Party (DP) received 46 percent of votes and twenty-four seats. Yet even these late, mostly competitive elections were not truly national; the *Lukiiko* (the parliament of Buganda) did not participate and instead appointed an additional twenty-one members to the legislature.[58] Initially, Uganda retained multi-party competition through a tenuous power-sharing deal between rivals: the leader of the UPC, Milton Obote, served as prime minister and the *Kabaka* (king) of Uganda served as president.[59] However, four years later, Obote consolidated power by exiling the *Kabaka*, arresting Bagandan cabinet officials, and taking the presidential title for himself. Obote himself lost power in a coup in 1971, and Uganda did not experience a postindependence election until 1980, and then not again until 1996.[60]

Reforms after the Cold War

Despite long periods of authoritarian rule, many countries with short colonial pluralism later experienced liberalization, including some full-blown democratization episodes. Most others introduced multi-party electoral competition. These changes reflected a general trend: the end of superpower competition during the Cold War positively influenced electoral competition. Many colonies in this category were unable to resist the growing pressure from Western aid providers to allow meaningful electoral competition, even if such reforms did not yield full democracies.[61]

6.3.3 No Colonial Pluralism

Twenty-six colonies experienced zero years of colonial pluralism. All had unambiguously authoritarian regimes at independence, and these

---

[58] Schmidt 1999, 932–934. The transition from a nominated to an elected legislative council was slow in part because elites within the Kingdom of Buganda used their privileged colonial status to delay national-oriented reforms that would dilute their special privileges; see Hailey 1957, 292–295; Dinwiddy 1981, 501–504.

[59] Dinwiddy 1981.

[60] Schmidt 1999, 933.

[61] Levitsky and Way 2010; Miller 2020.

Table 6.3 *Postcolonial outcomes: No colonial pluralism*

Country	Independence	Initial level of democracy	Regime change year (event)
Congo (DR)	1960	0.29	1960 (coup)
Kuwait	1961	0.29	none
Cambodia	1953	0.27	1970 (coup)
Indonesia	1949	0.26	1966 (coup)
Vietnam	1954	0.24	none
Tunisia	1956	0.20	2011 (demo.)
Algeria	1962	0.19	1992 (coup)
Djibouti	1977	0.18	none
Equatorial Guinea	1968	0.18	none
Maldives	1965	0.17	2008 (demo.)
Cape Verde	1975	0.17	1991 (demo.)
São Tomé and P.	1975	0.16	1991 (demo.)
Bahrain	1971	0.15	none
Iraq	1932	0.15	1958 (coup)
Nepal	1947	0.14	1990 (demo.)
Jordan	1946	0.13	none
Guinea-Bissau	1974	0.13	1980 (coup)
Egypt	1922	0.12	1953 (coup)
Libya	1951	0.11	1969 (coup)
Mozambique	1975	0.08	none
Angola	1975	0.07	none
Morocco	1956	0.07	none
Bhutan	1947	0.04	2008 (demo.)
Qatar	1971	0.02	none
UAE	1971	0.02	none
Oman	1951	0.01	none

Notes: This table lists every country from our core sample (see Appendix Table A.9) with zero years of colonial pluralism. The regime-change event "demo." is an abbreviation for democratization.

regimes have proved remarkably durable. Nineteen survived until 1990 and twelve are still intact as of 2024. Many of these regimes emerged either from rebel groups who fought for independence from an authoritarian metropole or were national monarchs to whom the colonizer (usually Britain) handed off power. Table 6.3 summarizes these colonies.

We also assess the histories of non-European countries not colonized by a Western power, which we expect to have similarly undemocratic histories. Non-Western colonies were uniformly authoritarian after independence, reflecting their lack of electoral competition under colonial rule. Never-colonized countries, by definition, did not experience *colonial* pluralism, although some initiated early constitutional and electoral reforms. However, monarchs and militaries unchecked by an external power often rolled back these advances.

Rebel Regimes and National Monarchs

Rebel groups seized power at independence in Angola, Mozambique, and Guinea-Bissau following anticolonial wars against Portugal, who never introduced meaningful electoral reforms. In Algeria, the National Liberation Front (FLN) gained power after a negotiated settlement with France in 1962, having never participated in a multi-party election under Arab majority rule before achieving independence. Territory-wide electoral institutions in Algeria were weak at independence due to racial restrictions and high centralization. Although elections dated back to the nineteenth century, most major decisions were made in Paris.[62]

The long-lasting authoritarian regimes in three of these cases fit a broader pattern by which regimes that gain power through rebellions are typically authoritarian and remarkably durable.[63] While vying for power, rebel groups usually create a political wing and a military wing. When a group wins control of the state, the political wing becomes the ruling party and the military wing becomes the new state military. The battle-hardened ruling party was usually strong (compared to typically weak parties in countries with late colonial electoral reforms), which fostered tight control over the military. However, because the leaders of rebel parties gained their positions from developing a competitive advantage in coercion rather than by mobilizing electoral support, the result was stable authoritarian governance.

Fifteen cases gained independence as monarchies. Determining executive succession by hereditary lineages eliminates the possibility of

---

[62] V-Dem codes a low democracy score in all these years, which is why Algeria is coded as having no years of colonial pluralism. Nonetheless, this case has similarities to Zimbabwe, discussed earlier with the lengthy pluralism cases.

[63] Lachapelle et al. 2020; Meng and Paine 2022.

modern, mass-based elections for the position of chief executive. Moreover, the political arena is confined mainly to the ruling family itself. In the dynastic monarchies of the Persian Gulf, monarchs share power within the ruling family. This lowers the stakes over who is the head of state by providing lucrative ministries to other family members. Thus, even during upheaval periods such as the Arab Spring of 2011, Middle Eastern monarchies have usually succeeded at channeling demands within the existing political system rather than reforming it.[64]

Countries with no exposure to colonial pluralism continue to be less democratic than other ex-colonies since the Cold War ended, although average democracy levels have risen steadily (see Figure 6.4). Cape Verde and São Tomé and Príncipe, small ex-Portuguese colonies that did not fight for independence, each democratized following the introduction of multi-party elections in the early 1990s. In Bhutan, the monarchy transformed from absolute to constitutional by delegating more powers to the prime minister and becoming subject to parliamentary impeachment.[65] In Mozambique, the governing party FRELIMO negotiated a settlement following a long-running civil war with the Mozambican National Resistance (RENAMO), which established multi-party elections. However, many of these cases remain closed authoritarian regimes, in contrast to their near absence among other postcolonial cases. Monarchies such as Qatar, the United Arab Emirates, and Bahrain lack any meaningful political competition even below the level of the executive.[66]

Other Non-European Countries

Non-Western powers colonized some non-European territories in the nineteenth and twentieth centuries, including parts of East Asia by Japan and Central Asia by the Soviet Union. Like Portugal (and some earlier Western metropoles), these regimes were authoritarian and did

---

[64] Herb 1999; Menaldo 2012; Gause III 2013.

[65] Hofmann 2006.

[66] In Morocco and Jordan, the same ruling family remains in power, but they have introduced multi-party competition in national legislatures that have some ability to influence policy. Jordan's democracy score rose from 0.15 in 1989 to an average of 0.24 since 1990; the figures in Morocco are nearly identical. Yet despite modest liberalizing reforms, even these countries remain categorized as closed authoritarian regimes because the chief executive is unelected.

not create plural institutions in their colonies.[67] Within the Soviet Union, symbolic single-party elections for the Congress of Soviets were held periodically until 1936. More competitive elections occurred only in 1989, to the Congress of People's Deputies of the Soviet Union, as the empire was disintegrating.[68] In Japanese-controlled Taiwan, city and township councils became partially elected in 1935 on tiny franchises circumscribed by high tax-paying requirements.

Never-colonized countries experienced more meaningful early electoral reforms, although these countries usually did not consolidate democratic regimes either. In six cases, constitutional reforms and elections occurred in the nineteenth century or early twentieth century, around the time that many non-white middle-class colonies gained representative institutions. However, as shown in Figure 6.5, these noncolonies have not attained comparable democracy levels as non-white middle-class colonies or, since 1990, settler-minority colonies. Although elites influenced by Western models achieved temporary electoral reforms, an external power was not present to prevent usurpation by the traditional ruling dynasty or the military.

Defensive modernization efforts to prevent Western occupation prompted early electoral reforms, usually amid broader reforms to create a constitutional monarchy, in the Ottoman Empire/Turkey (1876, 1908), Japan (1890), Persia/Iran (1906), China (1912), Afghanistan (1931), and Siam/Thailand (1933).[69] A common theme was Western-educated or inspired reformers (e.g., the Young Turks) who sought to modernize the military and implement Western-style parliamentary institutions, in part as an attempt to increase the regime's international legitimacy. These groups, sometimes in alliance with the military, either deposed the monarch or pressured him to adopt a constitution in which an elected legislature constrained his power, at least in theory.

---

[67] Between 1919 and 1945, the average V-Dem democracy score was 0.14 in Portugal, 0.19 in Japan, and 0.11 in the Russia/Soviet Union. These are roughly the same score as the average closed authoritarian regime in 2022 (0.15).

[68] White 2010. Mongolia, also under communist rule, followed a similar pattern as the Soviet Socialist Republics in Central Asia; see Gluchowski and Grotz 2002.

[69] Other noncolonized monarchies established elections to a national parliament either later (Ethiopia in 1957, Yemen in 1971) or never (Saudi Arabia).

These reforms yielded moderate increases in V-Dem democracy scores, albeit from a very low base. The average scores of these six countries increased from 0.05 in the ten years prior to the first election to 0.12 in the ten years afterward, which is still below the average score for a closed authoritarian regime in 2022 (0.15).[70] The low democracy scores reflected electoral restrictions similar to those we have discussed for many colonies. Less than 2 percent of the Japanese population was eligible to vote in 1890 because of high tax-paying requirements.[71] In Iran, property requirements severely constricted the electorate and the seats were heavily malapportioned to favor Teheran.[72] Suffrage was nominally universal in Thailand, but the monarch appointed half the parliament and elections were indirect.[73] The only role of the Afghan Parliament was to passively approve laws.[74]

Counterrevolutions and civil disorder posed even greater impediments to consolidating constitutional reforms. Western-inspired reformers were but one faction, and royalists often sought to reassert control. The Ottoman Empire's First Constitutional Era ended after two years when the sultan dissolved the elected Chamber of Deputies in 1878, yielding three decades of absolutist rule.[75] The Young Turks, after successfully pressing for constitutional reforms in 1908, immediately faced a counterrevolution and consolidated power only by manipulating parliamentary elections and repressing the opposition.[76] Constitutionalists in Iran successfully defeated a counterrevolution in 1909, but were unable to consolidate control in rural areas and succumbed to Russian pressure to suspend the constitution and the elected *Majlis* in 1911.[77] China's reforms occurred amid the collapse of the Qing Dynasty,[78] which was followed by a period of warlordism, and Thailand has experienced constant shuffling between constitutional

---

[70] We count 1908 as the first election in Turkey for this calculation, as the 1876 reforms were reversed almost immediately.

[71] Beasley 1989, 670; Meyer 2012, 144. See also Mason 1962; Fraser, Mason and Mitchell 2005; Sims 2019.

[72] Martin 2011, 468.

[73] Nelson 2002, 266.

[74] Sarabi 2002, 503–504.

[75] Cleveland 2004, 85–86.

[76] Cleveland 2004, 134–137.

[77] Keddie 1983; Cleveland 2004, 143–147.

[78] Wright 1968.

and authoritarian regimes. The power vacuum created by elite in-fighting and broader societal struggles also elevated the political impor-tance of the military. Western colonizers were not benevolent toward their dependent populations but generally succeeded at preventing vio-lent coups and rebellions, which enabled middle-class parliamentarians in select colonies to consolidate electoral competition.[79]

Liberia was a borderline noncolony with some similarities to settler-minority colonies, and failed to consolidate democracy despite early elections.[80] Formerly enslaved persons from the United States formed a coastal elite of Americo-Liberians who modeled their constitution after that of the United States and developed a two-party system in the mid-nineteenth century. However, similar to (white) settler mi-norities elsewhere, Americo-Liberians comprised a numerically small (less than 1 percent of the population in the 1960s) and racially distinct socioeconomic elite who monopolized political power. Suf-frage was highly restricted for a century with property requirements that favored the coastal elite. Even after moving to nominally uni-versal suffrage in 1948, Americo-Liberians retained their monopoly on power through corruption and repression in what was effectively a one-party state governed by the True Whig Party. In reaction to the unwillingness of the Americo-Liberian elites to share power, a faction of indigenous Liberian officers staged a coup in 1980 that vio-lently ended the settler regime and perpetuated authoritarian rule in a new form.

6.4 Postcolonial Legacies in Early Decolonization Colonies

Colonial institutions strongly influenced postcolonial outcomes in pre-1945 decolonization cases as well. In the neo-Britains (United States, Canada, Australia, and New Zealand), pluralist metropolitan institu-tions and large settler populations facilitated the early introduction of colonial elections for the white majority, which yielded stable

---

[79] Among Western dependencies, domestic reversals to constitutional reforms occurred in the indirectly ruled protectorates of Kuwait (1938–1939) and Maldives (1952–1954). In both cases, royalists re-established absolute monarchies after brief constitutional reforms; see Koch 2002, 155–156; Lehr 2002, 586.

[80] For the following, see Kilson 1963; Jones 1974; Okolo 1981.

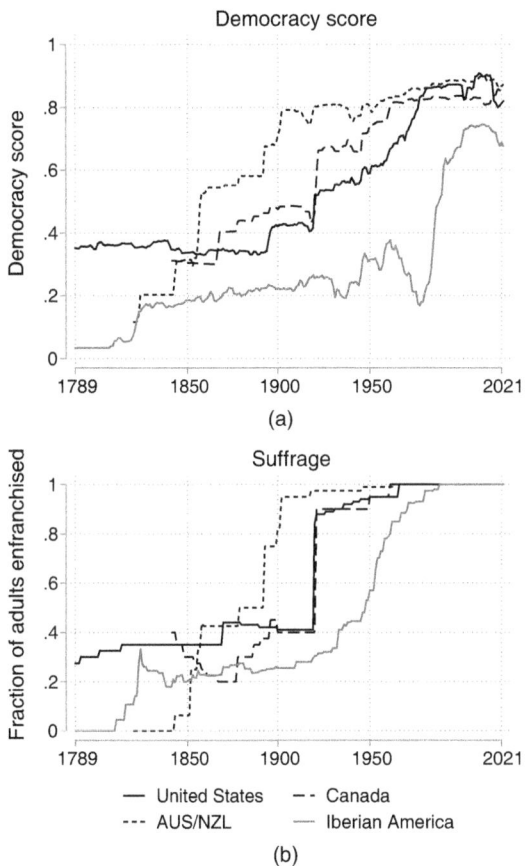

Figure 6.6 Democracy levels in the neo-Britains and Iberian America
Notes: The outcome variable in Figure 6.6(a) is the V-Dem electoral democracy index over time for a single country or group of countries. The outcome variable in Figure 6.6(b) is the V-Dem variable for the fraction of the adult population with the legal right to vote. The tables below list the full sample. Australia and New Zealand had nearly identical democracy scores throughout the entire period, which is why we combine them into one average line.

democracies after independence. Iberian American ex-colonies, with authoritarian colonial experiences, were unstable and mostly authoritarian for roughly a century-and-a-half after independence. We summarize trends over time in democracy scores and franchise size in Figure 6.6.

Table 6.4 *Postcolonial outcomes: Neo-Britains*

Country	Independence	Initial level of democracy	Regime change year (event)
New Zealand	1907	0.81	none
Australia	1901	0.78	none
Canada	1867	0.41	none
United States	1783	0.35	none

Notes: Year of independence for all but the United States is the year of dominion status. The first year for the United States in V-Dem is 1789. The V-Dem data set does not have long enough temporal coverage to calculate years of colonial pluralism for all these countries. However, given the low standard for pluralism we adopt, we presume that all four met our standard for lengthy colonial pluralism (at least twenty years of semi-competitive elections before gaining independence).

6.4.1 Democratic Legacies in the Neo-Britains

Australia and New Zealand had the highest democracy scores around independence of any Western colony. By the independence period, both countries had established fully or nearly universal suffrage for men and women.[81] Lower democracy scores in the United States and Canada at independence reflected their smaller franchises. Roughly half of adult men could vote in the United States and Canada in the late nineteenth century, as they were restricted by property, taxpaying, and racial restrictions; and all women were disenfranchised. After independence, all four colonies established stable democratic regimes with multi-party competition and rotation in office. Democracy scores increased in the United States and Canada over time as they expanded the franchise, and all four countries made improvements in the quality of elections with reforms such as introducing the secret ballot and reducing clientelism and patronage. Table 6.4 summarizes these cases.

As discussed in Chapter 3, each country had a history of locally elected colonial assemblies dating back decades or centuries. All four

---

[81] Starting in the 1850s, every Australian colony passed manhood suffrage laws, and the Commonwealth Franchise Act of 1902 passed shortly after independence enshrined universal male and female suffrage; see Waterhouse 2010, 239–241. In New Zealand, property-holding qualifications were low at the outset of elections and were further lowered in the 1880s, and women were enfranchised in 1893; see Belich 2010, 259, 263.

adopted constitutions that placed stringent constraints on the executive.[82] Nor was the military an important political actor, which reflected a conscious decision to avoid the perils of concentrating despotic powers in the national government. In the United States and Canada, whose institutions at independence were fairly nondemocratic by contemporary standards, voting rights expanded over time as officials responded to pressure from agitation and nonparticipation.[83]

The neo-Britains differed from the other settler colonies we have analyzed throughout the book because whites comprised an overwhelming majority of the population at the national level as well as in almost every subnational state or province. In the mid-nineteenth century, the average Canadian province was 99 percent white, with corresponding figures of 97 percent in Australian colonies, 96 percent in New Zealand, and 96 percent in US states excluding those in the South.[84] Thus, even if the national political regime was racially restrictive, it could nonetheless meet minimalist standards of democracy.[85] In the United States, national voting rights for Blacks did not become permanently enshrined until the Voting Rights Act of 1965. As late as 1934, Canada passed a federal statute that prevented Inuits and members of First Nations who lived on reserves from voting in federal elections, which was reversed in 1960.[86] In Australia, the same Commonwealth Franchise Act of 1902 that enshrined universal white suffrage simultaneously prevented indigenous Australians and various other non-white persons from voting in federal elections. In 1965, Queensland became the final state to grant indigenous voting rights.[87]

The US South is the only exception among the neo-Britains in which challenges from non-whites prompted a white reaction to create unambiguously authoritarian regimes (at the subnational level). Reflecting

---

[82] Dahl 2003; Waterhouse 2010, 240–247.

[83] Braun and Kvasnicka 2013 discuss attracting migrants to Western states (nonparticipation) and Teele 2018 examines the role of local organizations (agitation) in promoting female suffrage. Keyssar 2009 discusses these and other themes in his broad overview of franchise expansion in the United States. See McRae 2019 for the evolution of the franchise in Canada.

[84] Paine 2019*a*, 565.

[85] Boix, Miller and Rosato 2013, for example, adopt for their data set the commonplace standard that the minimum franchise size for a regime to potentially qualify as democratic is half the adult male population.

[86] Canadian Encyclopedia 2022.

[87] Australian Electoral Commission 2020.

Table 6.5 *Postcolonial outcomes: Iberian America*

Country	Independence	Initial level of democracy	Regime change year (event)
Brazil	1822	0.26	1889 (coup)
Peru	1824	0.24	1829 (coup)
Colombia	1819	0.21	1830 (coup)
Bolivia	1825	0.19	1828 (shuffling)
Chile	1818	0.18	1827 (shuffling)
Mexico	1821	0.18	1823 (coup)
Guatemala	1821	0.12	1829 (civil war)
Argentina	1816	0.09	1828 (coup)
Uruguay	1828	0.05	1838 (shuffling)
Paraguay	1811	0.04	1841 (coup)

Notes: Year of independence from Hensel 2014. We include only countries that gained independence directly from Spain or Portugal. Excluded countries: all that comprised the Federal Republic of Central America except for Guatemala (Costa Rica, El Salvador, Honduras, Nicaragua), all that comprised Gran Colombia except for Colombia (Ecuador, Panama, Venezuela), the Dominican Republic because it was militarily occupied by Haiti for more than two decades almost immediately after gaining independence from Spain, and Cuba because it gained independence from (and was intermittently occupied by) the United States. The regime-change event "shuffling" encompasses rapid shuffling of presidents within a short period and forced resignations.

the legacy of chattel slavery, the population was only 61 percent white in the average state in the US South as of 1850, and whites were a minority in South Carolina and Mississippi.[88] Like the British West Indies and settler parts of Africa, whites in the US South used coercion and unfair voting practices to establish subnational authoritarian regimes from the 1890s through 1960s, which reversed temporary gains in Black voting rights in the 1860s and 1870s.[89]

---

[88] Paine 2019*a*, 565. The South is defined as the eleven states that formed the Confederate States of America.

[89] Kousser 1974; Valelly 2009; Mickey 2015. Paine 2019*a*, 565, presents data on the discrepancy in voting restrictions between southern states and the rest of the Union during the Jim Crow era.

Table 6.6 **Voting population in Spanish America and US/Canada**

Countries/Years	1840–1880	1881–1920	1921–1940
U.S./Canada	13.0%	20.5%	39.5%
Spanish America	0.6%	5.7%	10.2%
ARG/CRI/URU	-	8.8%	16.3%
Rest of Sp.Am.	0.6%	4.2%	7.2%

Notes: Figures in the cells are the average percentage of the population voting in elections, based on averaging Engerman and Sokoloff's 2005 select data for various countries and years within each category. We follow these scholars by distinguishing Argentina, Costa Rica, and Uruguay from the rest of the region.

6.4.2 *Authoritarian Legacies in Iberian America*

In Iberian America, the colonial legacy was inauspicious for promoting democracy. Despite sizable populations of white settlers, authoritarian metropoles had blocked any moves toward representative institutions until the very end of the colonial era. These colonies not only failed to benefit from possible *pro*-democratic effects of settlers, but also suffered from the *anti*-democratic effects of landed European oligarchies. Landed elites engaged in constant political infighting (including coups and revolts) and resisted moves toward broadening the franchise and deepening electoral competition. Table 6.5 summarizes the colonies.

All the Iberian American countries had low democracy scores around independence. Their average score of 0.15 was the same as in Bahrain upon independence (see Table 6.3). As we showed in Figure 6.6, average democracy scores in the region remained fairly low until the late twentieth century. Table 6.6 shows that Spanish American countries had much smaller franchises than the United States and Canada. Democracy did not become consolidated in most of Latin America until the 1980s, more than 150 years after independence for most countries.

White settlers formed an entrenched landed class during the colonial era, dating back to the establishment of hereditary land titles over *haciendas*.[90] Many scholars argued that landed elites delayed

---

[90] Skidmore and Smith 2005, 22. Land inequality in Latin America remains strikingly high to the present day; see Frankema 2009*b*.

democratization by blocking the aspirations of the working class.[91] Only when the lower classes gained in size and organizational strength were they able to overcome landed elites and promote greater political competition and expanded franchises. Political regimes remained unstable throughout the early twentieth century even where more competitive political institutions existed, as in Argentina, Chile, Costa Rica, and Uruguay (see Table 6.6).[92] Scholars link the rise of democracy in the region in the 1980s and 1990s to successful popular mobilization by the working class,[93] and a foreign policy shift in the United States toward promoting democracy in the region.[94]

6.5 Conclusion

Nearly all ex-Western colonies experienced some form of elections prior to gaining independence, but few consolidated democratic rule afterward. Hasty electoral reforms usually failed to build strong institutions that would create propitious conditions for self-enforcing democracy. Colonies with early elections for non-European middle classes generally had the best prospects for establishing and maintaining postcolonial democratic regimes. In these colonies, electoral reforms usually occurred over the course of multiple decades, and political parties formed initially among elites and eventually established deep roots across society. Institutionalized political parties created a class of political elites with a comparative advantage in electoral competition, which created incentives for them to uphold democratic rule and provided a buffer against military intervention or incumbent consolidation.

---

[91] Rueschemeyer, Stephens and Stephens 1992, 155; Collier 1999, 34; Skidmore and Smith 2005, 50. See also Collier and Collier 1991 for a broad analysis of twentieth-century political regimes and the struggle between organized labor and landed elites, and cross-regional statistical evidence in Ansell and Samuels 2014 that links higher land inequality to a lower likelihood of democratic transitions.

[92] On early reforms in Chile, see Rueschemeyer, Stephens and Stephens 1992, 176; Valenzuela 1996; Collier 1999, 59; North, Summerhill and Weingast 2000, 30. On persistent instability in Argentina, see O'Donnell 1994; Levitsky and Murillo 2005a,b. More generally, see Engerman and Sokoloff 2005.

[93] Collier 1999; Haggard and Kaufman 2016, 110–116.

[94] Mainwaring and Pérez-Liñán 2014, 230–231; Levitsky and Way 2010.

Most countries did not enjoy these favorable conditions for post-colonial democracy. Often, colonial electoral reforms were rushed concessions to stave off revolts in many post-1945 colonies and in the early Iberian American empires. Parties gained little experience with mass political competition and often fell to military coups after independence. Other parties moved in a personalist direction and formally eliminated multi-party competition shortly after independence. Elsewhere, colonialism formed the foundation for a durable authoritarian regime, either because European resistance to political reforms bred a mass rebellion or because the metropole handed off power to an unelected monarch.

Countries with early elections for white settlers followed a more mixed path. In the historically unique neo-Britains, large white majorities were usually able to preserve a monopoly on political power without resorting to mass repression or extreme tactics to restrict the franchise. Elsewhere, white minorities eroded the quality of democratic competition by clinging to power, sometimes undermining the advantages otherwise created by early electoral competition.

Overall, the evidence in this chapter establishes that we cannot understand contemporary levels of democracy in much of the world without scrutinizing the colonial era. Colonial elections, *because* of their various flaws, put countries on divergent trajectories at independence that have largely reinforced themselves over time.

7 | Conclusion

Why are some countries more democratic than others? Existing theories and evidence focus almost exclusively on postindependence explanatory variables and cases. However, this approach overlooks the origins of democratic institutions in the non-European world. Almost all Western colonies held at least one national election prior to independence, and the overwhelming majority of contemporary non-European regimes with meaningful elections (either fully democratic or electoral authoritarian) held their first election under Western rule.

Colonies varied in the timing of their first election, the extent of policymaking autonomy, and the size of the franchise. In some colonies, democratic reforms occurred gradually and always in the direction of increasing democracy levels, whereas others incurred reversions to autocratic direct rule. At independence, some new countries met minimalist standards of democracy. Some postcolonial democracies were durable, but many fell to military coups or incumbent consolidation shortly after independence. Other cases experienced colonial elections but never achieved fully democratic competition – or never held any colonial elections at all.

7.1 Summary of Main Findings

7.1.1 Theory: Actors, Goals, and Strategic Options

Metropolitan actors sought to extract rents, broadly defined, from their colonies. The potential sources of rents included economic exploitation and trade, securing strategic bases, and enhancing national prestige. To achieve these benefits at minimal cost, leaders in the metropole preferred to confine decision-making power to themselves and their appointees. However, both whites and non-whites living in the colonies could pressure officials by lobbying, withdrawing participation, or revolting. Representation in political institutions secured

194

colonists' interests more effectively than temporary policy concessions, which could more easily be rolled back in the future.

7.1.2 Pluralism of Metropolitan Institutions

Pluralistic metropolitan institutions created a permissive condition for colonial elections to occur. Authoritarian metropoles denied representation to their colonies because they were skeptical of parliaments at home and faced higher transaction acts to managing unfamiliar institutions. When pushed, hybrid metropolitan regimes that combined some electoral competition with a small franchise permitted similar institutions in their colonies. Among fully democratic metropoles, the impetus for mass franchise expansion often occurred under left-wing governance coalitions and when special interests were weaker, whereas monarchies at home made this institution palatable in their colonies.

Confirming these ideas, electoral institutions were rare in colonies of authoritarian metropoles both in absolute and relative terms. Within the New World before 1850, colonies of parliamentary metropoles had electoral institutions in 72.7 percent of colony-years, compared to 1.5 percent for colonies with authoritarian metropoles. Nearly every British colony in North America and the West Indies had an elected legislature in the mid-eighteenth century. By contrast, electoral institutions were almost entirely absent in the French, Spanish, and Portuguese empires prior to the French Revolution.

Between 1850 and 1945, among a global sample, colonies of pluralistic metropoles had electoral institutions in 38.2 percent of colony-years, compared to 1.4 percent in the authoritarian metropole colonies. By 1965, democratic metropoles had deferred to the "wind of change" and implemented decolonization reforms. Electoral institutions were nearly universal among their colonies and ex-colonies (92 percent), and the franchise had grown large as well (average of 81 percent of the adult population who could vote). By contrast, economic and prestige rents encouraged Portugal's narrow ruling elite to hold on as long as possible, and their obstinate stance prompted major anticolonial revolts and ushered in rebel regimes at independence.

7.1.3 Dual Effects of White Settlers

White settlers exerted dual effects on democratic development. They usually succeeded at gaining early representation for themselves by pressuring pluralistic metropoles through lobbying, the prospect of crippling the economic productivity of the colony through nonpartic- ipation, or even revolting. Britain's earliest colonies, located in North America and the West Indies, had large populations of English set- tlers. Most gained representative assemblies within twenty years of settlement, in contrast to later-conquered colonies in the West In- dies and Canada where the white population was largely Catholic (a disenfranchised group at home). In the nineteenth century, Cana- dian, Australian, and New Zealand colonies gained high autonomy commensurate to the earlier US colonies. By the early twentieth cen- tury, electoral institutions also were common in parts of Africa with larger white settlements, both within the British empire (South Africa, Zimbabwe, Kenya) and French empire (Algeria).

But the same tools that enabled white settlers to gain represen- tation for themselves could also be used to deny representation to others. Settlers formed entrenched landed oligarchies which jealously guarded their monopoly over voting rights. When challenged, settlers responded with repression or authoritarian institutional change. In the British West Indies, this yielded a wave of reversals in electoral as- semblies in the nineteenth century. White minorities feared that Black freedmen would soon dominate their elected legislatures. In Africa af- ter World War II, colonies with large white settler populations resisted franchise expansion for Africans, which prompted decolonization wars. After independence, whites in the US South prevented eman- cipated blacks from gaining permanent voting rights for more than a century, and landed interests in Iberian America blocked franchise expansion throughout the nineteenth and twentieth centuries.

One consequence of these dual effects was that settlers promoted postcolonial democracy in relatively few cases. Settlers propelled early elections in the four neo-Britains, who consolidated democracy after- ward (albeit with the subnational exception of the US South). Within the West Indies, among countries that eventually gained independence, only the Bahamas and Barbados had uninterrupted experiences with electoral institutions originally created by white settlers. Europeans also developed electoral institutions in Israel, which became demo- cratic after independence, although this was an unusual case with a diaspora of settlers who did not originate from the metropole. South Africa (and its dependency of Namibia) are borderline cases with early settler elections and comparatively democratic regimes since transitioning to majority rule, but in between settlers coercively resisted franchise expansion.[1] Elsewhere, settlers dismantled early institutions to prevent majority rule (most of the British West Indies), violently repressed attempts to broaden the franchise (Algeria and Zimbabwe), or never developed electoral institutions in the first place under authoritarian metropoles (Spanish America, Brazil, and Angola).

7.1.4 Pressure from Non-Europeans

Non-Europeans faced pervasive discrimination but could gain concessions in three distinct circumstances. First, starting in the nineteenth century, emancipated Blacks in plantation colonies and non-European residents of select port cities formed middle classes educated in European languages who worked as lawyers, doctors, teachers, and journalists. Although small, they could effectively lobby and agitate for early representation; it was difficult to justify exclusion for colonists who would have met the franchise requirements at home and were otherwise like Europeans except for their skin color. This explains the early emergence of elections in the presidency cities of India and select port cities in West Africa (e.g., Saint-Louis in Senegal, Lagos in Nigeria, and Freetown in Sierra Leone), and the re-emergence of elections across the West Indies by the 1920s. These early elections were limited in both scale and scope but nonetheless distinguished these colonies from most of the colonial world.

Second, the threat of mass revolts rose across the colonial world after World War II. The balance of power shifted away from the major colonial powers and rising nationalism helped non-white leaders to organize opposition movements against oppressive rule. Democratic metropoles responded by implementing decolonization reforms, which included majority-elected assemblies with universal suffrage, followed by independence shortly afterward. Compared to colonies of authoritarian metropoles or with settler minorities, colonies of democratic metropoles had much larger franchises in the 1960s and were less likely to experience major decolonization wars.

Third, traditional rural elites were favored in subnational governance for much of the colonial period. In special cases, one monarch

---

[1] Most quantitative data sets characterize South Africa as a democracy since 1994 and Namibia as an electoral authoritarian regime.

corresponded with most or all of a colony's territory. National monarchs usually gained high levels of autonomy throughout the colonial period and created an alternative to mass elections for handing off power when decolonization became inevitable. Metropoles with a monarchy at home, in particular Britain, more frequently chose this path.

7.1.5 Postcolonial Persistence

Postcolonial democracy was not the only, or even the most frequent, product of colonial elections. Instead, colonial elections, *because* of their various flaws, put countries on divergent trajectories at independence that have largely reinforced themselves over time.

The relatively few countries with lengthy episodes of colonial pluralism usually became durable democracies. Politicians had sunk costs in democratic procedures such as competing in elections and navigating legislatures. Institutionalized parties helped to stabilize democratic competition and to create a buffer against military intervention. Colonies with non-white middle classes or very large settler populations often followed this path.

However, colonial elections were typically short-lived or flawed in various ways, which undermined postcolonial democracy. Countries with short periods of colonial pluralism were usually characterized by the absence of institutionalized parties or established norms of democratic competition. Consequently, electoral losers had incentives to seize power through military coups and rebellions, and electoral winners had incentives to consolidate their power by eliminating the possibility of losing their office in future elections. Many such cases had weak colonial-era elites and experienced hasty electoral reforms after World War II when the threat of mass revolt was imminent. The end of the Cold War prompted liberalizing reforms, but these countries remained less democratic than countries with longer exposure to colonial pluralism.

Most national monarchies and colonies of authoritarian metropoles gained no meaningful experience with colonial elections and were undemocratic at independence. Rebel regimes and monarchies each had institutional constellations that strengthened the regime against subversion by actors such as the military, and these regimes tended to survive for decades after independence. Many of these countries remain closed authoritarian regimes to the present day.

7.2 Broader Implications for Democracy and Dictatorship

Our findings carry implications for many segments of the democratization literature, including top-down democratic transitions, social classes and democratization, democratic sequencing, dominant-party democracies, non-Western institutions and democracy, and international democracy promotion. Greater attention to colonial cases will advance these research agendas.

7.2.1 Top-down Democratic Transitions

What prompts democratic transitions from above? This question is central to the colonial setting because of the importance of metropolitan decision-making. Existing research analyzes elite splits between hardliners and moderates, which create openings for voluntarist transitions.[2] This idea has limited relevance for understanding colonial reforms. Rather than analyzing a single country with an authoritarian regime that contemplates a transition, we are in effect considering distinct central (metropolitan) and regional (colonial) governments. Democratic institutions in the metropole created an opening for expanding pluralism in the colonial government, regardless of whether metropolitan elites were unified or divided. Moreover, unlike some prominent accounts of pro-British effects on democracy,[3] we do not take a purely top-down, voluntarist approach. Even if conditions in the metropole were favorable for permitting colonial reforms, a push from below was still needed. Understanding which actors are most likely to provide this push requires engaging with research on which social classes facilitate transitions from below.

7.2.2 Social Classes and Democratization

Which social classes routinely pressure for or block democratization? We identify three key domestic groups in the colonial context: white settlers, non-European majorities that posed a credible threat of revolt, and non-white middle classes. These groups have analogs to social classes studied in the broader literature but also challenge some well-established ideas.

---

[2] O'Donnell and Schmitter 1986.
[3] Weiner 1987.

White settlers resemble two very different types of actors in existing studies. In Ansell and Samuels' theory of intraelite competition, capitalist elites who are excluded from power leverage their relative wealth to push for political incorporation.[4] Casting metropolitan officials as the autocratic incumbent, white settlers correspond with this conceptualization of the capitalist class because they comprised a colonial economic elite who used their lobbying, agitation, and nonparticipation options to gain representation for themselves. But white settlers also resembled the canonical landlords, an actor derided as antithetical to democratization.[5] Settlers routinely blocked franchise expansion to perpetuate their dominance over the best land and economic opportunities. Existing theories do not explain how a single social group could exbihit such mixed effects.

Non-European majorities, when they posed a credible threat of revolt after 1945, resembled the generic masses actor posited by Acemoglu and Robinson as well as Boix.[6] In their accounts, the masses compel elites to democratize when they pose a credible threat of revolt.[7] Our evidence supports this implication for franchise expansion specifically, but not other aspects of democracy. Mass revolt threats routinely compelled colonizers to grant concessions such as universal suffrage and legislative majorities. However, hasty concessions in the run up to independence rarely consolidated durable postcolonial democracy because parties were not institutionalized and norms of electoral competition were not well established. Consequently, late-reforming countries with short episodes of colonial pluralism often experienced military coups and incumbent consolidation after independence.

Non-white colonial middle classes resemble the canonical prodemocratic actors in existing theories, which include the working class,[8] Moore's conception of the bourgeoisie,[9] or the middle class

---

[4] Ansell and Samuels 2014.

[5] Moore 1966*a*; Ansell and Samuels 2014; Albertus 2015.

[6] Boix 2003; Acemoglu and Robinson 2006.

[7] Acemoglu and Robinson 2006 also consider the alternative response of repression, which autocratic elites choose when income inequality is high. This aspect of their theory helps to explain why white settlers often fought to hold onto power; see also Paine 2019*b*.

[8] Rueschemeyer, Stephens and Stephens 1992.

[9] Moore 1966*a*.

generally.[10] In the colonial setting, such actors arose when early colonization of port cities fostered elites educated in European languages or after emancipated slaves gained metropolitan legal rights.[11] Contrary to expectations from some existing theories, these groups often gained early representation specifically because they were small and did not pose violent threats. After franchise expansion, early concessions often created an institutionalized foundation for durable postcolonial democracy. Moreover, unlike the commonly analyzed European experiences, the development of these middle classes was not a product of rapid economic growth, which raises questions about modernization accounts of democratization for colonial and postcolonial cases.[12]

7.2.3 Democratic Sequencing

Does the sequencing of electoral reforms matter for democracy promotion? Dahl distinguishes between contestation, the extent to which elections are free and fair; and participation, the scope of who can participate in politics, which corresponds with franchise size in polities where officials are chosen by elections.[13] He contends that establishing electoral competition among a small and cohesive elite followed later by mass franchise expansion should provide a favorable path to establishing full democracy. In such countries, "the rule, the practices, and the culture of competitive politics developed first among a small elite .... Later, as additional social strata were admitted into politics they were more easily socialized into the norms and practices of competitive politics already developed among the elites."[14] Bratton and van de Walle propose a similar hypothesis for settler regimes in Africa: "For all their fatal flaws, settler minority colonies (at least in South Africa, South West Africa, and Rhodesia) had the virtue of institutionalizing

---

[10] Collier 1999. More recent work highlights cases such as post-Soviet Eastern Europe, China, and Indonesia in which the middle class opposes democracy because of dependence on the state; see Bellin 2000; Wright 2010; Rosenfeld 2020; Lankina 2021. Although European-assimilated non-white middle classes were undoubtedly products of the colonial state, they lacked similar ties that would produce antidemocratic alliances.

[11] Owolabi 2015, 2023.

[12] For ongoing debates, see Lipset 1959; Przeworski et al. 2000; Acemoglu et al. 2008; Boix 2011; Miller 2012.

[13] Dahl 1971.

[14] Dahl 1971, 36.

political competition . . . . The process of liberalization would seem to be relatively easier in regimes where competition is tolerated; the main challenge is then the simpler one of expanding the franchise to allow political participation."[15]

Countries with early elections propelled by a non-white middle class support these arguments about democratic sequencing. In India and Jamaica, the leading parties began as small, elite-led institutions, and later developed mass bases. The establishment of internal party rules (India) and the experience of many elections with mass franchises prior to gaining independence (Jamaica) cemented elections as the only viable way to gain power after independence. Enlarging the franchise did not upset the balance that made democracy self-enforcing. The urban elite were neither in a position to block subsequent franchise expansion nor were they racially differentiated from the newly enfranchised.

By contrast, countries with early elections for white settler minorities provide weak support for the democratic sequencing idea. Across the British West Indies, white planters disbanded their early representative institutions rather than allow Black-majority rule. In Africa, repression by settlers to prevent majority rule usually prompted insurgencies; and when the majority eventually came to power, the early electoral foundations were severely weakened. South Africa and Namibia, highlighted by Bratton and van de Walle,[16] are two of the only exceptions. But in both countries, the same party – the political wing of the victorious rebel group – has nonetheless held power for the entire period since gaining majority rule.

7.2.4 Dominant-party Democracies

Does regular rotation in office or a single dominant party stabilize democracy? Rotation in office is a hallmark of democratic competition and, in Western democracies, long periods of hegemony by a single party are rare.[17] However, in many postcolonial countries with reasonably democratic regimes, one party has governed for long periods. Among countries in the V-Dem data set that gained independence or

[15] Bratton and van de Walle 1997, 179. See also Lindberg 2009; Diamond, Linz and Lipset 1989, 4; Miller 2015.
[16] Bratton and van de Walle 1997, 179.
[17] Pempel 1990.

majority rule after 1945, fourteen sustained pluralistic competition for at least three decades after gaining independence (or long enough for a peaceful electoral rotation in office to occur). For the average country in this sample, the party that governed at independence won the first four postcolonial elections and survived in power for twenty-two years.[18]

All else equal, democracy would appear to function better when rotation in office occurs somewhat regularly. This requires opposition parties to adjust their platforms to better compete for votes, which occasionally results in incumbent defeat. But even if true, this all-else-equal proposition presumes that democratic competition necessarily persists. Many postcolonial experiences belie this assumption. Instead, there may be a tradeoff between rotation in office and the durability of pluralistic competition. If one party is able to consistently win competitive elections over long periods, they have fewer incentives to engage in blatantly nondemocratic actions such as declaring emergency rule. And even when a dominant party loses, they can bide their time as an opposition party until the next election. This topic should receive more attention in future research.

7.2.5 Non-Western Institutions and Democracy

Can precolonial, non-Western institutions promote contemporary democracy? "Modern" institutions of direct democracy, such as elected representatives, legislatures, and political parties, are Western in origin. However, broader democratic elements are not, such as popular selection of leaders and collective decision-making.[19] The Western conquest of the world fundamentally restructured institutions, in particular the implantation of national-level electoral institutions. However, at the subnational level, it was often expedient to leave existing institutions

---

[18] Figures calculated by authors using the "Name of largest party" variable from the V-Party data set; see Lindberg et al. 2022 and Pemstein et al. 2023. Sustained pluralism is defined as a democracy score of at least 0.4. The colonies are Barbados, Botswana, Gambia, India, Israel, Jamaica, Mauritius, Namibia, Papua New Guinea, Solomon Islands, South Africa (post-1994), Sri Lanka, Trinidad and Tobago, and Vanuatu. Another case, Senegal, falls just below this pluralism threshold, and the same party won the first eight elections and survived in office for forty years.

[19] Manin 1997; Stasavage 2020; Gerring et al. 2022, 27–35.

in place. Sometimes this meant local authoritarian monarchies, but not always. Participatory institutions at the village level in Eastern Nigeria, for example, were the basis of local governance throughout much of the colonial period.[20] Traditional leaders throughout Africa and elsewhere remain influential in contemporary electoral politics.[21]

Even at the national level, precolonial institutions have survived in some countries. Frequently, these were more authoritarian institutions such as monarchies, as we have discussed. However, Botswana and Vanuatu highlight how traditional governance institutions can successfully interact with Western-style elections. These are two exceptions in which a relatively democratic postcolonial regime followed a short episode of colonial pluralism. In each, a combination of small populations and highly indirect European rule enabled pluralistic traditional institutions to persist at the national level.

In precolonial Botswana, various Tswana groups developed traditions of collective rule. Chiefs ruled alongside a general assembly of all adult males in the community, who met in the *kgotla* (council place). The traditional assembly met regularly and often overruled the desires of the chief.[22] Colonial Bechuanaland was largely an afterthought by British officials and settlers relative to neighboring South Africa and Rhodesia.[23] A Native Advisory Council comprised of traditional chiefs was the only territory-wide assembly for Africans for most of the colonial period, which perpetuated traditional institutions at the national level.[24] Traditional families and governance institutions form the basis of the Botswana Democratic Party, which has won every election since independence.

The Condominium of New Hebrides (Vanuatu) was an unusual case in which Britain and France jointly governed dozens of islands that comprised the colony, albeit with minimal official presence from either power. The French actively resisted electoral reforms because they feared that angophile elements would dominate, leaving the chiefs with substantial political power.[25] Traditional chiefs remain important to

---

[20] Hailey 1951, 147–187; Bolt et al. 2023.
[21] Baldwin 2015.
[22] Schapera 1940, 72.
[23] Acemoglu, Johnson and Robinson 2002*a*; Lange 2009, Ch. 7.
[24] Hailey 1953.
[25] Jupp 1983.

the present day for selecting, nominating, and endorsing political candidates. According to a recent survey of experts on politics in Vanuatu, "the absence of violence or crises in Vanuatu can be attributed to the role of chiefs and the *kastom*-inspired modes of dispute resolution."[26]

Social scientists have only recently begun to take seriously how precolonial participatory institutions have structured colonial and postcolonial institutions.[27] This is undoubtedly an important area for future research.

7.2.6 International Democracy Promotion

Does international influence promote democracy? Most existing research focuses on patterns of trade and foreign aid since the Cold War ended and episodes of direct occupation such as the United States in Iraq and Afghanistan.[28] In these accounts, democratic powers are more likely than authoritarian powers to promote electoral institutions in client states, although this is only one of various and potentially conflicting goals. After the West became hegemonic in international affairs in the 1990s and 2000s, the United States and the European Union became less likely to support dictators and more likely to demand electoral reforms in return for aid and prospects for joining organizations such as the EU. This form of international pressure has generally succeeded at inducing countries to adopt multi-party elections, but Western powers often look the other way when incumbents violate other aspects of the democratic process. Thus, external intervention has often yielded electoral authoritarian regimes rather than full democracies. Direct occupation entails additional problems of pacification that often undermine prospects for stable postoccupation democracy.

The colonial period is informative for understanding the broad failures of international democracy promotion and the underpinnings of

---

[26] Veenendaal 2021, 1341.

[27] Giuliano and Nunn 2013; Baldwin 2015; Bentzen, Hariri and Robinson 2019; Acemoglu and Robinson 2020; Ahmed and Stasavage 2020; Stasavage 2020; Bolt et al. 2023.

[28] For the former, see Dunning 2004; Pevehouse 2005; Levitsky and Way 2010; Boix 2011; Gunitsky 2014; Hyde and Marinov 2014; Escribà-Folch and Wright 2015; Bush 2016; Haggard and Kaufman 2016; Miller 2020. For the latter, see Dobbins 2003; Enterline and Greig 2005, 2008.

the rare successes. Under colonialism, Western powers were highly successful at introducing elections in their colonies, as nearly every colony experienced at least one election prior to gaining independence. Yet these regimes were rarely full democracies. Like contemporary electoral authoritarian regimes, many regimes at independence combined large franchises with tainted electoral competition. Given these similarities, we encourage research on international democracy promotion to take the colonial period into account for theory-building and empirical testing.

7.2.7 Political Regimes in the Twenty-First Century

As of 2024, widespread decolonization from Western empires began nearly eight decades ago. Yet processes that began then or even earlier continue to affect contemporary political regimes. Many regimes that originated in the colonial era are still in place: thirteen democracies, six monarchies, five rebel regimes, and seven other dictatorships.[29] Durable postcolonial democracies emerged almost exclusively from colonies with early elections, spurred by either non-European middle classes or white settlers, whereas stable postcolonial dictatorships emerged from authoritarian decolonization episodes. In countries where electoral reforms were instituted shortly before independence, competitive elections seldom lasted long afterward. The various flaws in the electoral process during decolonization have analogs to the more recent past, as Western democracy promotion in the 1990s and 2000s generally succeeded at inducing multi-party electoral competition but not full-blown democracy. Establishing competitive elections as the sole means of achieving political office is an enduring challenge that external intervention usually cannot solve.

---

[29] Numbers tallied from the tables in Chapter 6.

Appendix: Data and Regression Analysis

A.1 Chapter 3

A.1.1 Tables A.1 and A.2: Interimperial Comparisons

Table A.1 is a cross-section of all colonies in the sample for this chapter, and the dependent variable indicates whether any elections occurred within the colony's first twenty years of occupation. Table A.2 is a panel and the dependent variable equals 1 in any colony-year in which an electoral institution existed. Every column contains an indicator for British colonies. Column 1 is a baseline bivariate specification. Column 2 controls for year fixed effects and the following covariates:

- Labor coercion: coded by authors using information from Sokoloff and Engerman (2000), Engerman and Sokoloff (2011), Mahoney (2010, 116), Bruhn and Gallego (2012), and Arias and Girod (2014). We code indicator variables for coercion of a large population of enslaved Africans and for high labor coercion of indigenous persons; and in other regressions, we combine these into an aggregate indicator for high labor coercion. Our sources agree that labor coercion varied broadly by region. All the areas in the mid-Atlantic and New England regions of the present-day United States, all of present-day Canada, the Southern Cone of South America, and Oceania had low labor coercion. All areas of the southern United States, the West Indies, and Brazil had coercion of enslaved Africans. The remaining parts of Spanish America (i.e., not the Southern Cone) had high coercion of indigenous labor. Table A.3 lists the scoring for every case.
- Population density in 1500: data from McEvedy and Jones (1978). See Acemoglu, Johnson and Robinson (2002b) for previous usage in the literature.

- State antiquity in 1500: data from Bockstette, Chanda and Putterman (2002) and Putterman (2012) on the weighted number of years between 0 and 1500 that a territory had political institutions above the local level. See Hariri (2012) for previous usage in the literature. In Paine (2019*a*), we describe the additional sources used to fill in missing values for this and the previous variable.
- Precolonial democracy: data from Bentzen, Hariri and Robinson (2019). They measure the fraction of "large" ethnic groups within the borders of modern-day countries for which local headmen were selected by election or consensus, using ethnic-group level data from Murdock (1967). They expect that large groups would have the greatest effect on contemporary democracy levels because they were more likely to remain influential throughout the colonial period. They consider different thresholds for "large." In their preferred specification, "large" means societies with 1,000 inhabitants or more, which is the threshold we use. The original data set does not contain any values for West Indies plantation colonies. We imputed a value of 0 for all these colonies. Because of the decimation of indigenous populations following European colonization, their theory would not anticipate that the institutions of these groups would persist throughout the colonial period.

Column 3 interacts British colonialism with an indicator for either type of labor coercion to assess whether the effect of British colonialism is conditional on having low labor coercion. Column 4 adds the additional covariates to this specification.

Table A.1 *Interimperial comparisons (cross-section)*

DV: Electoral institutions within twenty years of colonization				
	(1)	(2)	(3)	(4)
British colony	0.684***	0.667***	0.760***	0.742***
	(0.0735)	(0.110)	(0.0877)	(0.106)
Labor coercion			0.0476	0.187
			(0.0477)	(0.154)
Br. col.*Labor coercion			−0.128	−0.142
			(0.138)	(0.162)
Labor coercion (Africans)		0.0914		
		(0.114)		
Labor coercion (indigenous)		0.230*		
		(0.135)		
Pop. density in 1500 (log)		−0.0403		−0.0338
		(0.0453)		(0.0440)
State antiquity in 1500		−0.699*		−0.599
		(0.403)		(0.410)
Precolonial democracy		2.289*		2.499*
		(1.227)		(1.304)
Intercept	0.0357	−0.0821	0.000	−0.179
	(0.0355)	(0.109)	(0.000)	(0.147)
Colonies	78	78	78	78
R-squared	0.432	0.476	0.437	0.477
Century-onset FE	NO	YES	YES	NO
Marginal effect estimates				
British colony | Low coercion			0.760***	0.742***
			(0.0877)	(0.106)
British colony | High coercion			0.632***	0.600***
			(0.107)	(0.140)

Notes: The sample consists of a cross-section of every colony listed in the tables throughout Chapter 3. Models estimated using OLS with robust standard errors. Models 2 and 3 contain fixed effects for the century in which colonization began. ***$p < 0.01$,** $p < 0.05$,* $p < 0.1$.

Table A.2 *Interimperial comparisons (panel)*

	DV: Electoral institutions exist			
	(1)	(2)	(3)	(4)
British colony	0.767***	0.743***	0.755***	0.727***
	(0.0365)	(0.0415)	(0.0536)	(0.0575)
Labor coercion			0.0170	0.0495
			(0.0242)	(0.0573)
Br. col.*Labor coercion			0.0243	0.0142
			(0.0704)	(0.0754)
Labor coercion (Africans)		0.0596		
		(0.0566)		
Labor coercion (indigenous)		0.107		
		(0.109)		
Pop. density in 1500 (log)		0.000133		0.000936
		(0.0189)		(0.0190)
State antiquity in 1500		−0.379		−0.306
		(0.309)		(0.219)
Precolonial democracy		0.924		0.940
		(0.648)		(0.666)
Intercept	0.0504***	0.0835	0.0353**	0.0962
	(0.0155)	(0.0931)	(0.0167)	(0.0991)
Colony-years	9,537	9,537	9,537	9,537
R-squared	0.599	0.626	0.600	0.625
Year FE	NO	YES	NO	YES
	Marginal effect estimates			
British colony │ Low coercion			0.755***	0.727***
			(0.0536)	(0.0575)
British colony │ High coercion			0.779***	0.741***
			(0.0457)	(0.0511)

Notes: The sample consists of a panel of every colony listed in the tables throughout Chapter 3 in years the territory was under colonial control (through 1850). Models estimated using OLS with robust standard errors clustered at the colony level.
***$p < 0.01$,** $p < 0.05$,* $p < 0.1$.

Table A.3 *Types of labor coercion*

Low labor coercion
Cape Breton (Nova Scotia), Chile, Connecticut, East/New Jersey, Louisiana-Illinois (French), Massachusetts Bay, New Brunswick, New Hampshire, New Haven (Connecticut), New South Wales, New York (British), New York (Dutch New Netherland), New Zealand, Newfoundland, Nova Scotia (British), Nova Scotia (French Acadia), Ontario, Pennsylvania, Placentia-Ile Royale (Nova Scotia), Plymouth (Massachusetts), Prince Edward Island, Quebec (British), Quebec (French Canada), Queensland, Rhode Island, Rio de la Plata, South Australia, Tasmania, Vancouver (British Columbia), Victoria, West Jersey (New Jersey), Western Australia

---

Slavery coercion
Antigua and Barbuda, Bahamas, Barbados, Berbice (Dutch Guiana), Bermuda, Brazil, British Honduras, British Virgin Islands, Cuba, Delaware, Demerara (Dutch Guiana), Dominica, East Florida, Essequibo (Dutch Guiana), French Guiana, Georgia, Grenada, Guadeloupe, Guyana (British), Jamaica, Martinique, Maryland, Montserrat, Netherlands Antilles, Nevis, North Carolina, Puerto Rico, Saint Domingue, Santo Domingo, South Carolina, St. Christopher (French), St. Kitts, St. Lucia, St. Vincent and the Grenadines, Suriname, Tobago, Trinidad, Virginia, West Florida

---

Indigenous coercion
Guatemala, New Granada, New Spain, Peru, Provincias Internas, Venezuela, Yucatan

---

A.1.2 Table A.4: Variation within the British Empire

In Table A.4, we examine a cross-section of British colonies to assess correlates of early electoral institutions. We proxy the relative power of the white community by settled versus conquered origins (Columns 1 and 2), and in the remaining columns, we further distinguish the dependence of the white population (for settled cases) and whether the previous colonizer was Catholic (for conquered cases). In the latter specifications, the reference category consists of both dependent settlements and colonies conquered from the French or the Spanish. This yields comparisons to a set of colonies for which our theory anticipates a lower prevalence of early electoral institutions.

In addition to the covariates used in the preceding regressions, we evaluate two sets of covariates unique to British colonies. First, the form of the original colonial charter. The earliest English-settled colonies were not directly controlled by the Crown, who instead delegated authority to either private corporates (e.g., the Virginia Company) or proprietors (e.g., Lord Baltimore). Most became royal colonies only later. Typically, this change occurred without an interruption in their elected legislatures; the Dominion of New England was an exception. Most conquered colonies, by contrast, began as royal colonies; the only exceptions were proprietary charters for some former Dutch colonies. Thus, the distinction among corporate (14 percent of all British colonies during this period), proprietary (31 percent), and royal charters (55 percent) largely aligns with the settled versus conquered distinction. Royal charters are the omitted reference category in the regressions. We coded both this and the settled/conquered variable from the secondary sources referenced throughout the book. A particularly useful source is Wight (1946a), especially his appendix.

Second, we include an indicator for colonies originally settled by religious minority groups. This addresses the possible concern that only these white groups routinely pressed for representative institutions, as opposed to profit-seeking plantation owners (see, e.g., Pitman 1917; although for qualitative critiques of this idea, see O'Shaughnessy 2000, 6–7, and Gailmard 2024). To determine which English-settled colonies were founded on ideas of religious freedom, we consulted www.loc.gov/exhibits/religion/rel01.html and www.libertarianism.org/columns/soul-liberty-toleration-emergence-religious-freedom-colonies.

Table A.4 *Variation within the British empire*

	DV: Electoral institutions within twenty years of colonization			
	(1)	(2)	(3)	(4)
Settled	0.0333	−0.208		
	(0.133)	(0.170)		
Settled			0.372**	0.502**
(nondependent)			(0.139)	(0.202)
Conquered			0.526***	0.737***
(non-Catholic)			(0.118)	(0.258)
Labor coercion		0.197		0.182
		(0.119)		(0.160)
Pop. density in		−0.0466		0.0394
1500 (log)		(0.101)		(0.0840)
State antiquity in		−1.099**		−1.275**
1500		(0.501)		(0.479)
Precolonial		7.469		10.31*
democracy		(6.527)		(5.099)
Corporate charter		0.122		−0.155
		(0.235)		(0.327)
Proprietary charter		−0.0978		−0.405
		(0.231)		(0.359)
Religious freedom		0.100		0.160
settlement		(0.102)		(0.116)
Intercept	0.700***	0.659**	0.474***	0.284
	(0.105)	(0.249)	(0.118)	(0.278)
Colonies	50	50	50	50
R-squared	0.001	0.245	0.194	0.361
Century-onset FE	NO	YES	NO	YES

Notes: The sample consists of a cross-section of every British colony listed in the tables throughout Chapter 3. Models estimated using OLS with robust standard errors. ***$p < 0.01$,** $p < 0.05$,* $p < 0.1$.

A.1.3 Table A.5: Disaggregating Dutch Colonies

Prior to the French Revolution, elections were nearly exclusive to the British empire. The only exceptions were two Dutch colonies that held elections (Essequibo and Demerara) starting in the eighteenth century and an abortive experiment with elections in French Canada in the seventeenth century. The Dutch empire had a parliamentary metropole, which may help to explain its greater openness to allowing elections compared to absolutist metropoles. In the pooled sample, we distinguish British and Dutch colonies from all others and examine the incidence of elections prior to 1787; in that year, the French Assembly of Notables met, which led to electoral reforms in its colonies. Dutch colonies had elected assemblies in 10.3 percent of colony-years. This figure is high compared to colonies in the absolutist empires (0.3 percent of colony-years), but much lower than British colonies during the pre-1787 period (86 percent of colony-years). In Table A.5, we add a Dutch-colony fixed effect to the specifications in Table A.1. Given the additional fixed effect for British colonies, this leaves Spanish, Portuguese, and French colonies as the reference category. The coefficient for Dutch colonies is positive but not statistically significant.

Table A.5 *Disaggregating Dutch colonies*

	DV: Electoral institutions exist	
	(1)	(2)
British colony	0.829***	0.812***
	(0.0381)	(0.0415)
Dutch colony	0.100	0.0879
	(0.0679)	(0.0673)
Labor coercion (Africans)		0.0281
		(0.0502)
Labor coercion (indigenous)		0.0438
		(0.0523)
Pop. density in 1500 (log)		−0.0214
		(0.0195)
State antiquity in 1500		−0.00547
		(0.0388)
Precolonial democracy		0.236
		(0.189)
Intercept	0.00306	0.0298
	(0.00304)	(0.0682)
Colony-years	7,121	7,121
R-squared	0.693	0.710
Year FE	NO	YES
Sample	Pre-1787	Pre-1787

Notes: The sample consists of a panel of every colony listed in the tables throughout Chapter 3 in years the territory was under colonial control (through 1787). Models estimated using OLS with robust standard errors clustered at the colony level.
***$p < 0.01$,** $p < 0.05$,* $p < 0.1$.

A.1.4 *Table A.6: British versus French Colonies*

Table A.6 compares only British and French colonies while controlling for and interacting with the level of legislative constraints in France. The interaction term between British colonies and legislative constraints in France is negative in sign and statistically significant, meaning that greater legislative constraints in France attenuate the positive British coefficient. Moreover, the marginal effect of British colonialism is positive and statistically significant only in years in which the French metropole was authoritarian.

Table A.6 *British versus French colonies*

	DV: Electoral institutions exist	
	(1)	(2)
British colony	0.995***	0.831***
	(0.0499)	(0.0820)
Executive constraints in France	1.562***	1.093***
	(0.202)	(0.309)
Br. col.*Exec. con. in France	−1.667***	−1.085***
	(0.270)	(0.285)
Labor coercion		0.0359
		(0.0528)
Pop. density in 1500 (log)		0.168***
		(0.0370)
State antiquity in 1500		−2.195***
		(0.176)
Precolonial democracy		18.46***
		(3.625)
Intercept	−0.158***	0.0695
	(0.0235)	(0.149)
Colony-years	6,109	6,109
R-squared	0.459	0.579
Year FE	NO	YES
	Marginal effect estimates	
British colony | Fr. authoritarian	0.814***	0.713***
	(0.0346)	(0.0623)
British colony | Fr. parliamentary	−0.112	0.110
	(0.146)	(0.139)

Notes: The sample consists of a panel of every British and Frency colony listed in the tables throughout Chapter 3 in years the territory was under colonial control (through 1850). Legislative constraints in France from V-Dem, a continuous variable measured annually. The first data point in V-Dem is 1789. For earlier years, we use the value that V-Dem assigns for the entire Napoleonic period (0.109). For the marginal effects, *French authoritarian* corresponds to the value during the Napoleonic period (0.109), and French parliamentary corresponds to the highest value during the pre-Napoleonic Revolutionary period (0.664). Models estimated using OLS with robust standard errors clustered at the colony level. ***$p < 0.01$,** $p < 0.05$,* $p < 0.1$.

A.1.5 Table A.7: Parliamentary Metropoles and Colony FE

Table A.7 replaces the colonizer-specific indicators with an indicator for parliamentary regimes. For the pre-1850 period covered in this chapter, we code all years as parliamentary for Britain, Netherlands in all years before 1796, France from 1789–1799 and 1848–1852, Spain from 1808–1813, and Portugal from 1820–1822. Unfortunately, due to missingness in V-Dem's legislative constraints variable (in particular because of its starting year of 1789), it is not possible to use a continuous variable while maintaining a meaningful sample. Column 1 is a baseline bivariate specification, Column 2 adds covariates, and Column 3 adds colony fixed effects (hence comparing colonies to themselves over time based on whether the metropole is parliamentary at the time).

Table A.7 *Parliamentary metropoles and colony FE*

	DV: Electoral institutions exist		
	(1)	(2)	(3)
Parliamentary metropole	0.712***	0.674***	0.405***
	(0.0512)	(0.0565)	(0.0794)
Labor coercion (Africans)		−0.0910	
		(0.112)	
Labor coercion (indigenous)		−0.0348	
		(0.142)	
Pop. density in 1500 (log)		0.0335	
		(0.0354)	
State antiquity in 1500		−0.474	
		(0.328)	
Precolonial democracy		1.381	
		(0.880)	
Intercept	0.0154**	0.221	0.941***
	(0.00698)	(0.148)	(0.109)
Colony-years	9,537	9,537	9,537
R-squared	0.502	0.533	0.814
Year FE	NO	YES	YES
Colony FE	NO	NO	YES

Notes: The sample consists of a panel of every colony listed in the tables throughout Chapter 3 in years the territory was under colonial control (through 1850). Models estimated using OLS with robust standard errors clustered at the colony level. ***$p < 0.01$,** $p < 0.05$,* $p < 0.1$.

A.1.6 Table A.8: Major Anticolonial Revolts before 1850

Table A.8 demonstrates that plantation colonies were less likely to experience major anticolonial revolts among a cross-section of New-World colonies before 1850. The sample is smaller than that in Table A.1 because we exclude colonies that were merged into others (various early British North American colonies) or that were conquered by another empire (various French and Dutch colonies). Column 1 does not contain any covariates, which enables us to back out percentages directly from the regression coefficients: 59.5 percent of nonplantation colonies had a major anticolonial revolt compared to 7.7 percent of plantation colonies. In the subsequent specifications, we add colonizer fixed effects and/or substantive covariates.

Table A.8 *Major anticolonial revolts before 1850*

	DV: Major anticolonial revolt			
Plantation colony	−0.518***	−0.497***	−1.288***	−1.322***
	(0.0977)	(0.0987)	(0.164)	(0.218)
Labor coercion			−0.382	−0.375
(indigenous)			(0.263)	(0.258)
Pop. density in 1500			0.255***	0.262***
(log)			(0.0492)	(0.0640)
State antiquity in			−0.658*	−0.661
1500			(0.382)	(0.405)
Precolonial			−0.742	−0.756
democracy			(1.671)	(1.781)
Intercept	0.595***	0.884***	2.229***	2.262***
	(0.0820)	(0.0986)	(0.154)	(0.205)
Colonies	63	63	63	63
R-squared	0.275	0.389	0.700	0.702
Colonizer FE	NO	YES	NO	YES
Century-onset FE	NO	NO	YES	YES

Notes: The sample consists of a cross-section of most colonies listed in the tables throughout Chapter 3, with the exceptions described above. Colonizer fixed effects include British, French, and Dutch, leaving Spanish and Portuguese colonies as the reference category. We omit a covariate for *Labor coercion (Africans)* because this category is a strict superset of *plantation colonies*. Models estimated using OLS with robust standard errors. ***$p < 0.01$,**$p < 0.05$,*$p < 0.1$.

A.2 Chapter 4

A.2.1 Categories of Colonies

The following describes how we grouped each colony into the different categories.

- From 1850 onward, we code the colonies of Portugal, Italy, Spain, Germany, and France (from 1852 to 1870) as *authoritarian metropoles*. Libya and Somalia were Italian colonies until 1945, which we code as authoritarian metropoles until that date. Burundi, Cameroon, Namibia, Papua New Guinea, Rwanda, Tanzania, and Togo were each German colonies until 1919, which we code as authoritarian metropoles until that date. Any colony that meets the criterion for authoritarian metropole is coded as such, even if it also meets any criteria in the following bullet points.
- A colony is *settler dominant* if Europeans comprised at least 25 percent of the population, and *settler minority* if Europeans comprised at least 5 percent of the population, using data from Gerring et al. (2022) and other sources cited throughout the text.
  - Most colonies fit into the same bin for European population share for the entire time period, at least after the initial decades of colonization: below 5 percent, between 5 percent and 25 percent, or more than 25 percent. Thus, we code the same category over time for most cases (except if the metropole switches to or away from authoritarian; see the previous bullet point).
  - The main exceptions are plantation colonies in the West Indies, where the European share of the population plummeted over time. At various times in the eighteenth, nineteenth, and (in some unusual cases) twentieth centuries, whites had dropped from previously high population shares to below 5 percent of the population. We code 1883 (fifty years after emancipation was announced in the British empire) as the year in which the following V-Dem cases switched categories from settler minority to non-white middle class: Barbados, Guyana, Jamaica, and Trinidad and Tobago. In Figure 4.2, this distinction is irrelevant because the line is the prevalence of electoral institutions across all British West Indies colonies (which includes many microcolonies not included in V-Dem), regardless of the size of the white population.

- Among the post-1945 decolonization cases, only Israel's European population share meets our threshold for settler dominance (at least 25 percent of the population is white). Israel is excluded from any figures or regression tables that use our discrete colonial categories, but is included in other tables and figures.
- In colonies with a *non-white middle class*, the colony was founded before 1850. Although this is an indirect proxy for the concept of interest, it has high face validity. Early colonies in Africa and Asia tended to be geographically circumscribed to major port cities; and, as discussed in Owolabi (2023), early colonies in the West Indies had large populations of formerly enslaved persons who gained metropolitan legal rights following emancipation. Olsson (2009) and Ertan, Fiszbein and Putterman (2016) each provide cross-national data sets measuring the onset of colonial rule. We consulted these sources as well as various maps depicting port cities (see Schwartzberg 1992, 49, for Asia and Ajayi and Crowder 1985, 43–51, for Africa) to verify that the colonizer had gained control of at least one port city by 1850. Colonies in the British West Indies meet the early-colonization distinction, which justifies the aforementioned decision to code them as non-white middle classes from 1883 onward.
- In *national monarchies*, the country had a national monarch at independence.
- All remaining colonies lacked powerful elites (either settlers or non-whites) and are grouped into the residual category, *weak elites*.

Table A.9 lists the core sample of countries for Chapters 4 through 6. This consists of every colony under Western colonial rule at some point in the twentieth century (except Australia and New Zealand, which we analyze only in Chapter 3) with data in V-Dem. Each unit enters the data set in its year of colonization, measured using Ertan, Fiszbein and Putterman (2016) (we use dates from Olsson 2009 for any countries not included in Ertan et al.'s data set).

Table A.9 Core sample of colonies in Chapters 4 through 6

Authoritarian metropole[a]	Settler minority	Weak elite	Non-white middle class	National monarchy
Angola	Algeria	Benin	Barbados[e]	Bahrain
Cape Verde	Israel[c-f]	Botswana	Gabon	Bhutan
Equatorial G.	Namibia[d]	Burkina Faso[f]	Gambia	Burundi[d]
Guinea-Bissau	South Africa	Cameroon[d-f]	Ghana	Cambodia
Libya[b-f]	Tunisia	Cen. Afr. Rep.	Guyana[e]	Egypt
Mozambique	Zimbabwe	Chad	India	Iraq
São Tomé and P.		Comoros[f]	Indonesia	Jordan
Somalia[b]		Congo (Rep.)	Ivory Coast	Kuwait
		Congo (DR)	Jamaica[e]	Laos
		Djibouti	Malaysia	Lesotho
		Fiji	Mauritius	Maldives
		Guinea	Nigeria	Morocco
		Kenya	Pakistan[g]	Nepal
		Lebanon	Philippines	Oman
		Madagascar	Senegal	Qatar
		Malawi	Seychelles	Swaziland
		Mali	Sierra Leone	UAE[f]
		Mauritania	Singapore	
		Myanmar	Sri Lanka	
		Niger	Suriname	
		Papua NG[d]	Trin. & Tob[e]	
		Rwanda[d]	Vietnam[f]	
		Solomon Isl.		
		South Yemen		
		Sudan		
		Syria		
		Tanzania[d]		
		Togo[d]		
		Uganda		
		Vanuatu		
		Zambia		

[a] Every French colony is coded as *authoritarian metropole* during the Second Empire (1852–1870).

[b] After 1945, Libya is *national monarchy* and Somalia is *weak elite*; both switched from Italian to British control.

[c] Israel is the only colony in this sample for which the European population is large enough to count as *settler dominant* (more than 25%). Because of the different theoretical implications for *settler dominant* and *settler minority* cases, we exclude Israel from any figures and regressions that use the discrete colonial categories.

[d] Coded as *authoritarian metropole* prior to 1919 (end of German colonial empire).

[e] Coded as *settler minority* prior to 1883 (fifty years after emancipation announced in British empire).

[f] These countries have missing V-Dem data for some later colonial years: Burkina Faso (missing 1932–47 when it did not exist as a separate colony), Cameroon (no data before independence), Comoros (missing 1914–45), Israel (no data before independence), Libya (missing 1942–50), United Arab Emirates (no data before independence), and Vietnam (no data until 1945). Thus, observations from these country-years are missing from the figures and regression estimates. We coded years of colonial pluralism for each based on available V-Dem data and other sources.

[g] Pakistan was not a distinct territorial entity until its split from India upon independence. Pakistan is in the statistical sample only for Chapter 6 (using the same colonial-era variables as India), but not Chapters 4 or 5.

A.2.2 Main Patterns

Tables A.10 to A.12 correspond with the figures at the beginning of Chapter 4. Each regression consists of a cross-section of colonies in 1945. Every specification contains indicators for four of our five colonial categories, leaving the omitted one as the reference category. Note that we do not model the sixth category, settler-dominant, because among the later colonies, only Israel meets the 25 percent European population share threshold; we omit Israel from these regressions. In each table, Panel A contains only the indicators and Panel B adds covariates.

In the appendix for Chapter 3, we describe every covariate except Protestant missionaries in 1923; we do not use this variable in the regressions for the previous chapter because of the late date at which it is measured. This variable, drawn from Woodberry (2012), is the number of Protestant missionaries per 10,000 people in each territory in 1923. In Paine (2019a), we describe the additional sources used to fill in missing values for this variable. Additionally, the precolonial democracy measure is missing values from some countries. For all of these, we impute a value of 0.

Table A.10 examines the existence of an elected assembly. The positive coefficient for settler minority colonies is robustly statistically significant relative to all other categories except non-white middle classes. The coefficient for non-white middle classes is positive relative to every category except settler minority colonies, and robustly statistically significant. The negative coefficient for authoritarian metropoles is robustly statistically significant relative to all other categories. Table A.11 examines franchise size. Non-white middle-class cases are distinguished from the others at the 10 percent significance level. Table A.12 examines V-Dem democracy score. Colonies with a non-white middle-class and settler-minority colonies are each statistically discernible from every other category, but not from each other.

Table A.10 *Electoral institutions in 1945*

	DV: Electoral institutions exist				
Panel A. Basic specifications					
	(1)	(2)	(3)	(4)	(5)
Authoritarian	−0.222**	−0.810***	−0.406***	−1.000***	
metropole	(0.101)	(0.0884)	(0.0896)	(0.000)	
Settler	0.778***	0.190**	0.594***		1.000***
minority	(0.101)	(0.0884)	(0.0896)		(0.000)
Weak elites	0.184	−0.403***		−0.594***	0.406***
	(0.135)	(0.126)		(0.0896)	(0.0896)
Non-white	0.587***		0.403***	−0.190**	0.810***
middle class	(0.134)		(0.126)	(0.0884)	(0.0884)
National		−0.587***	−0.184	−0.778***	0.222**
monarchy		(0.134)	(0.135)	(0.101)	(0.101)
Intercept	0.222**	0.810***	0.406***	1.000***	0.000
	(0.101)	(0.0884)	(0.0896)	(0.000)	(0.000)
Colonies	82	82	82	82	82
R-squared	0.312	0.312	0.312	0.312	0.312
Panel B. Add covariates					
	(1)	(2)	(3)	(4)	(5)
Authoritarian	−0.152	−0.750***	−0.347***	−0.940***	
metropole	(0.124)	(0.122)	(0.116)	(0.0898)	
Settler	0.788***	0.190*	0.593***		0.940***
minority	(0.123)	(0.103)	(0.105)		(0.0898)
Weak elites	0.195	−0.403***		−0.593***	0.347***
	(0.139)	(0.126)		(0.105)	(0.116)
Non-white	0.598***		0.403***	−0.190*	0.750***
middle class	(0.136)		(0.126)	(0.103)	(0.122)
National		−0.598***	−0.195	−0.788***	0.152
monarchy		(0.136)	(0.139)	(0.123)	(0.124)
Intercept	0.159	0.757***	0.354***	0.947***	0.00731
	(0.115)	(0.113)	(0.110)	(0.0982)	(0.0405)
Colonies	82	82	82	82	82
R-squared	0.324	0.324	0.324	0.324	0.324
Covariates	YES	YES	YES	YES	YES

Notes: The sample is a cross-section of colonies (listed in Table A.9) measured in 1945. Models estimated using OLS with robust standard errors. Panel B includes the following covariates in every model: state antiquity in 1500, population density in 1500 (logged), precolonial democracy, and Protestant missionaries in 1923.
***$p < 0.01$,** $p < 0.05$,* $p < 0.1$.

Table A.11 *Franchise size in 1945*

	DV: Fraction of adult population with suffrage		
Panel A. Basic specifications			
	(1)	(2)	(3)
Settler minority	−0.150*	0.00455	
	(0.0875)	(0.0501)	
Weak elites	−0.155*		−0.00455
	(0.0902)		(0.0501)
Non-white middle class		0.155*	0.150*
		(0.0902)	(0.0875)
Intercept	0.220**	0.0655	0.0700**
	(0.0815)	(0.0386)	(0.0318)
Colonies	33	33	33
R-squared	0.091	0.091	0.091
Panel B. Add covariates			
	(1)	(2)	(3)
Settler minority	−0.214*	−0.0318	
	(0.124)	(0.0787)	
Weak elites	−0.182*		0.0318
	(0.102)		(0.0787)
Non-white middle class		0.182*	0.214*
		(0.102)	(0.124)
Intercept	0.171	−0.0113	−0.0431
	(0.105)	(0.0666)	(0.126)
Colonies	33	33	33
R-squared	0.197	0.197	0.197
Covariates	YES	YES	YES

Notes: The sample is a cross-section of colonies measured in 1945. The core list is colonies in Table A.9 that had electoral institutions in 1945, which excludes all *authoritarian metropoles*. We additionally exclude all *national monarchies*; among those with electoral institutions, the former Ottoman territories were outliers with large franchises, and Swaziland was the only monarchy outside the Middle East with electoral institutions in 1945. Thus, the sample consists only of three colonial categories, with the reference category differing by column. Models estimated using OLS with robust standard errors. Panel B includes the following covariates in every model: state antiquity in 1500, population density in 1500 (logged), precolonial democracy, and Protestant missionaries in 1923. ***$p < 0.01$,** $p < 0.05$,* $p < 0.1$.

Table A.12 *Democracy score in 1945*

	DV: V-Dem electoral democracy index				
Panel A. Basic specifications					
	(1)	(2)	(3)	(4)	(5)
Authoritarian	−0.0419***	−0.117***	−0.0461***	−0.111**	
metropole	(0.0125)	(0.0195)	(0.0129)	(0.0457)	
Settler	0.0689	−0.00630	0.0647		0.111**
minority	(0.0471)	(0.0494)	(0.0472)		(0.0457)
Weak elites	0.00420	−0.0710***		−0.0647	0.0461***
	(0.0172)	(0.0228)		(0.0472)	(0.0129)
Non-white	0.0752***		0.0710***	0.00630	0.117***
middle class	(0.0226)		(0.0228)	(0.0494)	(0.0195)
National		−0.0752***	−0.00420	−0.0689	0.0419***
monarchy		(0.0226)	(0.0172)	(0.0471)	(0.0125)
Intercept	0.0599***	0.135***	0.0641***	0.129***	0.0180***
	(0.0120)	(0.0192)	(0.0124)	(0.0456)	(0.00368)
Colonies	77	77	77	77	77
R-squared	0.239	0.239	0.239	0.239	0.239
Panel B. Add covariates					
	(1)	(2)	(3)	(4)	(5)
Authoritarian	−0.0163	−0.0937***	−0.0214	−0.0829	
metropole	(0.0225)	(0.0228)	(0.0153)	(0.0499)	
Settler	0.0666	−0.0108	0.0615		0.0829
minority	(0.0482)	(0.0511)	(0.0476)		(0.0499)
Weak elites	0.00513	−0.0723***		−0.0615	0.0214
	(0.0169)	(0.0221)		(0.0476)	(0.0153)
Non-white	0.0774***		0.0723***	0.0108	0.0937***
middle class	(0.0254)		(0.0221)	(0.0511)	(0.0228)
National		−0.0774***	−0.00513	−0.0666	0.0163
monarchy		(0.0254)	(0.0169)	(0.0482)	(0.0225)
Intercept	0.0339*	0.111***	0.0390***	0.101**	0.0176*
	(0.0198)	(0.0212)	(0.0116)	(0.0495)	(0.00977)
Colonies	77	77	77	77	77
R-squared	0.349	0.349	0.349	0.349	0.349
Covariates	YES	YES	YES	YES	YES

Notes: The sample is a cross-section of colonies (listed in Table A.9) measured in 1945. Models estimated using OLS with robust standard errors. Panel B includes the following covariates in every model: state antiquity in 1500, population density in 1500 (logged), precolonial democracy, and Protestant missionaries in 1923.
***$p < 0.01$,** $p < 0.05$,* $p < 0.1$.

A.2.3 India

More disaggregated evidence at the level of district boards further showcases the importance of education for prompting electoral reforms in India. In Figure A.1, we summarize the positive and statistically significant relationship between the percentage of Indians literate in English and the percentage of seats on district boards that were elected, both logged. Many low-literacy districts located above the regression line are located in Punjab, where the colonial state viewed the agrarian elite as supportive; and high-literacy districts located below the regression line are concentrated in Bengal, where the anglophone elite was regarded as less loyal to the colonial project (Lee, 2011; Tan, 2009).

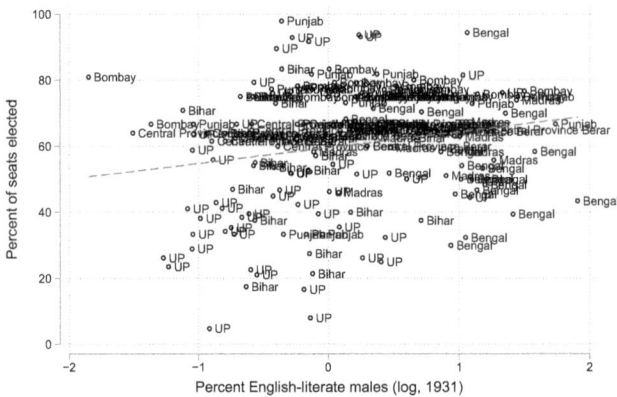

Figure A.1 Elected district boards in late colonial India

Notes: The units are 1931 districts (N = 190), labeled by province. The y-axis is the percent of the district board elected in 1931 (1929 for Punjab and 1934 for the Central Provinces and Bombay). The x-axis is the logged percentage of men literate in English less the percentage of Europeans. We present the linear regression line of the relationship between the two variables. The correlation coefficient is positive and statistically significant in an unreported bivariate regression specification (available in the replication data). Data from the Census of India 1931 (Hutton, 1933) and the *Reports of District and Local Boards* (various years). The presidency cities and Assam are missing.

A.2.4 West Africa

In the West Africa section of Chapter 4, we summarized a quantitative comparison of colonial districts based on data from Ricart-Huguet (2022). His unit of the analysis is the colonial district (or *cercle* in French colonies). The data set includes 312 districts across eight British and eight French colonies in West and East Africa: Benin (Dahomey), Burkina Faso (Upper Volta), Cote d'Ivoire, Ghana (Gold Coast), Guinea, Kenya, Malawi (Nyasaland), Mali (French Sudan), Mauritania, Niger, Nigeria, Senegal, Sierra Leone, Tanzania (Tanganyika), Uganda, and Zambia (Northern Rhodesia). Our sample consists of a cross-section of districts in these colonies. We include East Africa in the sample to avoid sampling on the dependent variable, although in some specifications we control for the West Africa region or for colony fixed effects.

As we discuss in Chapter 4, we count thirteen cities in West Africa that held direct elections to a territory-wide governing body prior to 1945:

- Dahomey (Benin): Abomey, Ouidah, Porto Novo
- Gold Coast (Ghana): Accra, Cape Coast, Sekondi
- Nigeria: Calabar, Lagos
- Senegal: Dakar, Gorée, Rufisque, Saint Louis
- Sierra Leone: Freetown

We matched each city with a corresponding colonial district to generate an indicator for early elections measured at the district level. In ten cases, the match was unambiguous because the district was named after the town. Appendix F of Ricart-Huguet (2022) states that Gorée was part of the Dakar district in Senegal. Gorée, therefore, has no effect on scoring the elections variable; elections in the town of Dakar sufficed to code the Dakar district as a 1. Based on matching towns with polygons for colonial districts (in consultation with the author of the data set), we code Rufisque as located within the Thies district in Senegal and Sekondi within the Ahanta district. Note that Ricart-Huguet's district-level maps are from 1925 for the French colonies and from 1938 for the British colonies.

Every variable in the following analysis besides the early elections indicator is from Ricart-Huguet's (2022) data set (see also Huillery 2009 for much of the French data). The main explanatory variables are indicators for early European penetration. The more exogenous measure of early European penetration is the presence of a natural harbor or cape. The one of more direct substantive relevance is a major center of precolonial European trading/slaving. This captures historical European economic activity in an area, which is closely associated with where European powers originally staked territorial claims in the form of formal protectorates and colonies. Ricart-Huguet codes a 1 on this binary variable for any district that meets either of two conditions: "(1) 250 or more slave ships sailed from pre-colonial trading posts/forts located in that district (for example, Ouidah in Benin) or (2) the district includes an important pre-colonial post that traded commodities (for example, Saint Louis in Senegal)" (p. 744).

In Table A.13, Columns 1 through 3 use the indicator for precolonial trade/slaving as the main explanatory variable. Column 1 is a bivariate specification, Column 2 adds substantive covariates, and Column 3 additionally includes colony fixed effects. Columns 4 through 6 use the indicator for a natural harbor or cape, but otherwise follow the same sequence of model specifications. The substantive covariates are those used in Table 1 of Ricart-Huguet (2022), plus an indicator for West African colonies: navigable river, rugged terrain, tsetse fly prevalence, malaria prevalence, soil quality, African population size (log), ethnic fractionalization, presence of Islam, intensity of agriculture, settlement patterns, indigenous slavery, and the presence of a precolonial state.

In Columns 1 and 4, the coefficient estimates from the bivariate regressions enable us to back out the cross-tabs. Of the twenty-four districts with a major precolonial European trading/slaving post, ten (41.7 percent) held early elections. By contrast, of the 288 districts without a major European trade post, only two (Abomey in Benin and Thies in Senegal) held an early election (0.7 percent).[1] Of the twenty-one districts with a natural harbor or cape, seven (33.3 percent) held early elections. By contrast, of the 291 districts without either a natural harbor or port, only five held early elections (1.7 percent). In three of the exceptions (Ouidah and Porto Novo in Benin, Accra in Ghana), a major trading/slaving center arose in an area that lacked the favorable geographical conditions of either a natural harbor or

---

[1] Thies is itself a "false negative" on the explanatory variable because this district contains Rufisque, a town within Four Communes that belonged to the trading network associated with Dakar.

Table A.13 *Early elections in West/East Africa: District-level regressions*

	DV: Early elections		
Panel A. Trading/slaving posts			
	(1)	(2)	(3)
Precolonial trade/slaving	0.410***	0.409***	0.387***
	(0.101)	(0.0955)	(0.0925)
Intercept	0.00694	−0.121	0.0420
	(0.00491)	(0.139)	(0.204)
Districts	312	312	312
R-squared	0.322	0.381	0.430
Covariates	NO	YES	YES
West Africa FE	NO	YES	NO
Colony FE	NO	NO	YES
Panel B. Natural harbors and capes			
	(1)	(2)	(3)
Natural harbor or cape	0.316***	0.295***	0.306***
	(0.103)	(0.0972)	(0.0980)
Intercept	0.0172**	−0.0238	0.162
	(0.00764)	(0.139)	(0.209)
Districts	312	312	312
R-squared	0.170	0.235	0.318
Covariates	NO	YES	YES
West Africa FE	NO	YES	NO
Colony FE	NO	NO	YES

Notes: The text describes the sample and data. Models estimated using OLS with robust standard errors. ***$p < 0.01$,** $p < 0.05$,* $p < 0.1$.

cape. These differences are statistically significant with and without the covariates.

The subnational unit of analysis is natural given our theoretical interest in the characteristics of individual *cities* that correspond with early elections. Disaggregating the units allows us not only to identify greater variation among a larger number of units, but it also avoids an obvious ecological inference problem with colony-level data. A

colony might simultaneously have early European colonial penetration and early elections, but the sites of these two activities could
occur in different parts of the colony. Such observations would confirm our hypothesis in the regression despite not, in fact, supporting
the hypothesis. Colonial districts mollify, but do not completely obvi-
ate, this ecological inference problem. As a check against ecological
inference concerns, we consulted the data coding notes in Ricart-
Huguet's (2022) Appendix F. There, to justify his scores at the district
level, he provides information on the specific sites within each district
where the major precolonial European trading/slaving posts, natural
harbors, and capes were located. For each case with early elections
and the presence of early European penetration, we assessed whether
the feature (either precolonial European trading/slaving post or natural harbor/cape) was indeed located within the city that held the
early elections. This was true in every case except one, the Ahanta
district in Ghana, in which Sekondi is located. Neither the major trading center (Fort St. Anthony in Axim) nor the cape (Cape Three Points)
were located in Sekondi. Although Sekondi, like many coastal areas in
modern-day Ghana, had an early European slaving castle (the British
built Fort Sekondi in 1682), the fort was burned in 1698 and the area
did not come under permanent British control until 1872.

A.2.5 References for Additional Early Election Cases

Here we discuss additional early election cases listed in the tables
throughout Chapter 4 but not discussed in the text. NB: The following
information draws from, but is intended to supplant, the coding notes
on these cases from the codebook to accompany Paine (2019a). The
information is largely the same, but we revised some onset years based
on new sources. We also provide additional sourcing for limitations on
the franchise and autonomy.

- Botswana and Swaziland: European mining interests in Bechuanaland and white landowners in Swaziland gained representation on
  European Advisory Councils in 1920 and 1921, respectively. These
  were largely powerless consolatory institutions designed to inform
  proclamations made by the High Commissioner. They existed alongside African councils comprised of unelected traditional elites, the
  Native Advisory Council in Bechuanaland and the Libandhla in

Swaziland. Bechuanaland and Swaziland gained legislative councils, in which Africans participated in elections, in 1961 and 1964, respectively. Even in these late elections, elected Africans did not comprise a majority of seats and the African representatives were chosen indirectly (Colonial Reports 1931, 6–7; Hailey 1957, 271–275; Stevens 1963; Spence 1964, 224; Proctor 1968, 60; Manungo 1999; Booth 2000, 104–105, 143–145, 247–248; Makgala 2010, 59).

- Egypt: prior to British colonization, Egypt had an independent army and a Western-style parliament dominated by the incumbent Turco-Circassian elites (Weipert-Fenner, 2020, 56–57). Although 1866 was the first year of elections to the precolonial parliament, we code 1882 as the first election year in our data set because we focus on colonial elections. Reflecting the precolonial precedent, the first colonial election returned nearly all the same representatives as the previous pre-British election (Abul-Magd, 2010, 697–699). "Under British rule, a bicameral system was installed that existed until 1912. It consisted of the Consultative Legislative Council (Majlis shura al-qawanin) with thirty members, fourteen of whom were appointed by the khedive and the government on a permanent basis, and sixteen of whom were elected every six years by provincial councils. Even though this council had only a consultative role on budgetary matters and legislation, the government had to justify its decisions to the council, which convened five times a year." On the second chamber, the General Assembly (al-Jamiyya al-umumiyya), forty-six of eighty-two members (which included all members of the Legislative Council) were directly elected by Egyptians on a limited franchise (approximately 13 percent of Egyptians). The second chamber had the right to vote on tax proposals, but this body met only once a year and lacked the right to propose legislation (Weipert-Fenner, 2020, 56–57). We code the restrictions based on the upper chamber because it appeared to be the more important body.
- Fiji: the first elections for seats on the Legislative Council occurred in 1905, but only Europeans participated in the elections. Indo-Fijians gained the right to elect three seats in 1929, compared to six for Europeans. In 1937, the number of elected seats for Europeans and Indo-Fijians was made equal (Ali, 1973). Property and income requirements remained in place until 1963, although literacy requirements persisted after this date (Hartmann, 2002, 647).

This is an unusual case in which the native population allied *with* Europeans and *against* majority rule. Migrant workers from India (Indo-Fijians) became the majority of the population over native Melanesians, and the latter saw Europeans as a buffer to protect their interests. When the franchise expanded in the 1960s, separate communal rolls were retained (Hartmann, 2002, 643–644).

- Indonesia: the Dutch East Indies gained minimal electoral representation starting in 1917. The electorate of the local Volksraad was tiny with separate electoral rolls by race; in 1939, there were only 2,228 eligible voters, of whom 1,452 were Indonesian. Europeans elected fifteen seats compared to twenty for Indonesians despite Europeans comprising only 0.47 percent of the population (seats from Nieuwenhuysen 1961; population percentage calculated by authors from Van Imhoff and Beets 2004, 52, and Epstein 1931, 1127). Even after expanding membership, only twenty of the sixty-one seats were (indirectly) elected by Indonesians, and the assembly had purely consolatory powers. Given these limitations, many nationalist leaders declined to participate entirely and instead pressed for a real parliament (Nieuwenhuysen, 1961).

- Mauritius: the first elections for seats on the Legislative Council occurred in 1886. As in the contemporaneous Jamaican constitution, the elected members were roughly in parity with official members, but there was effectively an official majority because the governor retained the right to appoint more official members if desired. The reforms, intended to empower Indians, included a low property qualification and an educational test that Indians could take in their own language (Will, 1966, 706). Nonetheless, only 1.1 percent of the total population was registered to vote in the mid-1880s; and only 7.3 percent of registered voters were Indians despite comprising 70 percent of the population.[2]

- Myanmar (Burma): the post-World War I electoral reforms in India spilled over to Burma, which was governed as part of India; and the introduction of elections also responded to the 1920 Rangoon

---

[2] Registration data from Will 1966, 706. Indian percentage of the population calculated by authors using census data from 1881 reported in Keltie 1887.

University Students' Boycott (Dudley, 1973, 598). The initial elections to the Legislative Council in 1923 were consciously patterned on the Indian model (Seekins, 2017, 187–88). These elections were held "under limited franchise depending on property and education. Moreover, these polls took place only on a communal basis with reserved seats for Europeans, Anglo-Indians, Karen, and other social groups" (Frasch, 2002, 600). Further reforms in both India and Burma in 1935 broadened the degree of policymaking autonomy under the new "dyarchy" regimes.

- Namibia: after becoming a Mandate under South African control in 1920, a proclamation in 1921 created an Advisory Council with nominated members only. A Commission recommended for South West Africa to have the same form of government as in the four provinces of the Union once "the population included at least 10,000 adult male British subjects of European descent" (Emmett, 1927, 121). The white population clamored for a greater degree of self-government, yielding a new constitution in 1925 with a legislative assembly "consist[ing] of twelve elected and six nominated members. All adults of European origin who were British subjects had a vote for the election of the twelve members." The first election for the assembly occurred in 1926. However, the Union reserved the right to legislate for the territory on all matters (Hailey, 1957, 268–271).
- Netherlands Antilles: see Suriname entry.
- Philippines: upon conquest from Spain in 1898, the United States declared its intention to prepare Filipinos for independence. Similar to the Middle Eastern Mandates, this early concession was a reaction to a major revolt. In the Philippine-American War, a large section of the elite had fought in favor of independence (Holden and Jacobson, 2012, 15). Secretary of War William Howard Taft, who urged Congress to pass the bill, wrote to Republican legislators that "there are some members of our party that are fearful that this gives too great power to an electorate, many of whom were lately in insurrection, but... I should very much regret having to go back to Manila without such a provision" (Cooper, 1902, 33). The first election occurred in 1907 and the legislature became bicameral in 1916. The initial franchise had religious (Christian), literacy, and property-owning requirements. Illiterates were enfranchised in 1924 but disenfranchised again in 1937, following a reform

in 1935 to abolish property qualifications and to extend suffrage to non-Christians and women (Hartmann, Hassall and Jr., 2002, 185, 188–189).

- Sri Lanka: like India, the non-white middle class was the main group that demanded elections in Ceylon. English-educated Sri Lankans founded organizations to articulate their demands for constitutional reform, including the Ceylon National Association. The reforms of 1910 addressed these demands, but only nominally, as the Ceylonese gained only one elected seat on the legislative council (amid the creation of four elected seats total, two of which were for the tiny European population). Ceylonese pushed for further reforms through "strictly peaceful and constitutional" means. Ceylon gained a majority of elected seats on the legislative council in 1923, four years behind India, albeit with continued franchise restrictions and separate communal rolls. In 1931, further reforms introduced universal suffrage for men and women and eliminated seats reserved for ethnic minority groups. This was the first grant of universal suffrage for a non-white population within the British empire, and was not repeated for more than a decade. Idiosyncratic concerns by British policymakers appeared to drive the decision. They contended that the Ceylonese were ready for additional autonomy but were concerned that restrictions on the franchise would enflame ethnic tensions between Sinhalese and Tamils (Namasivayam 1951, 16–20, 50–68; Howard 1960, 85–90; De Silva 1979).

- Suriname and Netherlands Antilles: in Suriname, electoral representation began in 1865 for the Colonial States (*Koloniale Staten*). A majority of seats were elected under a limited franchise, although the governor retained powers over finances (Ledgister, 1998, 138–139). A similar body was introduced in the other Dutch West Indian colony, the Netherlands Antilles, in 1936 (Oostindie and Klinkers, 2012, 61). The Netherlands reacted to failures in the East Indies by granting increased autonomy for its colonies in 1949. Under the Interim Orders, "Surinam received a larger measure of autonomy than any British colony in the region at the time," including parliamentary government and ministerial responsibility to the legislature, which was now elected under universal suffrage (Ledgister, 1998, 145).

- Swaziland: see Botswana entry.

- Tunisia: in an attempt to appease nationalist sentiments after World War I, France created a Grand Council with limited legislative capacity. There were separate European and Tunisian chambers. The European chamber had fifty-six members, more than half of whom were elected by Europeans. None of the forty Tunisian members were directly elected, and their section was suspended in 1934 (Perkins, 1997, 72).
- Vietnam: in 1880, Cochinchina (the southern part of modern-day Vietnam) gained a *conseil colonial* with six seats directly elected by French citizens with universal male suffrage, six seats for Vietnamese representatives who were selected through a two-step process in which delegates chosen by notables in each village (who were not themselves elected officials) served as an electoral college, and two additional *ex officio* European members. This body determined how taxes would be levied and spent. Members of the Vietnamese middle class pressed for reforms and France broadened the franchise for Vietnamese in 1922. However, representation was still heavily restricted: Vietnamese remained on a separate electoral roll with much more limited suffrage than for French voters, Vietnamese continued to control a minority of seats, and some Vietnamese members were appointed (Cook, 1977; Tai, 1984). We code the elections in Cochinchina as geographically circumscribed because the neighboring colonies of Annam and Tonkin, which were joined along with Cochinchina into the State of Vietnam within the French Union in 1949, lacked electoral representation.

A.3 Chapter 5

A.3.1 Main Patterns

The sample and setup of the first three tables are identical to those in the previous chapter, with the year of the analysis changed from 1945 to 1965. Table A.14 examines the existence of an elected assembly. Other than *authoritarian metropole* colonies having a lower prevalence of electoral institutions, there are no systematic differences across categories. Table A.15 examines franchise size. *Non-white middle-class* and *weak elite* colonies are each statistically distinguished (in a positive direction) from every other category but not from each other. Authoritarian metropoles have significantly smaller franchises than the other categories. Table A.16 examines V-Dem democracy score. *Non-white middle-class* colonies are statistically discernible from every other category, and *weak elites* have significantly higher scores than every category except non-white middle class.

Table A.14 *Electoral institutions in 1965*

	DV: Electoral institutions exist				
Panel A. Basic specifications					
	(1)	(2)	(3)	(4)	(5)
Authoritarian metropole	−0.111	−0.667***	−0.635***	−0.667***	
	(0.232)	(0.199)	(0.201)	(0.199)	
Settler minority	0.556***	0.000	0.0312		0.667***
	(0.121)	(0.000)	(0.0317)		(0.199)
Weak elites	0.524***	−0.0313		−0.0313	0.635***
	(0.125)	(0.0317)		(0.0317)	(0.201)
Non-white middle class	0.556***		0.0312	0.000	0.667***
	(0.121)		(0.0317)	(0.000)	(0.199)
National monarchy		−0.556***	−0.524***	−0.556***	0.111
		(0.121)	(0.125)	(0.121)	(0.232)
Intercept	0.444***	1.000	0.969***	1.000	0.333*
	(0.121)	(0.000)	(0.0317)	(0.000)	(0.199)
Colonies	82	82	82	82	82
R-squared	0.450	0.450	0.450	0.450	0.450
Panel B. Add covariates					
	(1)	(2)	(3)	(4)	(5)
Authoritarian metropole	−0.103	−0.673***	−0.650***	−0.734***	
	(0.256)	(0.219)	(0.218)	(0.225)	
Settler minority	0.631***	0.0609	0.0840		0.734***
	(0.136)	(0.0468)	(0.0592)		(0.225)
Weak elites	0.548***	−0.0231		−0.0840	0.650***
	(0.128)	(0.0288)		(0.0592)	(0.218)
Non-white middle class	0.571***		0.0231	−0.0609	0.673***
	(0.126)		(0.0288)	(0.0468)	(0.219)
National monarchy		−0.571***	−0.548***	−0.631***	0.103
		(0.126)	(0.128)	(0.136)	(0.256)
Intercept	0.461***	1.031***	1.008***	1.092***	0.358*
	(0.140)	(0.0565)	(0.0424)	(0.0916)	(0.210)
Colonies	82	82	82	82	82
R-squared	0.492	0.492	0.492	0.492	0.492
Covariates	YES	YES	YES	YES	YES

Notes: The sample is a cross-section of colonies (listed in Table A.9) measured in 1965. Models estimated using OLS with robust standard errors. Panel B includes the following covariates in every model: state antiquity in 1500, population density in 1500 (logged), precolonial democracy, and Protestant missionaries in 1923. ***$p < 0.01$,** $p < 0.05$,* $p < 0.1$.

Table A.15 *Franchise size in 1965*

	DV: Fraction of adult population with suffrage				
Panel A. Basic specifications					
	(1)	(2)	(3)	(4)	(5)
Authoritarian metropole	−0.561***	−0.936***	−0.921***	−0.460**	
	(0.112)	(0.0429)	(0.0441)	(0.205)	
Settler minority	−0.101	−0.476**	−0.461**		0.460**
	(0.234)	(0.210)	(0.210)		(0.205)
Weak elites	0.361***	−0.0145		0.461**	0.921***
	(0.120)	(0.0615)		(0.210)	(0.0441)
Non-white middle class	0.375***		0.0145	0.476**	0.936***
	(0.120)		(0.0615)	(0.210)	(0.0429)
National monarchy		−0.375***	−0.361***	0.101	0.561***
		(0.120)	(0.120)	(0.234)	(0.112)
Intercept	0.561***	0.936***	0.921***	0.460**	0.000
	(0.112)	(0.0429)	(0.0441)	(0.205)	(0.000)
Colonies	81	81	81	81	81
R-squared	0.463	0.463	0.463	0.463	0.463
Panel B. Add covariates					
	(1)	(2)	(3)	(4)	(5)
Authoritarian metropole	−0.495***	−0.917***	−0.909***	−0.498***	
	(0.142)	(0.0832)	(0.0642)	(0.181)	
Settler minority	0.00347	−0.418**	−0.410**		0.498***
	(0.213)	(0.180)	(0.180)		(0.181)
Weak elites	0.414***	−0.00789		0.410**	0.909***
	(0.130)	(0.0581)		(0.180)	(0.0642)
Non-white middle class	0.422***		0.00789	0.418**	0.917***
	(0.125)		(0.0581)	(0.180)	(0.0832)
National monarchy		−0.422***	−0.414***	−0.00347	0.495***
		(0.125)	(0.130)	(0.213)	(0.142)
Intercept	0.526***	0.947***	0.940***	0.529***	0.0307
	(0.140)	(0.0712)	(0.0519)	(0.186)	(0.0358)
Colonies	81	81	81	81	81
R-squared	0.523	0.523	0.523	0.523	0.523
Covariates	YES	YES	YES	YES	YES

Notes: The sample is a cross-section of colonies (listed in Table A.9) measured in 1965. Models estimated using OLS with robust standard errors. Panel B includes the following covariates in every model: state antiquity in 1500, population density in 1500 (logged), precolonial democracy, and Protestant missionaries in 1923. ***$p < 0.01$,** $p < 0.05$,* $p < 0.1$.

Table A.16 *Democracy score in 1965*

	DV: V-Dem electoral democracy index				
Panel A. Basic specifications					
	(1)	(2)	(3)	(4)	(5)
Authoritarian metropole	−0.106***	−0.345***	−0.200***	−0.127***	
	(0.0199)	(0.0368)	(0.0163)	(0.0239)	
Settler minority	0.0202	−0.218***	−0.0730**		0.127***
	(0.0302)	(0.0433)	(0.0280)		(0.0239)
Weak elites	0.0932***	−0.145***		0.0730**	0.200***
	(0.0246)	(0.0396)		(0.0280)	(0.0163)
Non-white middle class	0.238***		0.145***	0.218***	0.345***
	(0.0412)		(0.0396)	(0.0433)	(0.0368)
National monarchy		−0.238***	−0.0932***	−0.0202	0.106***
		(0.0412)	(0.0246)	(0.0302)	(0.0199)
Intercept	0.131***	0.369***	0.224***	0.151***	0.0248***
	(0.0192)	(0.0364)	(0.0154)	(0.0234)	(0.00519)
Colonies	81	81	81	81	81
R-squared	0.490	0.490	0.490	0.490	0.490
Panel B. Add covariates					
	(1)	(2)	(3)	(4)	(5)
Authoritarian metropole	−0.0906**	−0.328***	−0.183***	−0.116***	
	(0.0398)	(0.0405)	(0.0283)	(0.0410)	
Settler minority	0.0256	−0.211***	−0.0664**		0.116***
	(0.0345)	(0.0474)	(0.0327)		(0.0410)
Weak elites	0.0920***	−0.145***		0.0664**	0.183***
	(0.0263)	(0.0407)		(0.0327)	(0.0283)
Non-white middle class	0.237***		0.145***	0.211***	0.328***
	(0.0456)		(0.0407)	(0.0474)	(0.0405)
National monarchy		−0.237***	−0.0920***	−0.0256	0.0906**
		(0.0456)	(0.0263)	(0.0345)	(0.0398)
Intercept	0.121***	0.358***	0.213***	0.147***	0.0308**
	(0.0353)	(0.0391)	(0.0234)	(0.0401)	(0.0142)
Colonies	81	81	81	81	81
R-squared	0.516	0.516	0.516	0.516	0.516
Covariates	YES	YES	YES	YES	YES

Notes: The sample is a cross-section of colonies (listed in Table A.9) measured in 1965. Models estimated using OLS with robust standard errors. Panel B includes the following covariates in every model: state antiquity in 1500, population density in 1500 (logged), precolonial democracy, and Protestant missionaries in 1923. ***$p < 0.01$,** $p < 0.05$,* $p < 0.1$.

The sample in Table A.17 consists of 111 territories that gained independence no earlier than 1943, using data from Owolabi (2015). This is larger than our core V-Dem sample because it contains many microstates, some of which never gained independence. The dependent variable in Table A.17 indicates whether a country gained independence before 1965. The main explanatory variables are indicators for whether a colony belongs to a category that tended to have a negotiated decolonization process (any of the *weak elite, non-white middle class,* or *national monarchy*), and an indicator for whether the colony's population exceeded 1 million in 1960. All specifications contain these two variables and their interaction. Column 1 is a baseline specification with only these variables. Column 2 adds various covariates from Owolabi's data set: an indicator for major oil producer, an indicator for forced settlement colonies, a logged count of the number of years under Western colonial rule as of 1960, and fixed effects for British and French colonies. We cannot use the colonial covariates from the other tables because they have insufficient coverage for this expanded sample. Columns 3 and 4 present the same specifications while dropping nineteen territories that never gained independence, given possible concerns that such colonies are systematically different.

The findings support our expectations. In each specification, the effect of negotiated decolonization colonies is positive and statistically significant among colonies with populations exceeding one million. Thus, even when stratifying on population, a lack of vested interests to hold on yielded earlier independence. Conversely, the effect of a large population on earlier independence is positive and statistically significant among negotiated decolonization colonies. This confirms our theoretical expectation that democratic colonizers moved faster toward independence for larger colonies that posed a greater threat of revolt.

Table A.17 *Independence before 1965*

	DV: Independence before 1965			
	(1)	(2)	(3)	(4)
Negotiated decolonization	0.125***	0.104	0.184***	0.180
	(0.0450)	(0.108)	(0.0643)	(0.140)
Population exceeds 1M	0.400*	0.240*	0.400*	0.252*
	(0.223)	(0.144)	(0.224)	(0.142)
Interaction term	0.386*	0.505***	0.348	0.458***
	(0.232)	(0.150)	(0.236)	(0.160)
Intercept	0.000	0.282	0.000	0.0955
	(0.000)	(0.338)	(0.000)	(0.379)
Colonies	111	111	92	92
R-squared	0.601	0.696	0.575	0.677
Sample	Full	Full	Only indep.	Only indep.
Covariates	NO	YES	NO	YES
	Marginal effect estimates			
ND | Large pop.	0.511**	0.610***	0.532**	0.638***
	(0.227)	(0.127)	(0.227)	(0.122)
ND | Small pop.	0.125***	0.104	0.184***	0.180
	(0.0450)	(0.108)	(0.0643)	(0.140)
Large pop. | ND=1	0.786***	0.745***	0.748***	0.710***
	(0.0624)	(0.0825)	(0.0751)	(0.0965)
Large pop. | ND=0	0.400*	0.240*	0.400*	0.252*
	(0.223)	(0.144)	(0.224)	(0.142)

Notes: The text describes the sample and data. Models estimated using OLS with robust standard errors. In the marginal effects panel, "ND" abbreviates the variable *Negotiated decolonization*. ***$p < 0.01$,** $p < 0.05$,* $p < 0.1$.

A.3.2 Left-wing Metropolitan Governments

Table A.18 assesses the correlation between left-wing metropolitan governments and the onset of universal male suffrage. In all specifications, left-wing parties are the reference category. The first column contains only indicators for right-wing and center governments. The second column adds substantive covariates and year fixed effects. The third column has colony and year fixed effects. The distinction between left-wing parties and each of the other types of metropolitan governments is statistically significant and negative in all specifications.

Table A.18 *Left-wing metropolitan governments and universal male suffrage*

	DV: Onset of universal male suffrage		
	(1)	(2)	(3)
Right metro. government	−0.0548**	−0.123***	−0.124***
	(0.0242)	(0.0223)	(0.0233)
Center metro. government	−0.0878***	−0.0971***	−0.150***
	(0.0267)	(0.0263)	(0.0470)
Intercept	0.103***	0.101***	0.569***
	(0.0188)	(0.0287)	(0.0243)
Colony-years	604	604	604
R-squared	0.016	0.241	0.333
Covariates	NO	YES	NO
Year FE	NO	YES	YES
Colony FE	NO	NO	YES

Notes: Sample is annual observations of every *weak elite* and *non-white middle class* case (see Table A.9) during years of colonial rule between 1945 and 1965. Vanuatu is excluded because it had two colonizers simultaneously, which disables coding the metropolitan government variable. The dependent variable equals 1 in the first year with universal male suffrage, 0 in all previous years, and is set to missing after the first year. We coded the first year of universal male suffrage mainly using V-Dem. For the right/center metropolitan government variables (left-wing metropolitan government is the reference category), data from Brambor and Lindvall 2018. Models estimated using OLS with standard errors clustered at the colony level. Column 2 includes the following covariates: state antiquity in 1500, population density in 1500 (logged), precolonial democracy, and Protestant missionaries in 1923. ***$p < 0.01$,** $p < 0.05$,* $p < 0.1$.

A.3.3 Comparing British Colonialism: Contestation and Participation

In Table A.19, we compare British colonies to those of other democratic metropoles on different components of democracy in 1965. V-Dem's electoral democracy index consists of four main components: freedom of expression, freedom of association, franchise size, and clean elections (a fifth, ancillary, component indicates whether any national offices are elected). Another relevant measure we analyze is legislative constraints on the executive, a component of V-Dem's liberal democracy index.

In Panel A, the only regressor is an indicator for British colonies. In Panel B, we control for the same substantive covariates as in other regressions plus indicators for our different colonial types: settler minority, non-white middle class, and national monarchies, which leave weak elites as the reference category. British colonies score significantly higher on freedom of association, clean elections, and constraints on the executive, but significantly lower on franchise size. France moved all its colonies to universal suffrage in 1956, whereas the franchise expanded more gradually in British colonies. Reflecting higher contestation and lower participation, the coefficient estimate for the aggregate democracy score is positive but not statistically significant. The Panel B regressions are notable because we stratify on colonial categories, yet British colonies were still distinct from others.

Table A.19 *Comparing British colonialism: Contestation and participation in 1965*

DV:	Electoral democracy	Freedom of expression	Freedom of association	Franchise size	Clean elections	Executive constraints
	(1)	(2)	(3)	(4)	(5)	(6)
Panel A. Basic specifications						
British colony	0.0358	0.0841	0.121**	-0.172**	0.114**	0.154***
	(0.0314)	(0.0538)	(0.0557)	(0.0753)	(0.0513)	(0.0552)
Intercept	0.221***	0.297***	0.288***	0.919***	0.261***	0.314***
	(0.0171)	(0.0359)	(0.0356)	(0.0428)	(0.0311)	(0.0399)
Colonies	74	74	74	74	74	68
R-squared	0.016	0.031	0.058	0.062	0.060	0.105
Panel B. Add colonial categories and covariates						
	(1)	(2)	(3)	(4)	(5)	(6)
British colony	0.0408	0.0591	0.0944*	-0.111	0.108**	0.135**
	(0.0276)	(0.0517)	(0.0564)	(0.0726)	(0.0512)	(0.0591)
Settler minority	-0.0859**	-0.201***	-0.153***	-0.493***	-0.115	-0.182***
	(0.0327)	(0.0666)	(0.0506)	(0.181)	(0.0817)	(0.0607)
Non-white middle class	0.126***	0.189***	0.208***	0.0136	0.108*	0.0526
	(0.0374)	(0.0668)	(0.0608)	(0.0608)	(0.0593)	(0.0698)
National monarchy	-0.116***	-0.119*	-0.119	-0.391***	-0.152**	-0.0792
	(0.0318)	(0.0653)	(0.0734)	(0.130)	(0.0710)	(0.0816)
Intercept	0.179***	0.220***	0.230***	0.924***	0.230***	0.266***
	(0.0265)	(0.0448)	(0.0483)	(0.0495)	(0.0460)	(0.0614)
Colonies	74	74	74	74	74	68
R-squared	0.498	0.411	0.457	0.371	0.401	0.237
Covariates	YES	YES	YES	YES	YES	YES

Notes: Sample is all colonies with democratic metropoles in 1965 (hence excluding *authoritarian metropole* cases). Vanuatu is excluded because it was jointly colonized by Britain and France. Models estimated using OLS with robust standard errors. Panel B includes the following covariates in every model: state antiquity in 1500, population density in 1500 (logged), precolonial democracy, and Protestant missionaries in 1923. ***$p < 0.01$,** $p < 0.05$,* $p < 0.1$.

A.3.4 Decolonization in Africa

Table A.20 analyzes African colonies only. In particular, we assess whether *authoritarian metropole*, *settler minority*, and *national monarchy* cases experienced distinct decolonization paths from the other categories, *non-white middle-class* and *weak elite colonies* (which collectively comprise the reference category in every regression). Columns 1 and 2 resemble Table A.15 because suffrage is the dependent variable, Columns 3 and 4 resemble Table A.16 because democracy score is the dependent variable, and decolonization war is the dependent variable in Columns 5 and 6. Odd-numbered columns contain only the indicators for colonial categories and even-numbered columns add covariates.

Settler-minority colonies and authoritarian metropoles are each negatively correlated with franchise size in 1965 and positively correlated with having a major decolonization war. In Paine (2019*b*), we extend these results by instrumenting for the fraction of a colony's land that was suitable for European settlement. Authoritarian metropoles and settler-minority colonies are also significantly negatively correlated with V-Dem democracy scores in 1965 (as are national monarchies). These findings support our theoretical expectations that authoritarian metropoles should categorically prevent democratic gains; national monarchies should not experience meaningful electoral reforms; and, in settler-minority colonies, actions to resist broadening the political community can erode early democratic advantages.

Table A.20 *Decolonization in Africa*

	DV: Franchise size		DV: V-Dem electoral democracy index		DV: Decolonization war	
	(1)	(2)	(3)	(4)	(5)	(6)
Authoritarian metropole	−0.950***	−0.922***	−0.212***	−0.214***	0.653***	0.672***
	(0.0320)	(0.0356)	(0.0158)	(0.0182)	(0.234)	(0.242)
Settler minority	−0.490**	−0.463***	−0.0847***	−0.0708***	0.903***	0.869***
	(0.210)	(0.147)	(0.0274)	(0.0242)	(0.0557)	(0.0798)
National monarchy	0.0500	0.0210	−0.0631***	−0.0586**	0.153	0.131
	(0.0320)	(0.0840)	(0.0170)	(0.0221)	(0.234)	(0.189)
State antiquity in 1500		0.311*		−0.00295		0.237
		(0.125)		(0.0455)		(0.243)
Pop. density in 1500 (log)		0.0769**		0.0153***		0.00412
		(0.0301)		(0.00556)		(0.0167)
Precolonial democracy		−0.119		0.0285		−0.371*
		(0.104)		(0.0525)		(0.193)
Intercept	0.950***	0.863***	0.236***	0.228***	0.0968*	0.0676
	(0.0320)	(0.0435)	(0.0138)	(0.0136)	(0.0557)	(0.0711)
Colonies	46	46	46	46	44	44
R-squared	0.675	0.795	0.483	0.532	0.518	0.533

Notes: The sample consists of all countries in mainland Africa plus Madagascar. Franchise size and V-Dem democracy score are each measured in 1965. For decolonization war, we code a 1 for any country that experienced a decolonization war in the twentieth century; see Paine (2019b) for details on this variable. For the decolonization war samples, we exclude Libya and Somalia because it became impossible to fight Italy for independence after Italy lost its colonies following World War II. We omit the covariate Protestant missionaries in 1923 in all specifications, which is highly collinear with settler-minority colonies. When both are included in the same model, settler minority loses significance and Protestant missionaries is statistically significant in the *opposite* direction as anticipated in existing theories: more missionaries covary with smaller franchise sizes. ***$p < 0.01$, **$p < 0.05$, *$p < 0.1$.

A.3.5 Potential National Monarchs

The following entries provide details on the set of potential national monarchs and which ones held formal powers at the national level upon independence:

- Some cases were obvious because the colony was founded upon a protectorate treaty with a local ruler and the colonial borders were then drawn to largely correspond with the historical domain of the state. These cases are Bahrain, Bhutan, Burundi, Cambodia, Egypt, Kuwait, Laos, Lesotho, Maldives, Morocco, Nepal, Oman, Qatar, Rwanda, Swaziland, and Tunisia.[3] All these monarchs were intact at independence (some as ruling monarchies and some as constitutional) except Rwanda, where the Hutu Revolution overthrew the Tutsi monarchy shortly before independence.

- In two cases, Iraq and Jordan, Britain appointed a member of the loyalist Hashemite family to serve as a territory-wide monarch, despite the absence of a precolonial monarchy.

- In two states, a historical dynasty ruled over most of the corresponding colony, and we count these as territory-wide monarchs. In Libya, Italy recognized the leader of the Senussi Order as the ruler of Cyrenaica. Upon independence, Britain made him king of the United Kingdom of Libya, which unified Cyrenaica, Tripolitania, and Fezzan. We thus count this as a British national monarchy. In Vietnam, the Nguyen dynasty was the nominal head of state in the French protectorates of Annam and Tonkin (the other colonial component of modern-day Vietnam was Cochinchina, which was the only area to hold legislative elections; see Table 4.4). The Viet Minh overthrew the monarchy in the August Revolution of 1945.

- In some cases, a European power established control over an area by militarily defeating a precolonial state and deposing its ruling dynasty. We include such cases if the frontiers of the historical state encompassed a substantial portion of the ensuing colony. These cases are Burma (Konbaung dynasty/Third Burmese Empire), Mali (Tukulor Empire), and Sudan (Mahdist state). Thus, all of these

---

[3] Brunei and Zanzibar are similar cases, but neither is in our statistical sample. Brunei does not meet the V-Dem threshold and Zanzibar was merged with Tanganyika (Tanzania) shortly after independence.

are coded as deposed national monarchies. Sri Lanka (Kingdom of Kandy) was a borderline case that we exclude from the count because of prior long-term Dutch colonization of the island and interference with the monarchy.

- In numerous African cases, one or multiple precolonial states were amalgamated with other polities to create a larger colony. In such cases, we counted the colony as having a potential national monarchy if the ethnic group that corresponded with the precolonial state was at least a quarter of the population or was the plurality group (in all but two of the following cases, both conditions held). These cases are Benin (Dahomey state; Fon 25 percent of total population and plurality), Burkina Faso (Mossi states; Mossi 50 percent of total population), Ghana (Asante state; Asante 28 percent of population and plurality), Guinea (Futa Jalon state; Fulani 28 percent of population and near plurality), Madagascar (Merina state; Merina 27 percent of population and plurality), Nigeria (Sokoto Caliphate; Hausa-Fulani 27 percent of population and plurality), and Uganda (Buganda state; Baganda 16 percent of population and plurality). Of these, only Uganda had a national monarch at independence. This was an unusual case in which the *Kabaka* of Buganda served as the country's president at independence, but the country was a republic rather than a monarchy. All other cases are coded as deposed national monarchies either because the colonizer ended the dynasty or did not promote a monarch at independence. Botswana is a borderline case that we exclude from the count because the Tswana were fractured among distinct polities and traditional governance was highly participatory. Data on ethnicity from Scarritt and Mozaffar (1999).
- In two cases, distinct local monarchies were combined to create a federal monarchy, thus creating a national monarchy at or near independence. In the United Arab Emirates, the seven Trucial States combined at independence to create a federal electoral monarchy. Upon independence, Malaysia amalgamated nine distinct monarchies (previously part of the Federated Malay States and Unfederated Malay states) along with the former Straits Settlements, North Borneo/Sabah, and Sarawak. The nine monarchies elect a territory-wide monarch.

A.4 Chapter 6

Tables A.21 to A.27 correspond with the figures presented in Chapter 6 and provide details on various robustness checks. All contain a panel of all postindependence years between 1945 and 2022 for every country in Table A.9. In some specifications, we include additional non-European countries in any postindependence years between 1945 and 2022: colonized by a non-Western power (North/South Korea, Taiwan, Kazakhstan, Kyrgyzstan, Tajikistan, Turkmenistan, and Uzbekistan) or never colonized (Afghanistan, China, Ethiopia, Iran, Japan, Liberia, Mongolia, Saudi Arabia, Thailand, Turkey, and Yemen).

We include covariates that are standard in postcolonial democracy regressions:

- GDP per capita (log): data from the Maddison project (Bolt et al. 2018). Data points for 2019 onward are imputed using data from 2018, and data points before 1950 are imputed using data from 1950. Missing data for Bhutan, Fiji, Guyana, Maldives, North Korea, Papua New Guinea, Solomon Islands, Somalia, South Yemen, Suriname, and Vanuatu.
- Population (log): data points for 2019 onward are imputed using data from 2018, and data points before 1950 are imputed using data from 1950. Data from the Maddison project (Bolt et al. 2018). Missing data for all the same countries as GDP per capita except North Korea.
- Oil/gas per capita (log): measured in real 2014 dollars. Data points for 2015 onward are imputed using data from 2014. For some countries, the first data point occurs after the date of independence. For those, we fill in values of 0 for all previous years if the value was 0 in the first year with data, and otherwise we take the average of the first ten years with data. Data from Ross and Mahdavi (2015). Missing data for São Tomé and Príncipe, Seychelles, and Vanuatu.
- Ethnic fractionalization: data from Alesina et al. (2003). Missing data for Maldives, São Tomé and Príncipe, and South Yemen.
- Muslim percentage of the population: data from La Porta et al. (1999). No missing data.

In Tables A.26 and A.27, we analyze different versions of the colonial pluralism variable. Both tables are identical except the first contains ex-colonies only and the second contains all non-Western countries. Following Figure 6.4, we distinguish cases by high colonial pluralism (at least twenty years), short (between one and nineteen years), and no years of colonial pluralism; changing the basis category and adding covariates across the various specifications in Columns 1 through 4. In Columns 5 and 6, we model a logged version of years of colonial pluralism (adding 0.1 to cases with 0 years). In Columns 7 and 8, we modify the years of colonial pluralism variable as follows. The V-Party data set (Lindberg et al. 2022; Pemstein et al. 2023) measures attributes of political parties in years when elections are held. For every country, we record the first year in which a political party existed. For the modified colonial pluralism variable, we subtract any years from the original variable in which no political party existed. Thus, for example, South Africa continues to have forty years of pluralism on the modified variable because parties existed for all forty years coded as plural for the original measure. By contrast, Jamaica's count drops to 18 because political parties competed in elections only between 1944 and 1962, when the country gained independence. As with the original variable, for the regressions, we take the log and add 0.1 to cases with 0 years.

Table A.21 Persistent democratic differences: Ex-colonies only

	(1)	(2)	(3)	(4)	(5)	(6)	(7)	(8)
				DV: V-Dem electoral democracy index				
Demo. at independence	0.787***	0.797***			0.868***	0.889***	0.690***	0.702***
	(0.0544)	(0.0940)			(0.0584)	(0.0642)	(0.0747)	(0.135)
Demo. 20 years before			1.092***	1.245***				
			(0.205)	(0.345)				
GDP p.c. (log)		0.00972		0.0237		0.0385***		0.00480
		(0.0120)		(0.0215)		(0.0132)		(0.0170)
Population (log)		−0.000732		−0.00832		0.00355		−0.00238
		(0.00752)		(0.0136)		(0.00555)		(0.0110)
Oil/gas p.c. (log)		−0.00524		−0.0129**		−0.00390		−0.00914
		(0.00435)		(0.00604)		(0.00358)		(0.00617)
Ethnic fractionalization		0.000732		0.0716		−0.0542*		0.0610
		(0.0381)		(0.0613)		(0.0295)		(0.0598)
Muslim population		4.73e−05		−0.000892**		0.000171		−0.000121
		(0.000353)		(0.000410)		(0.000211)		(0.000537)
Intercept	0.0798***	−0.00686	0.232***	0.0275	−0.0226	−0.285**	0.177***	0.0236
	(0.0182)	(0.112)	(0.0200)	(0.193)	(0.0145)	(0.128)	(0.0287)	(0.167)
Country-years	5,015	4,405	4,901	4,291	2,312	2,066	2,703	2,339
R-squared	0.426	0.594	0.174	0.426	0.690	0.746	0.353	0.447
Year FE	NO	YES	NO	YES	NO	YES	NO	YES
Years	All	All	All	All	Pre-1990	Pre-1990	Post-1990	Post-1990

Notes: Countries consist of those in Table A.9. Models estimated using OLS with robust standard errors clustered at the country level.
$***p < 0.01, **p < 0.05, *p < 0.1$.

Table A.22 *Persistent democratic differences: All non-Western colonies*

				DV: V-Dem electoral democracy index				
	(1)	(2)	(3)	(4)	(5)	(6)	(7)	(8)
Demo. at independence	0.779***	0.678***			0.855***	0.825***	0.668***	0.530***
	(0.0566)	(0.0867)			(0.0573)	(0.0614)	(0.0797)	(0.129)
Demo. 20 years before			1.087***	0.993***				
			(0.209)	(0.270)				
GDP p.c. (log)		0.0476*		0.0526**		0.0648***		0.0489**
		(0.0189)		(0.0211)		(0.0227)		(0.0226)
Population (log)		0.00637		−0.00396		0.0105		0.00331
		(0.00869)		(0.0120)		(0.00749)		(0.0112)
Oil/gas p.c. (log)		−0.0151***		−0.0202***		−0.00967**		−0.0217***
		(0.00510)		(0.00603)		(0.00427)		(0.00719)
Ethnic fractionalization		−0.0198		0.00680		−0.0684**		0.0457
		(0.0406)		(0.0566)		(0.0291)		(0.0659)
Muslim population		−0.000371		−0.00100***		−2.64e−05		−0.000727
		(0.000324)		(0.000363)		(0.000239)		(0.000470)
Intercept	0.0929***	−0.345*	0.225***	−0.251	−0.00286	−0.543**	0.192***	−0.246
	(0.0181)	(0.186)	(0.0202)	(0.205)	(0.0113)	(0.228)	(0.0302)	(0.216)
Country-years	6,257	5,605	5,908	5,298	2,932	2,644	3,325	2,961
R-squared	0.379	0.550	0.150	0.438	0.622	0.709	0.289	0.409
Year FE	NO	YES	NO	YES	NO	YES	NO	YES
Years	All	All	All	All	Pre-1990	Pre-1990	Post-1990	Post-1990

Notes: Countries consist of those in Table A.9 plus the additional non-European countries listed above. For never-colonized countries, we use 1945 as the year of independence. Models estimated using OLS with robust standard errors clustered at the country level.
***$p < 0.01$, ** $p < 0.05$, * $p < 0.1$.

Table A.23 *Postcolonial democracy by colonial categories: All years*

					DV: V-Dem electoral democracy index					
	(1)	(2)	(3)	(4)	(5)	(6)	(7)	(8)	(9)	(10)
Not Western colonized	0.0646	0.0595*	-0.107	-0.0870	-0.0383	-0.0321	-0.177***	-0.157***		
	(0.0525)	(0.0351)	(0.0915)	(0.0533)	(0.0521)	(0.0304)	(0.0588)	(0.0458)		
Non-white middle class	0.242***	0.217***	0.0706	0.0703	0.139***	0.125***			0.177***	0.157***
	(0.0415)	(0.0431)	(0.0856)	(0.0576)	(0.0410)	(0.0384)			(0.0588)	(0.0458)
Weak elites	0.103***	0.0916***	-0.0684	-0.0549			-0.139***	-0.125***	0.0383	0.0321
	(0.0313)	(0.0312)	(0.0812)	(0.0531)			(0.0410)	(0.0384)	(0.0521)	(0.0304)
Settler minority	0.171**	0.146***			0.0684	0.0549	-0.0706	-0.0703	0.107	0.0870
	(0.0815)	(0.0494)			(0.0812)	(0.0531)	(0.0856)	(0.0576)	(0.0915)	(0.0533)
Auth. metro./ monarchies			-0.171**	-0.146***	-0.103***	-0.0916***	-0.242***	-0.217***	-0.0646	-0.0595*
			(0.0815)	(0.0494)	(0.0313)	(0.0312)	(0.0415)	(0.0431)	(0.0525)	(0.0351)
Intercept	0.202***	-0.281	0.373***	-0.134	0.305***	-0.189	0.444***	-0.0641	0.266***	-0.221
	(0.0226)	(0.226)	(0.0783)	(0.236)	(0.0216)	(0.224)	(0.0348)	(0.240)	(0.0474)	(0.224)
Country-years	6,257	5,605	6,257	5,605	6,257	5,605	6,257	5,605	6,257	5,605
R-squared	0.154	0.464	0.154	0.464	0.154	0.464	0.154	0.464	0.154	0.464
Covariates	NO	YES	NO	YES	NO	YES	NO	YES	NO	YES
Year FE	NO	YES	NO	YES	NO	YES	NO	YES	NO	YES

Notes: Countries consist of those in Table A.9 plus the additional non-European countries listed above (these comprise the category *Not Western colonized*). Models estimated using OLS with robust standard errors are clustered at the country level.

$***p < 0.01$, $**p < 0.05$, $*p < 0.1$.

Table A.24 *Postcolonial democracy by colonial categories: Pre-1990*

	(1)	(2)	(3)	(4)	(5)	(6)	(7)	(8)	(9)	(10)
					DV: V-Dem electoral democracy index					
Not Western colonized	0.0698	0.0142	0.00254	-0.0417	-0.0352	-0.0841**	-0.176***	-0.192***		
	(0.0512)	(0.0376)	(0.0544)	(0.0474)	(0.0536)	(0.0341)	(0.0633)	(0.0508)		
Non-white middle class	0.245***	0.206***	0.178***	0.150***	0.140***	0.108**			0.176***	0.192***
	(0.0410)	(0.0446)	(0.0450)	(0.0493)	(0.0439)	(0.0442)			(0.0633)	(0.0508)
Weak elites	0.105***	0.0983***	0.0377	0.0424			-0.140***	-0.108**	0.0352	0.0841**
	(0.0233)	(0.0274)	(0.0298)	(0.0395)			(0.0439)	(0.0442)	(0.0536)	(0.0341)
Settler minority	0.0673***	0.0560*			-0.0377	-0.0424	-0.178***	-0.150***	-0.00254	0.0417
	(0.0252)	(0.0295)			(0.0298)	(0.0395)	(0.0450)	(0.0493)	(0.0544)	(0.0474)
Auth. metro/monarchies			-0.0673***	-0.0560*	-0.105***	-0.0983***	-0.245***	-0.206***	-0.0698	-0.0142
			(0.0252)	(0.0295)	(0.0233)	(0.0274)	(0.0410)	(0.0446)	(0.0512)	(0.0376)
Intercept	0.116***	-0.539*	0.183***	-0.483	0.221***	-0.441	0.361***	-0.333	0.186***	-0.525*
	(0.0120)	(0.296)	(0.0221)	(0.305)	(0.0199)	(0.298)	(0.0392)	(0.319)	(0.0497)	(0.300)
Country-years	2,932	2,644	2,932	2,644	2,932	2,644	2,932	2,644	2,932	2,644
R-squared	0.231	0.470	0.231	0.470	0.231	0.470	0.231	0.470	0.231	0.470
Covariates	NO	YES	NO	YES	NO	YES	NO	YES	NO	YES
Year FE	NO	YES	NO	YES	NO	YES	NO	YES	NO	YES

Notes: Countries consist of those in Table A.9 plus the additional non-European countries listed above (these comprise the category *Not Western colonized*). Years are pre-1990. Models estimated using OLS with robust standard errors clustered at the country level.
***p < 0.01, **p < 0.05, *p < 0.1.

Table A.25 *Postcolonial democracy by colonial categories: Post-1990*

		DV: V-Dem electoral democracy index								
	(1)	(2)	(3)	(4)	(5)	(6)	(7)	(8)	(9)	(10)
Not Western colonized	0.0702	0.0966**	-0.111	-0.0821	-0.0301	0.00607	-0.173**	-0.124**		
	(0.0662)	(0.0486)	(0.0990)	(0.0675)	(0.0614)	(0.0446)	(0.0667)	(0.0554)		
Non-white middle class	0.243***	0.220***	0.0615	0.0417	0.143***	0.130***			0.173**	0.124**
	(0.0513)	(0.0547)	(0.0897)	(0.0707)	(0.0450)	(0.0478)			(0.0667)	(0.0554)
Weak elites	0.100**	0.0905**	-0.0811	-0.0881			-0.143***	-0.130***	0.0301	-0.00607
	(0.0442)	(0.0450)	(0.0858)	(0.0671)			(0.0450)	(0.0478)	(0.0614)	(0.0446)
Settler minority	0.182*	0.179***			0.0811	0.0881	-0.0615	-0.0417	0.111	0.0821
	(0.0893)	(0.0654)			(0.0858)	(0.0671)	(0.0897)	(0.0707)	(0.0990)	(0.0675)
Auth. metro./monarchies			-0.182**	-0.179***	-0.100**	-0.0905**	-0.243***	-0.220***	-0.0702	-0.0966**
			(0.0893)	(0.0654)	(0.0442)	(0.0450)	(0.0513)	(0.0547)	(0.0662)	(0.0486)
Intercept	0.276***	-0.160	0.458***	0.0182	0.377***	-0.0699	0.519***	0.0599	0.347***	-0.0638
	(0.0358)	(0.250)	(0.0818)	(0.261)	(0.0259)	(0.242)	(0.0368)	(0.258)	(0.0557)	(0.254)
Country-years	3,325	2,961	3,325	2,961	3,325	2,961	3,325	2,961	3,325	2,961
R-squared	0.150	0.398	0.150	0.398	0.150	0.398	0.150	0.398	0.150	0.398
Covariates	NO	YES	NO	YES	NO	YES	NO	YES	NO	YES
Year FE	NO	YES	NO	YES	NO	YES	NO	YES	NO	YES

Notes: Countries consist of those in Table A.9 plus the additional non-European countries listed above (these comprise the category *Not Western colonized*). Years are post-1990. Models estimated using OLS with robust standard errors clustered at the country level.
***$p < 0.01$, **$p < 0.05$, *$p < 0.1$.

Table A.26 *Postcolonial democracy by colonial pluralism: Ex-colonies only*

				DV: V-Dem electoral democracy index				
	(1)	(2)	(3)	(4)	(5)	(6)	(7)	(8)
Panel A. All years								
Short colonial pluralism	−0.140***	−0.128***	0.0539*	0.0165				
	(0.0404)	(0.0465)	(0.0307)	(0.0299)				
No colonial pluralism	−0.226***	−0.182***						
	(0.0399)	(0.0453)						
Long colonial pluralism			0.247***	0.222***				
			(0.0483)	(0.0617)				
Years of pluralism (log)					0.0409***	0.0328***		
					(0.00690)	(0.00815)		
Years of pluralism with party (log)							0.0387***	0.0301***
							(0.00777)	(0.00864)
Intercept	0.440***	0.0640	0.246***	0.0574	0.291***	−0.0402	0.315***	−0.112
	(0.0337)	(0.198)	(0.0210)	(0.172)	(0.0141)	(0.190)	(0.0157)	(0.194)
Country-years	5,015	4,405	5,015	4,405	5,015	4,405	5,015	4,405
R-squared	0.188	0.428	0.194	0.433	0.190	0.419	0.153	0.397
Covariates	NO	YES	NO	YES	NO	YES	NO	YES
Year FE	NO	YES	NO	YES	NO	YES	NO	YES

DV: V-Dem electoral democracy index

Panel B. Pre-1990

	(1)	(2)	(3)	(4)	(5)	(6)	(7)	(8)
Short colonial pluralism	-0.168***	-0.139***	0.0416*	0.0107				
	(0.0420)	(0.0432)	(0.0228)	(0.0259)				
No colonial pluralism	-0.241***	-0.202***						
	(0.0412)	(0.0397)						
Long colonial pluralism			0.272***	0.224***				
			(0.0528)	(0.0610)				
Years of pluralism (log)					0.0441***	0.0368***		
					(0.00689)	(0.00704)		
Years of pluralism with party (log)							0.0367***	0.0326***
							(0.00752)	(0.00795)
Intercept	0.369***	-0.218	0.160***	-0.233	0.203***	-0.322	0.231***	-0.511**
	(0.0390)	(0.199)	(0.0166)	(0.194)	(0.0119)	(0.210)	(0.0159)	(0.213)
Country-years	2,312	2,066	2,312	2,066	2,312	2,066	2,312	2,066
R-squared	0.326	0.484	0.358	0.463	0.328	0.471	0.204	0.426
Covariates	NO	YES	NO	YES	NO	YES	NO	YES
Year FE	NO	YES	NO	YES	NO	YES	NO	YES

Table A.26 *(cont.)*

Panel C. Post-1990

	DV: V-Dem electoral democracy index							
	(1)	(2)	(3)	(4)	(5)	(6)	(7)	(8)
Short colonial pluralism	−0.114**	−0.111*	0.0625	0.0211				
	(0.0459)	(0.0563)	(0.0414)	(0.0419)				
No colonial pluralism	−0.209***	−0.160***						
	(0.0474)	(0.0569)						
Long colonial pluralism			0.221***	0.203***				
			(0.0524)	(0.0705)				
Years of pluralism (log)					0.0375***	0.0284***		
					(0.00852)	(0.0103)		
Years of pluralism with party (log)							0.0380***	0.0280**
							(0.00936)	(0.0107)
Intercept	0.499***	0.0789	0.322***	0.116	0.366***	−0.0161	0.386***	−0.0730
	(0.0343)	(0.260)	(0.0281)	(0.239)	(0.0191)	(0.248)	(0.0187)	(0.254)
Country-years	2,703	2,339	2,703	2,339	2,703	2,339	2,703	2,339
R-squared	0.157	0.305	0.154	0.315	0.159	0.297	0.146	0.290
Covariates	NO	YES	NO	YES	NO	YES	NO	YES
Year FE	NO	YES	NO	YES	NO	YES	NO	YES

Notes: Countries consist of those in Table A.9. Models estimated using OLS with robust standard errors clustered at the country level.
***$p < 0.01$, ** $p < 0.05$, * $p < 0.1$.

Table A.27 *Postcolonial democracy by colonial pluralism: All non-Western colonies*

				DV: V-Dem electoral democracy index				
	(1)	(2)	(3)	(4)	(5)	(6)	(7)	(8)
Panel A. All years								
Short colonial pluralism	-0.140***	-0.113**	0.0467	0.0168				
	(0.0404)	(0.0441)	(0.0313)	(0.0276)				
No colonial pluralism	-0.203***	-0.159***						
	(0.0415)	(0.0418)						
Long colonial pluralism			0.239***	0.179***				
			(0.0486)	(0.0582)				
Years of pluralism (log)					0.0349***	0.0269***		
					(0.00717)	(0.00721)		
Years of pluralism with party (log)							0.0353***	0.0276***
							(0.00791)	(0.00805)
Intercept	0.440***	-0.282	0.254***	-0.353	0.305***	-0.386*	0.321***	-0.431*
	(0.0336)	(0.226)	(0.0219)	(0.220)	(0.0155)	(0.220)	(0.0163)	(0.217)
Country-years	6,257	5,605	6,257	5,605	6,257	5,605	6,257	5,605
R-squared	0.141	0.425	0.151	0.420	0.137	0.418	0.117	0.409
Covariates	NO	YES	NO	YES	NO	YES	NO	YES
Year FE	NO	YES	NO	YES	NO	YES	NO	YES

Table A.27 (cont.)

				DV: V-Dem electoral democracy index				
Panel B. Pre-1990								
	(1)	(2)	(3)	(4)	(5)	(6)	(7)	(8)
Short colonial pluralism	−0.168***	−0.127***	0.0318	0.0259				
	(0.0420)	(0.0435)	(0.0267)	(0.0248)				
No colonial pluralism	−0.215***	−0.195***						
	(0.0458)	(0.0420)						
Long colonial pluralism			0.263***	0.205***				
			(0.0545)	(0.0621)				
Years of pluralism (log)					0.0364***	0.0336***		
					(0.00765)	(0.00724)		
Years of pluralism with party (log)							0.0333***	0.0343***
							(0.00805)	(0.00775)
Intercept	0.369***	−0.536*	0.170***	−0.622**	0.221***	−0.657**	0.237***	−0.766***
	(0.0390)	(0.279)	(0.0217)	(0.293)	(0.0157)	(0.272)	(0.0170)	(0.252)
Country-years	2,932	2,644	2,932	2,644	2,932	2,644	2,932	2,644
R-squared	0.235	0.464	0.268	0.437	0.221	0.456	0.152	0.432
Covariates	NO	YES	NO	YES	NO	YES	NO	YES
Year FE	NO	YES	NO	YES	NO	YES	NO	YES

DV: V-Dem electoral democracy index

Panel C. Post-1990

	(1)	(2)	(3)	(4)	(5)	(6)	(7)	(8)
Short colonial pluralism	-0.114**	-0.0950*	0.0539	0.00894				
	(0.0458)	(0.0543)	(0.0405)	(0.0398)				
No colonial pluralism	-0.185***	-0.123**						
	(0.0458)	(0.0514)						
Long colonial pluralism			0.212***	0.143**				
			(0.0516)	(0.0660)				
Years of pluralism (log)					0.0320***	0.0203**		
					(0.00823)	(0.00893)		
Years of pluralism with party (log)							0.0341***	0.0220**
							(0.00915)	(0.0100)
Intercept	0.499***	-0.179	0.331***	-0.211	0.379***	-0.269	0.394***	-0.290
	(0.0343)	(0.251)	(0.0267)	(0.242)	(0.0186)	(0.248)	(0.0187)	(0.251)
Country-years	3,325	2,961	3,325	2,961	3,325	2,961	3,325	2,961
R-squared	0.115	0.332	0.118	0.330	0.113	0.324	0.108	0.324
Covariates	NO	YES	NO	YES	NO	YES	NO	YES
Year FE	NO	YES	NO	YES	NO	YES	NO	YES

Notes: Countries consist of those in Table A.9 plus the additional non-European countries listed above. Models estimated using OLS with robust standard errors clustered at the country level. ***$p < 0.01$, **$p < 0.05$, *$p < 0.1$.

References

Abernethy, David B. 2000. *The Dynamics of Global Dominance: European Overseas Empires, 1415–1980.* Yale University Press.

Abrams, Larry and David J. Miller. 1976. "Who Were the French Colonialists? A Reassessment of the Parti Colonial, 1890–1914." *The Historical Journal* 19(3):685–725.

Abramson, Scott F. and Carles Boix. 2019. "Endogenous Parliaments: The Domestic and International Roots of Long-Term Economic Growth and Executive Constraints in Europe." *International Organization* 73(4): 793–837.

Abul-Magd, Zeinab. 2010. "Rebellion in the Time of Cholera: Failed Empire, Unfinished Nation in Egypt, 1840–1920." *Journal of World History* 21(4):691–719.

Acemoglu, Daron and James A. Robinson. 2006. *Economic Origins of Dictatorship and Democracy.* Cambridge University Press.

Acemoglu, Daron and James A. Robinson. 2012. *Why Nations Fail: The Origins of Power, Prosperity, and Poverty.* Currency.

Acemoglu, Daron and James A. Robinson. 2020. *The Narrow Corridor: States, Societies, and the Fate of Liberty.* Penguin Books.

Acemoglu, Daron, Simon Johnson and James A. Robinson. 2001. "The Colonial Origins of Comparative Development: An Empirical Investigation." *American Economic Review* 91(5):1369–1401.

Acemoglu, Daron, Simon Johnson and James A. Robinson. 2002*a*. An African Success Story. In *In Search of Prosperity: Analytic Narratives on Economic Growth*, ed. Dani Rodrik. Princeton University Press pp. 80–119.

Acemoglu, Daron, Simon Johnson and James A. Robinson. 2002*b*. "Reversal of Fortune: Geography and Institutions in the Making of the Modern World Income Distribution." *Quarterly Journal of Economics* 117(4):1231–1294.

Acemoglu, Daron, Simon Johnson, James A. Robinson and Pierre Yared. 2008. "Income and Democracy." *American Economic Review* 98(3): 808–842.

Afigbo, A.E. 1972. *Warrant Chiefs Indirect Rule in Southeastern Nigeria, 1891–1929.* Longman.

Ahmed, Ali T. and David Stasavage. 2020. "Origins of Early Democracy." *American Political Science Review* 114(2):502–518.

Ajayi, J.F. Ade and Michael Crowder. 1985. *Historical Atlas of Africa*. Longman.

Albertus, Michael. 2015. *Autocracy and Redistribution: The Politics of Land Reform*. Cambridge University Press.

Aldrich, Robert. 1996. *Greater France: A History of French Overseas Expansion*. Bloomsbury Publishing.

Aldrich, Robert. 2000. "French Colonies." Encyclopedia of 1848 Revolutions. Available at www.ohio.edu/chastain/dh/frenchco.htm.

Aldrich, Robert and John Connell. 1992. *France's Overseas Frontier: Départements et territoires d'outre-mer*. Cambridge University Press.

Alesina, Alberto, Arnaud Devleeschauwer, William Easterly, Sergio Kurlat and Romain Wacziarg. 2003. "Fractionalization." *Journal of Economic Growth* 8(2):155–194.

Alexandrowicz, C.H. 1973. The Partition of Africa by Treaty. In *Foreign Relations of African States*, ed. Kenneth Ingham. Butterworths pp. 129–155

Ali, Ahmed. 1973. Fiji and the Franchise: A History of Political Representation, 1900–1937. Ph.D. thesis. Australian National University.

Altman, Ida. 1987. "Spanish Hidalgos and America: The Ovandos of Cáceres." *The Americas* 43(3):323–346.

Aluko, Olajide. 1974. Politics of Decolonisation in British West Africa, 1945–1960. In *History of West Africa Vol. II*, ed. J.F. Ade Ajayi and Michael Crowder. Cambridge University Press pp. 622–663.

Anene, J.C. 1966. *Southern Nigeria in Transition 1885–1906: Theory and Practice in a Colonial Protectorate*. Cambridge University Press.

Anna, Timothy E. 1983. *Spain and the Loss of America*. University of Nebraska Press.

Ansell, Ben W. and David J. Samuels. 2014. *Inequality and Democratization: An Elite Competition Approach*. Cambridge University Press.

Anstey, Roger. 1970. Belgian Rule in the Congo and the Aspirations of the 'Evolue' Class. In *Colonialism in Africa 1870–1960, Volume 2: The History and Politics of Colonialism 1914–1960*, ed. L.H. Gann and Peter Duignan. Cambridge University Press pp. 194–225.

Antonius, George. 1934. "Syria and the French Mandate." *International Affairs (Royal Institute of International Affairs 1931–1939)* 13(4): 523–539.

Argov, Daniel. 1964. The Ideological Differences between Moderates and Extremists in the Indian National Movement with Special Reference to Surendranath Banerjea and Lajpat Rai 1883–1919. Ph.D. thesis. School of Oriental and African Studies, University of London.

Arias, Luz Marina and Desha Girod. 2014. "Indigenous Origins of Colonial Institutions." *Quarterly Journal of Political Science* 9:371–406.

Arnold, James R. and Roberta Wiener. 2015. *Understanding US Military Conflicts through Primary Sources [4 volumes]*. ABC-CLIO.

Arriola, Leonardo R., Jed DeVaro and Anne Meng. 2021. "Democratic Subversion: Elite Cooptation and Opposition Fragmentation." *American Political Science Review* 115(4):1358–1372.

Australian Electoral Commission. 2020. "Electoral Milestones for Indigenous Australians." Available at www.aec.gov.au/indigenous/milestones .htm.

Axtmann, Dirk. 2002. Iraq. In *Elections in Asia and the Pacific: A Data Handbook. Volume 1: Middle East, Central Asia, and South Asia*, ed. Dieter Nohlen, Florian Grotz and Christof Hartmann. Oxford University Press pp. 85–108.

Baldwin, Kate. 2015. *The Paradox of Traditional Chiefs in Democratic Africa*. Cambridge University Press.

Banerjea, Surendranath. 1925. *A Nation in Making, Being the Reminiscences of Fifty Years of Public Life*. Oxford University Press.

Basu, Aparna. 2008. "Women's Struggle for the Vote: 1917–1937." *Indian Historical Review* 35(1):128–143.

Bateman, David A. 2018. *Disenfranchising Democracy: Constructing the Electorate in the United States, the United Kingdom, and France*. Cambridge University Press.

Bates, Robert H. and Da-Hsiang Donald Lien. 1985. "A Note on Taxation, Development, and Representative Government." *Politics & Society* 14(1):53–70.

Beasley, W.G. 1989. Meiji Political Institutions. In *The Cambridge History of Japan, Volume 5: The Nineteenth Century*, ed. Marius B. Jansen. Cambridge University Press pp. 618–673.

Beck, J. Murray. 2009. "Nova Scotia." Available at www.thecanadianency clopedia.ca/en/article/nova-scotia.

Beik, Paul H. 1965. *Louis Philippe and the July Monarchy*. D. Van Nostrand Company.

Belich, James. 2010. How Much Did Institutions Matter? Cloning Britain in New Zealand. In *Exclusionary Empire: English Liberty Overseas, 1600–1900*, ed. Jack P. Greene. Cambridge University Press pp. 248–268.

Bellin, Eva. 2000. "Contingent Democrats: Industrialists, Labor, and Democratization in Late-Developing Countries." *World Politics* 52(2): 175–205.

Belloc, Hilaire. 1898. *The Modern Traveller*. E. Arnold.

Bendel, Petra. 1999. Nigeria. In *Elections in Africa: A Data Handbook*, ed. Dieter Nohlen, Bernard Thibaut and Michael Krennerich. Oxford University Press pp. 697–726.

Bender, Gerald. 1974. "Portugal and Her Colonies Join the Twentieth Century: Causes and Initial Implications of the Military Coup." *Ufahamu: A Journal of African Studies* 4(3):121–162.

Bentzen, Jeanet Sinding, Jacob Gerner Hariri and James A Robinson. 2019. "Power and Persistence: The Indigenous Roots of Representative Democracy." *Economic Journal* 129(618):678–714.

Berry, Sara. 1992. "Hegemony on a Shoestring: Indirect Rule and Access to Agricultural Land." *Africa* 62(3):327–355.

Bienen, Henry and Nicolas Van De Walle. 1989. "Time and Power in Africa." *American Political Science Review* 83(1):19–34.

Billings, Warren M. 2004. *A Little Parliament: The Virginia General Assembly in the Seventeenth Century*. Library of Virginia.

Blake, Robert. 1978. *A History of Rhodesia*. Alfred A. Knopf.

Blaydes, Lisa. 2010. *Elections and Distributive Politics in Mubarak's Egypt*. Cambridge University Press.

Bockstette, Valerie, Areendam Chanda and Louis Putterman. 2002. "States and Markets: The Advantage of an Early Start." *Journal of Economic Growth* 7(4):347–369.

Boix, Carles. 2003. *Democracy and Redistribution*. Cambridge University Press.

Boix, Carles. 2011. "Democracy, Development, and the International System." *American Political Science Review* 105(4):809–828.

Boix, Carles, Michael Miller and Sebastian Rosato. 2013. "A Complete Data Set of Political Regimes, 1800–2007." *Comparative Political Studies* 46(12):1523–1554.

Bolland, O. Nigel. 1992. Belize: Historical Setting. In *Guyana and Belize: Country Studies*, ed. Tim Merrill. Federal Research Division, Library of Congress pp. 155–186.

Bolt, Jutta, Leigh Gardner, Jennifer Kohler, Jack Paine and James A. Robinson. 2023. "African Political Institutions and the Impact of Colonialism." NBER Working Paper 30582.

Bolt, Jutta, Robert Inklaar, Herman de Jong and Jan Luiten van Zanden. 2018. "Rebasing 'Maddison'." Maddison Project Working paper 10. Available at www.rug.nl/ggdc/historicaldevelopment/maddison.

Boone, Catherine. 2003. *Political Topographies of the African State: Territorial Authority and Institutional Choice*. Cambridge University Press.

Boone, Catherine. 2014. *Property and Political Order in Africa: Land Rights and the Structure of Politics*. Cambridge University Press.

Booth, Alan R. 2000. *Historical Dictionary of Swaziland*. Scarecrow Press.

Boughton, James M. 2001. "Northwest of Suez: the 1956 Crisis and the IMF." *IMF Staff Papers* 48(3):425–446.

Bowen, John Richard. 2007. *Why the French Don't Like Headscarves: Islam, the State, and Public Space*. Princeton University Press.

Boxer, C.R. 1965. *Portuguese Society in the Tropics: The Municipal Councils of Goa, Macao, Bahia, and Luanda, 1510–1800*. University of Wisconsin Press.

Boxer, C.R. 1969. *The Portuguese Seaborne Empire: 1415–1825*. Hutchinson & Co.

Boxer, C.R. 1977. *The Dutch Seaborne Empire: 1600–1800*. Hutchinson & Co.

Bradshaw, Frederick. 1909. *Self-Government in Canada, and How It Was Achieved: The Story of Lord Durham's Report*. PS King & Son.

Bradshaw, Richard and Juan Fandos-Rius. 2016. *Historical Dictionary of the Central African Republic*. Rowman & Littlefield.

Brambor, Thomas and Johannes Lindvall. 2018. "The Ideology of Heads of Government, 1870–2012." *European Political Science* 17(2):211–222.

Brancati, Dawn. 2016. *Democracy Protests: Origins, Features, and Significance*. Cambridge University Press.

Bratton, Michael and Nicholas van de Walle. 1997. *Democratic Experiments in Africa: Regime Transitions in Comparative Perspective*. Cambridge University Press.

Braun, Sebastian and Michael Kvasnicka. 2013. "Men, Women, and the Ballot: Gender Imbalances and Suffrage Extensions in the United States." *Explorations in Economic History* 50(3):405–426.

Brook, Sir N. 1957. "'Future Constitutional Development in the Colonies': Report (CO, Print, GEN 174/012) of the Officials' Committee." In *The Conservative Government and the End of Empire 1957–1964. Part of the British Documents on the End of Empire Project*. Available at https://core.ac.uk/download/pdf/33337446.pdf, ed. Ronald Hyam and Wm. Roger Louis. Institute of Commonwealth Studies in the University of London pp. 4–28.

Brown, Robert E. 1952. "Democracy in Colonial Massachusetts." *New England Quarterly* 25(3):291–313.

Brownlee, Jason. 2007. *Authoritarianism in an Age of Democratization*. Cambridge University Press.

Bruhn, Miriam and Francisco A. Gallego. 2012. "Good, Bad, and Ugly Colonial Activities: Do They Matter for Economic Development?" *Review of Economics and Statistics* 94(2):433–461.

Burbank, Jane and Frederick Cooper. 2010. *Empires in World History: Power and the Politics of Difference*. Princeton University Press.

Burkholder, Mark A. and D.S. Chandler. 1977. *From Impotence to Authority: The Spanish Crown and the American Audiencias, 1687–1808*. University of Missouri Press.

Burns, E. Bradford. 1993. *A History of Brazil*. Columbia University Press.

Bush, Sarah Sunn. 2016. *The Taming of Democracy Assistance: Why Democracy Promotion Does Not Confront Dictators.* Cambridge University Press.

Bustin, Edouard. 1963. The Congo. In *Five African States: Responses to Diversity*, ed. Gwendolen M. Carter. Cornell University Press pp. 9–159.

Cahall, Raymond Du Bois. 1915. *The Sovereign Council of New France: A Study in Canadian Constitutional History.* Columbia University Press.

Cairo, Heriberto. 2006. "'Portugal is Not a Small Country': Maps and Propaganda in the Salazar Regime." *Geopolitics* 11(3):367–395.

Canadian Encyclopedia, The. 2022. "Voting Rights in Canada." www.thecanadianencyclopedia.ca/en/timeline/voting-rights-in-canada.

Carvalho, Jean-Paul and Christian Dippel. 2020. "Elite Identity and Political Accountability: A Tale of Ten Islands." *Economic Journal* 130(631):1995–2029.

Census. 1865. "Census of the Colony of the Cape of Good Hope: 1865." Available at https://babel.hathitrust.org/cgi/pt?id=uc1.l0074071051&view=1up&seq=7.

Census of India. 1922. *Census of India, 1921.* Census of India, 1921 Superintendent Government Printing. Available at https://books.google.com/books?id=h3kHcreR1VAC.

Chandler, Julian A.C. 1901. *The History of Suffrage in Virginia.* Johns Hopkins Press.

Chanock, Martin. 1977. *Unconsummated Union: Britain, Rhodesia and South Africa, 1900–45.* Manchester University Press.

Chenoweth, Erica, Maria J. Stephan and Maria Stephan. 2011. *Why Civil Resistance Works: The Strategic Logic of Nonviolent Conflict.* Columbia University Press.

Cichon, Deborah. 1989. The Leeward Islands – British Dependencies: British Virgin Islands, Anguilla, and Montserrat. In *Islands of the Commonwealth Caribbean: A Regional Study*, ed. Sandra W. Meditz and Dennis W. Hanratty. Federal Research Division, Library of Congress pp. 487–514.

Clementi, Sir Cecil. 1937. *A Constitutional History of British Guiana.* Macmillan.

Cleveland, William L. 2004. *A History of the Modern Middle East.* 3rd ed. Westview Press.

Cobban, Alfred. 1950. "The 'Parlements' of France in the Eighteenth Century." *History* 35(123/124):64–80.

Coggins, Richard. 2006. "Wilson and Rhodesia: UDI and British Policy Towards Africa." *Contemporary British History* 20(3):363–381.

Cohen, Andrew. 2009. "'Voice and Vision' – The Federation of Rhodesia and Nyasaland's Public Relations Campaign in Britain: 1960–1963." *Historia* 54(2):113–123.

Coleman, J.S. 1963. *Nigeria: Background to Nationalism*. University of California Press.

Collier, Ruth Berins. 1982. *Regimes in Tropical Africa*. University of California Press.

Collier, Ruth Berins. 1999. *Paths Toward Democracy: The Working Class and Elites in Western Europe and South America*. Cambridge University Press.

Collier, Ruth Berins and David Collier. 1991. *Shaping the Political Arena*. Princeton University Press.

Collins, Robert O. 2008. *A History of Modern Sudan*. Cambridge University Press.

Colonial Reports. 1931. *Bechuanaland Protectorate: Report for 1930, No. 1554*.

Compagnon, Daniel. 2011. *A Predictable Tragedy: Robert Mugabe and the Collapse of Zimbabwe*. University of Pennsylvania Press.

Congleton, Roger D. 2010. *Perfecting Parliament: Constitutional Reform, Liberalism, and the Rise of Western Democracy*. Cambridge University Press.

Conklin, Alice L. 1997. "'Democracy' Rediscovered: Civilization through Association in French West Africa (1914–1930)." *Cahiers d'études africaines* 37(Cahier 145): 59–84.

Cook, Megan. 1977. *The Constitutionalist Party in Cochinchina: The Years of Decline, 1930–1942*. Monash University Publishing.

Cooper, Frederick. 2014. *Citizenship Between Empire and Nation: Remaking France and French Africa, 1945–1960*. Princeton University Press.

Cooper, Henry Allen 1902. *Our Policy in the Philippines and the Philippine Civil Government Bill*. Available at https://books.google.com/books?id=sFdBAQAAMAAJ&printsec=frontcover&source=gbs_ge_summary_r&cad=0#v=onepage&q&f=false.

Coppedge, Michael, John Gerring, Carl Henrik Knutsen, Staffan I. Lindberg, Jan Teorell, David Altman, Michael Bernhard, Agnes Cornell, M. Steven Fish, Lisa Gastaldi, Haakon Gjerløw, Adam Glynn, Ana Good God, Sandra Grahn, Allen Hicken, Katrin Kinzelbach, Joshua Krusell, Kyle L. Marquardt, Kelly McMann, Valeriya Mechkova, Juraj Medzihorsky, Natalia Natsika, Anja Neundorf, Pamela Paxton, Daniel Pemstein, Josefine Pernes, Oskar Rydn, Johannes von Römer, Brigitte Seim, Rachel Sigman, Svend-Erik Skaaning, Jeffrey Staton, Aksel Sundstrm, Eitan Tzelgov, Yi-ting Wang, Tore Wig, Steven Wilson and Daniel Ziblatt. 2023a. "'V-Dem [Country-Year/Country-Date] Dataset v13' Varieties of Democracy (V-Dem) Project." Available at www.v-dem.net/data/the-v-dem-dataset.

Coppedge, Michael, John Gerring, Carl Henrik Knutsen, Staffan I. Lindberg, Jan Teorell, David Altman, Michael Bernhard, Agnes Cornell, M. Steven Fish, Lisa Gastaldi, Haakon Gjerløw, Adam Glynn, Sandra Grahn, Allen Hicken, Katrin Kinzelbach, Kyle L. Marquardt, Kelly McMann, Valeriya Mechkova, Anja Neundorf, Pamela Paxton, Daniel Pemstein, Oskar Rydn, Johannes von Römer, Brigitte Seim, Rachel Sigman, Svend-Erik Skaaning, Jeffrey Staton, Aksel Sundstrm, Eitan Tzelgov, Luca Uberti, Yi-ting Wang, Tore Wig and Daniel Ziblatt. 2023*b*. ""V-Dem Codebook v13" Varieties of Democracy (V-Dem) Project." Available at www.v-dem.net/data/reference-documents.

Coulon, Christian. 1989. Senegal: The Development and Fragility of Semidemocracy. In *Democracy in Developing Countries, Volume 2: Africa*, ed. Larry Jay Diamond, Juan José Linz and Seymour Martin Lipset. Lynne Rienner.

Cox, Gary W. 2016. *Marketing Sovereign Promises: Monopoly Brokerage and the Growth of the English State*. Cambridge University Press.

Cox, Gary W. and Mark Dincecco. 2021. "The Budgetary Origins of Fiscal-Military Prowess." *Journal of Politics* 83(3):851–866.

Craig, Hewan. 1952. *The Legislative Council of Trinidad and Tobago*. Faber & Faber Limited.

Cross, Cecil Merne Putnam. 1922. *The Development of Self-government in India, 1858–1914*. University of Chicago Press.

Crowder, Michael. 1967. *Senegal: A Study of French Assimilation Policy*. Methuen & Co Ltd.

Crowder, Michael. 1968. *West Africa under Colonial Rule*. Northwestern University Press.

Crowder, Michael and Donal Cruise O'Brien. 1974. French West Africa, 1945–1960. In *History of West Africa Vol. II*, ed. J.F. Ade Ajayi and Michael Crowder. Cambridge University Press pp. 664–699.

Crowder, Michael and Obaro Ikime. 1970. *West African Chiefs: Their Changing Status under Colonial Rule and Independence*. University of Ife Press.

Cruise O'Brien, Rita. 1972. *White Society in Black Africa: The French of Senegal*. Faber and Faber Limited.

Crystal, Jill. 1995. *Oil and Politics in the Gulf: Rulers and Merchants in Kuwait and Qatar*. Cambridge University Press.

Curtin, Philip D. 1955. *Two Jamaicas: The Role of Ideas in a Tropical Colony, 1830–1865*. Harvard University Press.

Dahl, Robert A. 1971. *Polyarchy: Participation and Opposition*. Yale University Press.

Dahl, Ronald A. 2003. *How Democratic Is the American Constitution?* Yale University Press.

David, Paul A. 1985. "Clio and the Economics of QWERTY." *American Economic Review* 75(2):332–337.

Davidson, J.W. 1948. *The Northern Rhodesian Legislative Council*. Faber & Faber Limited.

De Silva, G.P.S.H. 1979. *A Statistical Survey of Elections to the Legislatures of Sri Lanka, 1911–1977*. Marga Institute.

Decalo, Samuel. 1980. "Chad: The Roots of Centre-Periphery Strife." *African Affairs* 79(317):491–509.

Decalo, Samuel. 1990. *Coups and Army Rule in Africa*. Yale University Press.

Delivagnette, Robert L. 1970. French Colonial Policy in Black Africa, 1945 to 1960. In *Colonialism in Africa 1870–1960, Volume 2: The History and Politics of Colonialism 1914–1960*, ed. L.H. Gann and Peter Duignan. Cambridge University Press pp. 450–502.

Demélas-Bohy, M.-D. and F.-X. Guerra. 1996. The Hispanic Revolutions: The Adoption of Modern Forms of Representation in Spain and America (1808–1810). In *Elections Before Democracy: The History of Elections in Europe and Latin America*, ed. Eduardo Posada-Carbó. Springer pp. 33–60.

Diamond, Jared M. 1998. *Guns, Germs and Steel: A Short History of Everybody for the Last 13,000 Years*. Random House.

Diamond, Larry Jay, Juan José Linz and Seymour Martin Lipset. 1989. *Democracy in Developing Countries, Volume 4: Latin America*. Lynne Rienner.

Dieterich, Renate. 2002. Jordan. In *Elections in Asia and the Pacific: A Data Handbook. Volume 1: Middle East, Central Asia, and South Asia*, ed. Dieter Nohlen, Florian Grotz and Christof Hartmann. Oxford University Press pp. 141–154.

Dinwiddy, Hugh. 1981. "The Search for Unity in Uganda: Early Days to 1966." *African Affairs* 80(321): 501–518.

Dislère, Paul. 1906. *Traité de Législation Coloniale*. Librairie Administrative Paul Dupont.

Disney, A.R. 2009a. *A History of Portugal and the Portuguese Empire: Volume 1, Portugal*. Cambridge University Press.

Disney, A.R. 2009b. *A History of Portugal and the Portuguese Empire: Volume 2, The Portuguese Empire*. Cambridge University Press.

Dobbins, James F. 2003. "America's Role in Nation-building: From Germany to Iraq." *Survival* 45(4):87–110.

Doebbler, Curtis F. and Helga Fleischhacker. 1999. Sudan. In *Elections in Africa: A Data Handbook*, ed. Dieter Nohlen, Bernard Thibaut and Michael Krennerich. Oxford University Press pp. 843–862.

Dudley, Guilford A. 1973. *A History of Eastern Civilizations*. Wiley.

Duffy, James. 1962. *Portugal in Africa*. Penguin Books.

Dunn, Richard S. 2012. *Sugar and Slaves: The Rise of the Planter Class in the English West Indies, 1624–1713*. University of North Carolina Press.

Dunning, Thad. 2004. "Conditioning the Effects of Aid: Cold War Politics, Donor Credibility, and Democracy in Africa." *International Organization* 58(2):409–423.

Dutt, Srikant. 1981. "Bhutan's International Position." *International Studies* 20(3–4):601–623.

Easterly, William and Ross Levine. 2016. "The European Origins of Economic Development." *Journal of Economic Growth* 21(3):225–257.

Elliott, J.H. 2007. *Empires of the Atlantic World: Britain and Spain in America, 1492–1830*. Yale University Press.

Eluwa, G.I.C. 1971. "The National Congress of British West Africa: A Study in African Nationalism." *Présence Africaine* 77: 131–149.

Emmett, E. 1927. "The Mandate over South-West Africa." *Journal of Comparative Legislation and International Law* 9(1):111–122.

Engerman, Stanley L. and Kenneth L. Sokoloff. 2005. "The Evolution of Suffrage Institutions in the New World." *Journal of Economic History* 65(4):891–921.

Engerman, Stanley L. and Kenneth L. Sokoloff. 2011. *Economic Development in the Americas Since 1500: Endowments and Institutions*. Cambridge University Press.

Enterline, Andrew J. and J. Michael Greig. 2005. "Beacons of Hope? The Impact of Imposed Democracy on Regional Peace, Democracy, and Prosperity." *Journal of Politics* 67(4):1075–1098.

Enterline, Andrew J. and J. Michael Greig. 2008. "Against All Odds?: The History of Imposed Democracy and the Future of Iraq and Afghanistan." *Foreign Policy Analysis* 4(4):321–347.

Epstein, Mortimer. 1931. *The Statesman's Year-book: Statistical and Historical Annual of the States of the World for the Year 1931*. Macmillan.

Ertan, Arhan, Martin Fiszbein and Louis Putterman. 2016. "Who was Colonized and When? A Cross-country Analysis of Determinants." *European Economic Review* 83:165–184.

Escribà-Folch, Abel and Joseph Wright. 2015. *Foreign Pressure and the Politics of Autocratic Survival*. Oxford University Press.

Fails, Matthew D. and Jonathan Krieckhaus. 2010. "Colonialism, Property Rights and the Modern World Income Distribution." *British Journal of Political Science* 40(3):487–508.

Fall, Bernard B. 1967. *Hell in a Very Small Place: The Siege of Dien Bien Phu*. Lippincott.

Fearon, James. 2011. "Self-enforcing Democracy." *Quarterly Journal of Economics* 126(4):1661–1708.

Ferguson, Niall. 2012. *Empire: How Britain Made the Modern World*. Penguin Books.

Ferraz, Ricardo. 2022. "The Financial Costs of the Portuguese Colonial War, 1961–1974: Analysis and Applied Study." *Revista de Historia Economica-Journal of Iberian and Latin American Economic History* 40(2): 243–272.

Fieldhouse, D.K. 1982. *The Colonial Empires: A Comparative Survey from the Eighteenth Century*. Macmillan.

Fieldhouse, D.K. 1986. *Black Africa 1945–1980: Economic Decolonization and Arrested Development*. Routledge.

Finer, Samuel E. 2002. *The Man on Horseback*. Transaction Publishers.

Fisher, John. 1969. "The Intendant System and the Cabildos of Peru, 1784–1810." *Hispanic American Historical Review* 49(3): 430–453.

Forbes, Ernest R. 2008. "New Brunswick." Available at www.thecanadianencyclopedia.ca/en/article/new-brunswick.

Forbes, Urias. 1970. "The West Indies Associated States: Some Aspects of the Constitutional Arrangements." *Social and Economic Studies* 19(1): 57–88.

Fradera, Josep M. 2018. *The Imperial Nation: Citizens and Subjects in the British, French, Spanish, and American Empires*. Princeton University Press.

Franco-Vivanco, Edgar. 2021. "Justice as Checks and Balances: Indigenous Claims in the Courts of Colonial Mexico." *World Politics* 73(4): 712–773.

Frankema, Ewout. 2009a. "The Colonial Roots of Land Inequality: Geography, Factor Endowments, or Institutions?" *Economic History Review* 63(2):418–451.

Frankema, Ewout. 2009b. *Has Latin America Always Been Unequal? A Comparative Study of Asset and Income Inequality in the Long Twentieth Century*. Brill.

Fransee, Emily Lord. 2018. Without Distinction: Women's Suffrage in the French Empire, 1943–1962. Ph.D. thesis. Department of History, University of Chicago.

Frasch, Tilman. 2002. Myanmar (Burma). In *Elections in Asia and the Pacific: A Data Handbook. Volume 1: Middle East, Central Asia, and South Asia*, ed. Dieter Nohlen, Florian Grotz and Christof Hartmann. Oxford University Press pp. 597–620.

Fraser, Andrew, R.H.P. Mason and Philip Mitchell. 2005. *Japan's Early Parliaments, 1890–1905: Structure, Issues, and Trends*. Routledge.

Freedom House. 2022. "Freedom in the World: Comparative and Historical Data Files." Available at https://freedomhouse.org/report/freedom-world.

Gailmard, Sean. 2024. *Agents of Empire: English Imperial Governance and the Making of American Political Institutions.* Cambridge University Press.

Gandhi, Jennifer. 2008. *Political Institutions under Dictatorship.* Cambridge University Press.

Gandhi, Jennifer, Ben Noble and Milan Svolik. 2020. "Legislatures and Legislative Politics Without Democracy." *Comparative Political Studies* 53(9):1359–1379.

Gann, Lewis H. and Peter Duignan. 1962. *White Settlers in Tropical Africa.* Penguin Books.

Gann, Lewis H. and Peter Duignan. 1970. "Changing Patterns of a White Elite: Rhodesian and Other Settlers." In *Colonialism in Africa 1870-1960, Volume 2: The History and Politics of Colonialism 1914–1960,* ed. Peter Duignan and L.H. Gann. Cambridge University Press pp. 92–170.

Gardner, Leigh A. 2012. *Taxing Colonial Africa: The Political Economy of British Imperialism.* Oxford University Press.

Garfias, Francisco and Emily A. Sellars. 2021. "From Conquest to Centralization: Domestic Conflict and the Transition to Direct Rule." *Journal of Politics* 83(3):992–1009.

Gause, F. Gregory. 1994. *Oil Monarchies: Domestic and Security Challenges in the Arab Gulf States.* Council on Foreign Relations.

Gause III, F. Gregory. 2013. "Kings for All Seasons." *Brookings Doha Center Analysis Paper* 8.

Geddes, Barbara. 1999. "What Do We Know About Democratization After Twenty Years?" *Annual Review of Political Science* 2(1):115–144.

Geddes, Barbara, Joseph Wright and Erica Frantz. 2018. *How Dictatorships Work: Power, Personalization, and Collapse.* Cambridge University Press.

Gelabert, Juan. 1999. Castile, 1504–1808. In *The Rise of the Fiscal State in Europe,* ed. Richard Bonney. Oxford University Press pp. 201–241.

Gerring, John, Brendan Apfeld, Tore Wig and Andreas Forø Tollefsen. 2022. *The Deep Roots of Modern Democracy.* Cambridge University Press.

Gerring, John, Daniel Ziblatt, Johan Van Gorp and Julian Arevalo. 2011. "An Institutional Theory of Direct and Indirect Rule." *World Politics* 63(3):377–433.

Girard, Philip. 2010. Liberty, Order, and Pluralism: The Canadian Experience. In *Exclusionary Empire: English Liberty Overseas, 1600–1900,* ed. Jack P. Greene. Cambridge University Press pp. 160–190.

Giuliano, Paola and Nathan Nunn. 2013. "The Transmission of Democracy: From the Village to the Nation-State." *American Economic Review, Papers and Proceedings* 103(3):86–92.

Gleijeses, Piero. 1997. "The First Ambassadors: Cuba's Contribution to Guinea-Bissau's War of Independence." *Journal of Latin American Studies* 29(1):45–88.

Gluchowski, Peter M. and Florian Grotz. 2002. Mongolia. In *Elections in Asia and the Pacific: A Data Handbook. Volume 2: South East Asia, East Asia, and the Pacific,* ed. Dieter Nohlen, Florian Grotz and Christof Hartmann. Oxford University Press pp. 481–524.

Gokhale, Dinker Vishnu. 1895. *Inaugural Addresses by Presidents of the Indian National Congress: With Mr. Charles Bradlaugh's Speech.* Ripon Printing Press Company, Limited.

Góngora, Mario. 1975. *Studies in the Colonial History of Spanish America.* Cambridge University Press.

Good, Kenneth. 1976. "Settler Colonialism: Economic Development and Class Formation." *Journal of Modern African Studies* 14(4):597–620.

Goodwin, Jeff. 2001. *No Other Way Out: States and Revolutionary Movements, 1945–1991.* Cambridge University Press.

Government of India. 1936. *Statistical Abstract for British India, with Statistics, Where Available, Relating to Certain Indian States from 1923–24 to 1932–33. Sixty-Seventh Number.* Her Majesty's Stationery Office.

Graham, Aaron. 2018. "Legislatures, Legislation and Legislating in the British Atlantic, 1692–1800." *Parliamentary History* 37(3):369–388.

Green, William A. 1976. *British Slave Emancipation: The Sugar Colonies and the Great Experiment, 1830–1865.* Oxford University Press.

Greene, Jack P. 1963. *The Quest for Power: The Lower Houses of Assembly in the Southern Royal Colonies, 1689–1776.* University of North Carolina Press.

Greene, Jack P. 1986. *Peripheries and Center: Constitutional Development in the Extended Polities of the British Empire and the United States, 1607–1788.* University of Georgia Press.

Greene, Jack P. 2010a. Introduction: Empire and Liberty. In *Exclusionary Empire: English Liberty Overseas, 1600–1900,* ed. Jack P. Greene. Cambridge University Press pp. 1–24.

Greene, Jack P. 2010b. Liberty and Slavery: The Transfer of British Liberty to the West Indies, 1627–1865. In *Exclusionary Empire: English Liberty Overseas, 1600–1900,* ed. Jack P. Greene. Cambridge University Press pp. 50–76.

Greenwood, Frank Murray. 1993. *Legacies of Fear: Law and Politics in Quebec in the Era of the French Revolution.* University of Toronto Press.

Greif, Avner and David D. Laitin. 2004. "A Theory of Endogenous Institutional Change." *American Political Science Review* 98(4):633–652.

Grenier, John. 2008. *The Far Reaches of Empire: War in Nova Scotia, 1710–1760.* University of Oklahoma Press.

Guardado, Jenny. 2022. "Hierarchical Oversight and the Value of Public Office: Evidence from Colonial Peru." *Journal of Politics* 84(3):1353–1369.

Gunitsky, Seva. 2014. "From Shocks to Waves: Hegemonic Transitions and Democratization in the Twentieth Century." *International Organization* 68(03):561–597.

Hadenius, Axel. 1992. *Democracy and Development*. Cambridge University Press.

Haggard, Stephan and Robert R. Kaufman. 2012. "Inequality and Regime Change: Democratic Transitions and the Stability of Democratic Rule." *American Political Science Review* 106(3):495–516.

Haggard, Stephan and Robert R. Kaufman. 2016. *Dictators and Democrats: Masses, Elites, and Regime Change*. Princeton University Press.

Hailey, Lord. 1950*a*. *Native Administration in the British African Territories. Part. I. East Africa: Uganda, Kenya, Tanganyika*. His Majesty's Stationary Office.

Hailey, Lord. 1950*b*. *Native Administration in the British African Territories. Part. II. Central Africa: Zanzibar, Nyasaland, Northern Rhodesia*. His Majesty's Stationary Office.

Hailey, Lord. 1951. *Native Administration in the British African Territories. Part. III. West Africa: Nigeria, Gold Coast, Sierra Leone, Gambia*. His Majesty's Stationary Office.

Hailey, Lord. 1953. *Native Administration in the British African Territories. Part. V. The High Commission Territories: Basutoland, Bechuanaland, Swaziland*. His Majesty's Stationary Office.

Hailey, Lord. 1957. *An African Survey, Revised 1956*. Oxford University Press.

Hansard. 1934. "Indian Constitutional Reform." Available at https://api .parliament.uk/historic-hansard/lords/1934/dec/18/indian-constitutional-r eform.

Hansard. 1935. "Government of India Bill." Available at https://api.parliam ent.uk/historic-hansard/commons/1935/jun/05/government-of-india-bill.

Hargreaves, John D. 1996. *Decolonization in Africa*. Longman.

Haring, Clarence Henry. 1947. *The Spanish Empire in America*. Oxford University Press.

Hariri, Jacob Gerner. 2012. "The Autocratic Legacy of Early Statehood." *American Political Science Review* 106(3):471–494.

Hariri, Jacob Gerner. 2015. "A Contribution to the Understanding of Middle Eastern and Muslim Exceptionalism." *Journal of Politics* 77(2):477–490.

Harris, Coleridge. 1960. "The Constitutional History of the Windwards." *Caribbean Quarterly* 6(2–3):160–176.

Hartmann, Christof. 2002. Fiji Islands. In *Elections in Asia and the Pacific: A Data Handbook. Volume 2: South East Asia, East Asia, and the*

Pacific, ed. Dieter Nohlen, Florian Grotz and Christof Hartmann. Oxford University Press pp. 643–672.

Hartmann, Christof, Graham Hassall and Soliman M. Santos Jr. 2002. Philippines. In *Elections in Asia and the Pacific: A Data Handbook. Volume 2: South East Asia, East Asia, and the Pacific*, ed. Dieter Nohlen, Florian Grotz and Christof Hartmann. Oxford University Press pp. 185–238.

Hartwell, Edward M. 1911. Primary Elections in Massachusetts 1640–1694. *Proceedings of the American Political Science Association* 7: 210–224.

Hartwig, Charles W. and Samir Ghali. 1979. "France and the Lebanese Conflict." *Journal of South Asian and Middle Eastern Studies* 3(1):78.

Hartz, Louis. 1955. *The Liberal Tradition in America: An Interpretation of American Political Thought since the Revolution*. Houghton Mifflin Harcourt.

Henneman, John Bell Jr. 1999. France in the Middle Ages. In *The Rise of the Fiscal State in Europe*, ed. Richard Bonney. Oxford University Press pp. 101–122.

Hensel, Paul R. 2014. "The ICOW Colonial History Data Set." Available at www.paulhensel.org/icowcol.html.

Herb, Michael. 1999. *All in the Family: Absolutism, Revolution, and Democracy in Middle Eastern Monarchies*. SUNY Press.

Herbst, Jeffrey. 1989. "The Creation and Maintenance of National Boundaries in Africa." *International Organization* 43(4):673–692.

Herbst, Jeffrey. 2000. *States and Power in Africa*. Princeton University Press.

Higham, C.S.S. 1926. "The General Assembly of the Leeward Islands: Part II." *English Historical Review* 41(163):366–388.

Hirschman, Albert O. 1970. *Exit, Voice, and Loyalty: Responses to Decline in Firms, Organizations, and States*. Harvard University Press.

Hirschman, Albert O. 1978. "Exit, Voice, and the State." *World Politics* 31(1):90–107.

Hofmann, Klaus. 2006. "Democratization from Above: The Case of Bhutan." Available at www.mehr-demokratie.de/fileadmin/pdf/di-bhutan.pdf.

Holden, William N. and R. Daniel Jacobson. 2012. *Mining and Natural Hazard Vulnerability in the Philippines: Digging to Development or Digging to Disaster?* Anthem Press.

Homans, H.W. 1870. "France under the Second Empire." *The North American Review* 111(229):402–444.

House of Assembly of the Virgin Islands. n.d. "Constitutional & Political Development in the Virgin Islands 1950–2000." https://web.archive.org/web/20140502172134/www.legco.gov.vg/index.php?pageid=6.

House of Commons. 1946. "Eighth Volume of session 1945–46." Parliamentary Debates. First session of the Thirty-Eighth Parliament of the United Kingdom of Great Britain and Northern Ireland. No 420; fifth series. His Majesty's Stationery Office pp. 1415–1423.

Howard, William. 1960. *Ceylon: Dilemmas of a New Nation*. Princeton University Press.

Huillery, Elise. 2009. "History Matters: The Long-term Impact of Colonial Public Investments in French West Africa." *American Economic Journal: Applied Economics* 1(2):176–215.

Hull, Isabel V. 2013. *Absolute Destruction: Military Culture and the Practices of War in Imperial Germany*. Cornell University Press.

Huntington, Samuel P. 1984. "Will More Countries Become Democratic?" *Political Science Quarterly* 99(2):193–218.

Hutton, J.H. 1933. "Census of India, 1931." Manager of Publications.

Hyam, Ronald. 2007. *Britain's Declining Empire: The Road to Decolonisation, 1918–1968*. Cambridge University Press.

Hyde, Susan D. and Nikolay Marinov. 2014. "Information and Self-enforcing Democracy: The Role of International Election Observation." *International Organization* 68(2):329–359.

Idowu, H. Oludare. 1968. "The Establishment of Elective Institutions in Senegal, 1869–1880." *Journal of African History* 9(2):261–277.

Jackson, Julian. 2018. *De Gaulle*. Harvard University Press.

Jensen, Nathan M., Edmund Malesky and Stephen Weymouth. 2014. "Unbundling the Relationship between Authoritarian Legislatures and Political Risk." *British Journal of Political Science* 44(3): 655–684.

Johnson, Cecil. 1943. *British West Florida, 1763–1783*. Yale University Press.

Johnson, G. Wesley Jr. 1971. *The Emergence of Black Politics in Senegal: The Struggle for Power in the Four Communes, 1900–1920*. Stanford University Press.

Jones, Abeodu Bowen. 1974. The Republic of Liberia. In *History of West Africa Vol. II*, ed. J.F. Ade Ajayi and Michael Crowder. Cambridge University Press pp. 308–343.

Jupp, James. 1983. "Elections in Vanuatu." *Political Science* 35(1):1–15.

Kahler, Miles. 1981. "Political Regime and Economic Actors: The Response of Firms to the End of Colonial Rule." *World Politics* 33(3): 383–412.

Kammen, Michael. 1969. *Deputyes & Libertyes: The Origins of Representative Government in Colonial America*. Alfred A. Knopf.

Keddie, Nikki R. 1983. "Iranian Revolutions in Comparative Perspective." *The American Historical Review* 88(3):579–598.

Keesing's. 1973. "Enactment of 'Organic Law for the Overseas Territories' – Election of Legislative Assemblies and Consultative Councils in Overseas Territories." *Keesing's Record of World Events* 19(6):25948.

Keith, Arthur Berriedale. 1912. *Responsible Government in the Dominions*. Vol. 1. Clarendon Press.

Keltie, J. Scott. 1887. *The Statesman's Year-book: Statistical and Historical Annual of the States of the World for the Year 1887*. Macmillan.

Keltie, J. Scott. 1905. *The Statesman's Year-book: Statistical and Historical Annual of the States of the World for the Year 1905*. Macmillan.

Keltie, J. Scott. 1921. *The Statesman's Year-book: Statistical and Historical Annual of the States of the World for the Year 1921*. Macmillan.

Keltie, J. Scott. 1925. *The Statesman's Year-book: Statistical and Historical Annual of the States of the World for the Year 1925*. Macmillan.

Kenkel, Brenton and Jack Paine. 2023. "A Theory of External Wars and European Parliaments." *International Organization* 77(1):102–143.

Keyssar, Alexander. 2009. *The Right to Vote: The Contested History of Democracy in the United States*. Basic Books.

Khan, Roedad. 2002. *The British Papers: Secret and Confidential, India, Pakistan, Bangladesh Documents 1958–1969*. Oxford University Press.

Kiewiet, C.W. De. 1936. The Establishment of Responsible Government in Cape Colony, 1870–1872. In *Cambridge History of the British Empire, Volume 8*, ed. J. Holland Rose. Cambridge University Press pp. 429–448.

Kilson, Martin L. 1963. "Authoritarian and Single-party Tendencies in African Politics." *World Politics* 15(2):262–294.

Kirk-Greene, A.H.M. 1980. "The Thin White Line: The Size of the British Colonial Service in Africa." *African Affairs* 79(314):25–44.

Koch, Christian. 2002. Kuwait. In *Elections in Asia and the Pacific: A Data Handbook. Volume 1: Middle East, Central Asia, and South Asia*, ed. Dieter Nohlen, Florian Grotz and Christof Hartmann. Oxford University Press pp. 155–168.

Koenigsberger, H.G. 1995. Parliaments in the Sixteenth Century and Beyond. In *Uncommon Democracies: The One-Party Dominant Regimes*, ed. R.W. Davis. Stanford University Press pp. 269–311.

Kothari, Rajni. 1964. "The Congress 'System' in India." *Asian Survey* 4(12):1161–1173.

Kousser, J. Morgan. 1974. *The Shaping of Southern Politics: Suffrage Restriction and the Establishment of the One-Party South, 1880–1910*. Yale University Press.

Kraines, Oscar. 1953. "Israel: The Emergence of a Polity Part I." *Western Political Quarterly* 6(3):518–542.

Krishna, Gopal. 1966. "The Development of the Indian National Congress as a Mass Organization, 1918–1923." *The Journal of Asian Studies* 25(3):413–430.

La Porta, Rafael, Florencio Lopez-de-Silanes, Andrei Shleifer, and Robert W. Vishny. 1998. "Law and Finance." *Journal of Political Economy* 106(6):1113–1155.

La Porta, Rafael, Florencio Lopez-de-Silanes, Andrei Shleifer and Robert Vishny. 1999. "The Quality of Government." *Journal of Law, Economics, and Organization* 15(1):222–279.

Labaree, Leonard Woods. 1930. *Royal Government in America: A Study of the British Colonial System Before 1783*. Frederick Ungar.

Lachapelle, Jean, Steven Levitsky, Lucan A. Way and Adam E. Casey. 2020. "Social Revolution and Authoritarian Durability." *World Politics* 72(4):557–600.

Lanctot, Gustove. 1934. "The Elective Council of Quebec of 1657." *Canadian Historical Review* 15(2):123–132.

Landau, Jacob M. 1961. "Elections in Lebanon." *Western Political Quarterly* 14(1):120–147.

Lange, Matthew. 2009. *Lineages of Despotism and Development: British Colonialism and State Power*. University of Chicago Press.

Lange, Matthew, James Mahoney and Matthias vom Hau. 2006. "Colonialism and Development: A Comparative Analysis of Spanish and British Colonies." *American Journal of Sociology* 111(5):1412–1462.

Lange, Matthew K. 2004. "British Colonial Legacies and Political Development." *World Development* 32(6):905–922.

Lankina, Tomila and Lullit Getachew. 2012. "Mission or Empire, Word or Sword? The Human Capital Legacy in Postcolonial Democratic Development." *American Journal of Political Science* 56(2):465–483.

Lankina, Tomila V. 2021. *The Estate Origins of Democracy in Russia*. Cambridge University Press.

Lawrence, Adria. 2013. *Imperial Rule and the Politics of Nationalism: Anticolonial Protest in the French Empire*. Cambridge University Press.

Ledgister, F.S.J. 1998. *Class Alliances and the Liberal-Authoritarian State: The Roots of Post-colonial Democracy in Jamaica, Trinidad & Tobago, and Surinam*. Africa World Press, Inc.

Lee, Alexander. 2011. "Who Becomes a Terrorist?: Poverty, Education, and the Origins of Political Violence." *World Politics* 63(2):203–245.

Lee, Alexander. 2017. "Redistributive Colonialism: The Long Term Legacy of International Conflict in India." *Politics & Society* 45(2):173–224.

Lee, Alexander. 2018. "Ethnic Diversity and Ethnic Discrimination: Explaining Local Public Goods Provision." *Comparative Political Studies* 51(10):1351–1383.

Lee, Alexander and Jack Paine. 2019. "British Colonialism and Democracy: Divergent Inheritances and Diminishing Legacies." *Journal of Comparative Economics* 47(3):487–503.

Lee, Alexander and Jack Paine. 2023. "The Great Revenue Divergence." *International Organization* 77(2):363–404.

Lee, Alexander and Kenneth A. Schultz. 2012. "Comparing British and French Colonial Legacies: A Discontinuity Analysis of Cameroon." *Quarterly Journal of Political Science* 7(4):365–410.

Lee, M. Elaine. 1975. "The Origins of the Rhodesian Responsible Government Movement." *Rhodesian History* 6:33–52.

Lehr, Peter. 2002. Maldives. In *Elections in Asia and the Pacific: A Data Handbook. Volume 1: Middle East, Central Asia, and South Asia*, ed. Dieter Nohlen, Florian Grotz and Christof Hartmann. Oxford University Press pp. 585–596.

Lemarchand, René. 1964. Congo (Leopoldville). In *Political Parties and National Integration in Tropical Africa*, ed. James S. Coleman and Jr. Carl G. Rosberg. University of California Press pp. 560–596.

Letsa, Natalie Wenzell and Martha Wilfahrt. 2020. "The Mechanisms of Direct and Indirect Rule: Colonialism and Economic Development in Africa." *Quarterly Journal of Political Science* 15(4):539–577.

Levitsky, Steven and Lucan A. Way. 2010. *Competitive Authoritarianism: Hybrid Regimes after the Cold War*. Cambridge University Press.

Levitsky, Steven and Maria Victoria Murillo. 2005a. Building Castles in the Sand? The Politics of Institutional Weakness in Argentina. In *Argentine Democracy: The Politics of Institutional Weakness*, ed. Steven Levitsky and Maria Victoria Murillo. Penn State University Press pp. 21–44.

Levitsky, Steven and Maria Victoria Murillo. 2005b. Introduction. In *Argentine Democracy: The Politics of Institutional Weakness*, ed. Steven Levitsky and Maria Victoria Murillo. Penn State University Press pp. 1–20.

Lewis, Janet I. 2020. *How Insurgency Begins: Rebel Group Formation in Uganda and Beyond*. Cambridge University Press.

Liebesny, Herbert J. 1943. *Government of French North Africa*. University of Pennsylvania Press.

Lindberg, Staffan I. 2009. *Democratization by Elections: A New Mode of Transition*. Johns Hopkins University Press.

Lindberg, Staffan I., Nils Dupont, Masaaki Higashijima, Yaman Berker Kavasoglu, Kyle L. Marquardt, Michael Bernhard, Holger Döring, Allen Hicken, Melis Laebens, Juraj Medzihorsky, Anja Neundorf, Ora John Reuter, Saskia Ruth-Lovell, Keith R. Weghorst, Nina Wiesehomeier, Joseph Wright, Nazifa Alizada, Paul Bederke, Lisa Gastaldi, Sandra Grahn, Garry Hindle, Nina Ilchenko, Johannes von Römer Steven Wilson, Daniel Pemstein and Brigitte Seim. 2022. "Varieties of Party Identity and Organization (V-Party) Dataset V2. Varieties of Democracy (V-Dem) Project." Available at https://doi.org/10.23696/vpartydsv2.

Lipset, Seymour Martin. 1959. "Some Social Requisites of Democracy: Economic Development and Political Legitimacy." *American Political Science Review* 53(1):69–105.

Logevall, F. 2014. *Embers of War: The Fall of an Empire and the Making of America's Vietnam*. Random House.

Lords of Trade. 1727. "Recommendations for a Number of Inducements to Attract Settlers." Available at https://nslegislature.ca/about/history/time line#event-letter-lords-of-trade-to-lords-of-privy-council-recommendatio ns-for-a-number-of-inducements-to-attract-settlers.

Lovejoy, Paul E. 1992. Historical Setting. In *Nigeria: A Country Study*, ed. Helen Chapin Metz. Federal Research Division, Library of Congress pp. 1–84.

Loveman, Mara. 2014. *National Colors: Racial Classification and the State in Latin America*. Oxford University Press.

Lucas, C.P. 1912. *Lord Durham's Report on the Affairs of British North America*. Clarendon Press.

Lugard, F.D. 1922. *The Dual Mandate in British Tropical Africa*. William Blackwood and Sons.

Lührmann, Anna, Marcus Tannenberg and Staffan I Lindberg. 2018. "Regimes of the World (RoW): Opening New Avenues for the Comparative Study of Political Regimes." *Politics and Governance* 6(1):60–77.

Lust-Okar, Ellen. 2005. *Structuring Conflict in the Arab World: Incumbents, Opponents, and Institutions*. Cambridge University Press.

Lutzelschwab, Claude. 2013. Settler Colonialism in Africa. In *Settler Economies in World History*, ed. Jacob Metzer Christopher Lloyd and Richard Sutch. Brill pp. 141–167.

Lynch, John. 1992. "The Institutional Framework of Colonial Spanish America." *Journal of Latin American Studies* 24(S1):69–81.

Macaulay, Thomas Babington. 1835. "Minute upon Indian Education." Available at https://franpritchett.com/00generallinks/macaulay/ txt_minute_education_1835.html.

MacMillan, Hugh. 1985. "Swaziland: Decolonisation and the Triumph of 'Tradition'." *The Journal of Modern African Studies* 23(4): 643–666.

MacRae, Lachlan Farquhar. 1937. Some Aspects of the Native Problem of Kenya Colony. Ph.D. thesis. University of British Columbia.

Maguet, Edgard M. 1911. *Des conseils généraux dans les colonies françaises autres que l'algérie*. Georges Crès et Cie.

Mahoney, James. 2000. "Path Dependence in Historical Sociology." *Theory and Society* 29(4):507–548.

Mahoney, James. 2010. *Colonialism and Postcolonial Development: Spanish America in Comparative Perspective*. Cambridge University Press.

Mahoney, James and Richard Snyder. 1999. "Rethinking Agency and Structure in the Study of Regime Change." *Studies in Comparative International Development* 34(2):3.

Mainwaring, Scott and Aníbal Pérez-Liñán. 2014. *Democracies and Dictatorships in Latin America: Emergence, Survival, and Fall.* Cambridge University Press.

Mainwaring, Scott and Timothy Scully. 1995. Introduction: Party Systems in Latin America. In *Building Democratic Institutions: Party Systems in Latin America*, ed. Scott Mainwaring and Timothy Scully. Stanford University Press pp. 1–36.

Makgala, Christian John. 2010. "Limitations of British Territorial Control in Bechuanaland Protectorate, 1918–1953." *Journal of Southern African Studies* 36(1):57–71.

Mamdani, Mahmood. 1996. *Citizen and Subject: Contemporary Africa and the Legacy of Late Colonialism.* Princeton University Press.

Manin, Bernard. 1997. *The Principles of Representative Government.* Cambridge University Press.

Manning, Patrick. 1982. *Slavery, Colonialism and Economic Growth in Dahomey, 1640–1960.* Cambridge University Press.

Mansingh, Surjit. 2006. *Historical Dictionary of India.* Scarecrow Press.

Manungo, Kenneth R.D. 1999. "The Role of the Native Advisory Council in the Bechuanaland Protectorate, 1919–1960." *Botswana Journal of African Studies* 13(1–2):24–45.

Marcum, John A. 1969. *The Angolan Revolution. Vol. 1. The Anatomy of An Explosion (1950–1962).* MIT Press.

Marks, Thomas A. 1976. "Spanish Sahara–Background to Conflict." *African Affairs* 75(298):3–13.

Marongiu, Antonio. 1968. *Medieval Parliaments: A Comparative Study.* Eyre & Spottiswoode.

Marshall, Bernard. 1972. "Attempts at Windward/Leeward Federation." *Caribbean Quarterly* 18(2):9–15.

Marshall, Monty G. and Ted Robert Gurr. 2014. "Polity IV Project: Political Regime Characteristics and Transitions, 1800–2013." Available at www.systemicpeace.org/polity/polity4.htm.

Martin, Atherton. 1989. Historical Setting. In *Islands of the Commonwealth Caribbean: A Regional Study*, ed. Sandra W. Meditz and Dennis W. Hanratty. Federal Research Division, Library of Congress pp. 261–290.

Martin, Frederick. 1865. *The Statesman's Year-book: Statistical and Historical Annual of the States of the World for the Year 1865.* Macmillan.

Martin, Philip A. 2021. "Insurgent Armies: Military Obedience and State Formation after Rebel Victory." *International Security* 46(3): 87–127.

Martin, Vanessa. 2011. "State, Power and Long-term Trends in the Iranian Constitution of 1906 and its Supplement of 1907." *Middle Eastern Studies* 47(3):461–476.

Mason, R.H.P. 1962. *Japan's First General Election, 1890.* Cambridge University Press.

Mather, Cotton. 1689. "The Boston Declaration of Grievances." Available at http://nationalhumanitiescenter.org/pds/amerbegin/power/text5/Boston Declaration.pdf.

Maxon, Robert M. 1993. *Struggle for Kenya: The Loss and Reassertion of Imperial Initiative, 1912–1923.* Fairleigh Dickinson University Press.

Maxwell, Kenneth R. 1984. "Portuguese America." *International History Review* 6(4):529–550.

McCann, Frank D. 1997. Historical Setting. In *Brazil: A Country Study*, ed. Rex A. Hudson. Federal Research Division, Library of Congress pp. 1–86.

McCann, L.D. 2012. "Halifax." Available at www.thecanadianency clopedia.ca/en/article/halifax.

McEvedy, Colin and Richard Jones. 1978. *Atlas of World Population History.* Penguin Books.

McKinley, Albert Edward. 1905. *The Suffrage Franchise in the Thirteen English Colonies in America.* University of Pennsylvania.

McRae, Kenneth D. 1964. The Structure of Canadian History. In *The Founding of New Societies: Studies in the History of the United States, Latin America, South Africa, Canada, and Australia*, ed. Louis Hartz. Mariner Books pp. 219–274.

McRae, Matthew. 2019. "The Chaotic Story of the Right to Vote in Canada." Available at https://humanrights.ca/story/the-chaotic-story-of-the-right-to-vote-in-canada.

Meinhardt, Heiko. 1999. Malawi. In *Elections in Africa: A Data Handbook*, ed. Dieter Nohlen, Bernard Thibaut and Michael Krennerich. Oxford University Press pp. 549–566.

Menaldo, Victor. 2012. "The Middle East and North Africa's Resilient Monarchs." *Journal of Politics* 74(3):707–722.

Meng, Anne. 2020. *Constraining Dictatorship: From Personalized Rule to Institutionalized Regimes.* Cambridge University Press.

Meng, Anne and Jack Paine. 2022. "Power Sharing and Authoritarian Stability: How Rebel Regimes Solve the Guardianship Dilemma." *American Political Science Review* 116(4):1208–1225.

Meng, Anne, Jack Paine and Robert Powell. 2023. "Authoritarian Power Sharing: Concepts, Mechanisms, and Strategies." *Annual Review of Political Science* 26:153–173.

Meyer, Milton W. 2012. *Japan: A Concise History.* Rowman & Littlefield Publishers.

Mickey, Robert. 2015. *Paths Out of Dixie: The Democratization of Authoritarian Enclaves in America's Deep South, 1944–1972*. Princeton University Press.

Miller, Michael K. 2012. "Economic Development, Violent Leader Removal, and Democratization." *American Journal of Political Science* 56(4):1002–1020.

Miller, Michael K. 2015. "Democratic Pieces: Autocratic Elections and Democratic Development Since 1815." *British Journal of Political Science* 45(3):501–530.

Miller, Michael K. 2020. "The Strategic Origins of Electoral Authoritarianism." *British Journal of Political Science* 50(1):17–44.

Miller, Michael K. 2021. *Shock to the System: Coups, Elections, and War on the Road to Democratization*. Princeton University Press.

Misra, B.B. 1970. *Administrative History of India 1834–1947*. Oxford University Press.

Mlambo, Alois S. 2014. *A History of Zimbabwe*. Cambridge University Press.

Moore, Barrington. 1966a. *Social Origins of Democracy and Dictatorship*. Beacon Press.

Moore, John Preston. 1954. *The Cabildo in Peru under the Hapsburgs: A Study in the Origins and Powers of the Town Council in the Viceroyalty of Peru; 1530–1700*. Duke University Press.

Moore, John Preston. 1966b. *The Cabildo in Peru under the Bourbons: A Study in the Decline and Resurgence of Local Government in the Audencia of Lima, 1700–1824*. Duke University Press.

Morgan, Edmund S. 1989. *Inventing the People: The Rise of Popular Sovereignty in England and America*. WW Norton & Company.

Morgenthau, Ruth Schachter. 1964. *Political Parties in French-speaking West Africa*. Clarendon Press.

Morrell, W.P. 1930. *British Colonial Policy in the Age of Peel and Russell*. Clarendon Press.

Mosley, Paul. 1983. *The Settler Economies: Studies in the Economic History of Kenya and Southern Rhodesia 1900–1963*. Cambridge University Press.

Mowat, Charles Loch. 1943. *East Florida as a British Province, 1763–1784*. University of California Press.

Müller-Crepon, Carl. 2020. "Continuity or Change? (In)direct Rule in British and French Colonial Africa." *International Organization* 74(4):707–741.

Murdock, George Peter. 1967. *Ethnographic Atlas*. University of Pittsburgh Press.

Myrup, Erik Lars. 2010. "Kings, Colonies, and Councilors: Brazil and the Making of Portugal's Overseas Council, 1642–1833." *The Americas* 67(2):185–218.

Namasivayam, S. 1951. *The Legislatures of Ceylon.* Faber & Faber Limited.

Naoroji, Dadabhai. 1901. *Poverty and Un-British Rule in India.* S. Sonnen-schein.

Narain, Frank A. 2007. "Historical Information, Events, & Dates on the Parliament of Guyana from 1718 to 2006." Available at https://parliament.gov.gy/GUYANA%20PARLIAMENT%20HISTORY%20200 9-1.pdf.

Narizny, Kevin. 2012. "Anglo-American Primacy and the Global Spread of Democracy: An International Genealogy." *World Politics* 64(2):341–373.

Naylor, Phillip C. 2006. *Historical Dictionary of Algeria.* Rowman & Littlefield.

Nelson, Harold D. 1974. "Area Handbook for Senegal." Handbook prepared by Foreign Area Studies of the American University.

Nelson, Harold D. 1975. "Area Handbook for Guinea." Handbook prepared by Foreign Area Studies of the American University.

Nelson, Michael H. 2002. Thailand. In *Elections in Asia and the Pacific: A Data Handbook. Volume 2: South East Asia, East Asia, and the Pacific,* ed. Dieter Nohlen, Florian Grotz and Christof Hartmann. Oxford University Press pp. 261–320.

Nieuwenhuysen, J.P. 1961. "Indonesia's Constitutional Development Before Independence." *Theoria: A Journal of Social and Political Theory* 16: 50–57.

Nikolova, Elena. 2017. "Destined for Democracy? Labour Markets and Political Change in Colonial British America." *British Journal of Political Science* 47(1):19–45.

Nikolova, Elena and Jakub Polansky. 2021. "Conversionary Protestants Do Not Cause Democracy." *British Journal of Political Science* 51(4): 1723–1733.

Nogueira da Silva, Cristina. 2011. Political Representation and Citizenship Under the Empire. In *Res Publica 1820–1926: Citizenship and Political Representation in Portugal,* ed. Fernando Catroga and Pedro Tavares de Almeida. Assembly of the Republic: National Library of Portugal pp. 90–111.

North, Douglass C. 1991. "Institutions." *Journal of Economic Perspectives* 5(1):97–112.

North, Douglass C., William Summerhill and Barry R. Weingast. 2000. Order, Disorder and Economic Change: Latin America Versus North America. In *Governing for Prosperity,* ed. Bruce Bueno de Mesquita and Hilton L. Root. Yale University Press pp. 17–58.

Nova Scotia Legislature. 2017. "History of Voting in Nova Scotia." Available at https://nslegislature.ca/about/history/history-voting-nova-scotia.

Novati, Giampaolo Calchi. 2008. "Italy and Africa: How to Forget Colonialism." *Journal of Modern Italian Studies* 13(1):41–57.

O'Donnell, Guillermo A. 1994. "Delegative Democracy." *Journal of Democracy* 5(1):55–69.

O'Donnell, Guillermo and Philippe C. Schmitter. 1986. *Transitions from Authoritarian Rule: Tentative Conclusions About Uncertain Democracies.* Johns Hopkins University Press.

O'Gorman, Frank. 1986. "The Unreformed Electorate of Hanoverian England: The Mid-eighteenth Century to the Reform Act of 1832." *Social History* 11(1):33–52.

Okolo, Julius Emeka. 1981. "Liberia: The Military Coup and Its Aftermath." *The World Today* 37(4):149–157.

Oliver, Roland and Anthony Atmore. 2005. *Africa Since 1800.* 5th ed. Cambridge University Press.

Olsson, Ola. 2009. "On the Democratic Legacy of Colonialism." *Journal of Comparative Economics* 37(4):534–551.

Oostindie, Gert and Inge Klinkers. 2012. *Decolonising the Caribbean: Dutch Policies in a Comparative Perspective.* Amsterdam University Press.

Opello Jr., Walter C. 1994. Historical Setting. In *Portugal: A Country Study*, ed. Eric Solsten. Federal Research Division, Library of Congress pp. 1–62.

O'Shaughnessy, Andrew Jackson. 2000. *An Empire Divided: The American Revolution and the British Caribbean.* University of Pennsylvania Press.

Owen, Nicholas. 2003. "The Conservative Party and Indian Independence, 1945–1947." *The Historical Journal* 46(2):403–436.

Owen, Nicholas. 2007. *The British Left and India: Metropolitan Anti-Imperialism, 1885–1947.* Oxford University Press.

Owolabi, Olukunle P. 2014. "Colonialism, Development and Democratization: Beyond National Colonial Legacies." *APSA-Comparative Democratization Newsletter* pp. 2, 12–15.

Owolabi, Olukunle P. 2015. "Literacy and Democracy Despite Slavery: Forced Settlement and Postcolonial Outcomes in the Developing World." *Comparative Politics* 48(1):43–78.

Owolabi, Olukunle P. 2023. *Ruling Emancipated Slaves and Indigenous Subjects: The Divergent Legacies of Forced Settlement and Colonial Occupation in the Global South.* Oxford University Press.

Page, Scott E. 2006. "Path Dependence." *Quarterly Journal of Political Science* 1(1):87–115.

Paine, Jack. 2019*a*. "Democratic Contradictions in European Settler Colonies." *World Politics* 71(3):542–585.

Paine, Jack. 2019*b*. "Redistributive Political Transitions: Minority Rule and Liberation Wars in Colonial Africa." *Journal of Politics* 81(2):505–523.

Paine, Jack, Xiaoyan Qiu and Joan Ricart-Huguet. 2023. "Endogenous Colonial Borders: Precolonial States and Geography in the Partition of Africa." *American Political Science Review*, forthcoming.

Paping, Richard. 2014. General Dutch Population Development 1400-1850: Cities and Countryside. In *1st ESHD conference, Alghero, Italy.*

Parkman, Francis. 1875. *The Old Régime in Canada: France and England in North America.* Little, Brown, and Company.

Parry, J.H. 1966. *The Spanish Seaborne Empire.* Alfred A. Knopf.

Patel, Dinyar. 2020. *Naoroji: Pioneer of Indian Nationalism.* Harvard University Press.

Peemans, Jean-Philippe. 1975. Capital Accumulation in the Congo under Colonialism: The Role of the State. In *Colonialism in Africa 1870–1960,* Volume 4: The Economics of Colonialism, ed. L.H. Gann and Peter Duignan. Cambridge University Press pp. 165–212.

Peers, Douglas M. 2013. *India under Colonial Rule: 1700–1885.* Pearson Education.

Pempel, T.J. 1990. Introduction. Uncommon Democracies: The One-party Dominant Regimes. In *Uncommon Democracies: The One-Party Dominant Regimes,* ed. T.J. Pempel. Cornell University Press.

Pemstein, Daniel, Kyle L. Marquardt, Eitan Tzelgov, Yi-ting Wang, Juraj Medzihorsky, Joshua Krusell, Farhad Miri, Johannes von Römer. 2023. "The V-Dem Measurement Model: Latent Variable Analysis for Cross national and Cross temporal Expert coded Data." V-Dem Working Paper No. 21. 8th edition. University of Gothenburg: Varieties of Democracy Institute.

Perkins, Kenneth J. 1997. *Historical Dictionary of Tunisia,* 2nd ed. Scarecrow Press.

Pevehouse, Jon C. 2005. *Democracy from Above: Regional Organizations and Democratization.* Cambridge University Press.

Pierson, Paul. 2000. "Increasing Returns, Path Dependence, and the Study of Politics." *American Political Science Review* 94(2):251–267.

Pimenta, Fernando Tavaras. 2016. "Decolonisation Postponed: The Failure of the Colonial Politics of Marcelo Caetano (1968–1974)." *Social Dynamics* 42(1):12–30.

Pimlott, Ben. 1977. "Socialism in Portugal: Was it a Revolution?" *Government and Opposition* 12(3):332–350.

Pincus, Steven C.A and James A. Robinson. 2014. What Really Happened During the Glorious Revolution? In *Institutions, Property Rights, and Economic Growth: The Legacy of Douglass North,* ed. Sebastian Galiani and Itai Sened. Cambridge University Press.

Pitman, F.W. 1917. *The Development of the British West Indies: 1700–1763.* Archon Books.

Pole, J.R. 1957. "Suffrage and Representation in Massachusetts: A Statistical Note." *William and Mary Quarterly* 14(4):560–592.

Pole, J.R. 1966. *Political Representation in England and the Origins of the American Republic.* Macmillan.

Post, Ken. 1981. *Strike the Iron, Vol. I: A Colony at War: Jamaica, 1939–1945*. Humanities Press International.

Price, John Leslie. 1994. *Holland and the Dutch Republic in the Seventeenth Century: The Politics of Particularism*. Oxford University Press.

Priestley, Herbert Ingram. 1938. *France Overseas: A Study of Modern Imperialism*. Appleton-Century Company.

Pritchard, James. 2004. *In Search of Empire: The French in the Americas, 1670–1730*. Cambridge University Press.

Proctor, J.H. 1968. "The House of Chiefs and the Political Development of Botswana." *The Journal of Modern African Studies* 6(1):59–79.

Przeworski, Adam. 1991. *Democracy and the Market: Political and Economic Reforms in Eastern Europe and Latin America*. Cambridge University Press.

Przeworski, Adam. 2018. *Why Bother with Elections?* John Wiley & Sons.

Przeworski, Adam, Michael E. Alvarez, José Antonio Cheibub and Fernando Limongi. 2000. *Democracy and Development: Political Institutions and Well-being in the World, 1950–1990*. Cambridge University Press.

Putterman, L. 2012. "State Antiquity Index, Version 3.1." *Brown University*. Available at https://sites.google.com/brown.edu/louis-putterman.

Quinn, Frederick. 2000. *The French Overseas Empire*. Praeger Publishers.

Rabb, Theodore K. 2002. Institutions and Ideas: Planting the Roots of Democracy in Early Modern Europe. In *The Making and Unmaking of Democracy: Lessons from History and World Politics*, ed. Theodore K. Rabb and Ezra N. Suleiman. Routledge. pp. 41–58.

Ray, Rajat K. 1979. "Historical Roots of the Crisis of Calcutta, 1876–1939." *Economic and Political Weekly* 14(29):1206–1211.

Reno, William. 2011. *Warfare in Independent Africa*. Cambridge University Press.

Ricart-Huguet, Joan. 2022. "The Origins of Colonial Investments in Former British and French Africa." *British Journal of Political Science* 52(2): 736–757.

Ries, Matthias. 2002. Israel. In *Elections in Asia and the Pacific: A Data Handbook. Volume 1: Middle East, Central Asia, and South Asia*, ed. Dieter Nohlen, Florian Grotz and Christof Hartmann. Oxford University Press pp. 109–140.

Roberts, Stephen Henry. 1963. *The History of French Colonial Policy: 1870–1925*. Frank Cass & Company.

Robinson, James A. and Ragnar Torvik. 2016. "Endogenous Presidentialism." *Journal of the European Economic Association* 14(4):907–942.

Rogers, Howard Aston. 1970. "The Fall of the Old Representative System in the Leeward and Windward Islands, 1854–1877." Ph.D. thesis, Department of History, University of Southern California.

Rogoziński, Jan. 2000. *A Brief History of the Caribbean: From the Arawak and the Carib to the Present.* Plume Books.

Rosenfeld, Bryn. 2020. *The Autocratic Middle Class: How State Dependency Reduces the Demand for Democracy.* Princeton University Press.

Ross, Michael L. 2001. "Does Oil Hinder Democracy?" *World Politics* 53(3):325–361.

Ross, Michael L. 2012. *The Oil Curse: How Petroleum Wealth Shapes the Development of Nations.* Princeton University Press.

Ross, Michael L. and Paasha Mahdavi. 2015. "Oil and Gas Data, 1932–2014. Harvard Dataverse." Harvard Dataverse. Available at https://dataverse.harvard.edu/dataset.xhtml?persistentId=doi:10.7910/DVN/ZTPW0Y.

Rueschemeyer, Dietrich, Evelyne Huber Stephens and John D. Stephens. 1992. *Capitalist Development and Democracy.* Cambridge University Press.

Russell-Wood, A.J.R. 1974. "Local Government in Portuguese America: A Study in Cultural Divergence." *Comparative Studies in Society and History* 16(2):187–231.

Russell-Wood, A.J.R. ed. 1999. Introduction. In *Local Government in European Overseas Empires, 1450–1800: Part I.* Ashgate pp. xx–lxxxi.

Sacks, David. 1994. The Paradox of Taxation: Fiscal Crises, Parliament, and Liberty in England, 1450–1640. In *Fiscal Crises, Liberty, and Representative Government 1450–1789,* ed. Philip T. Hoffman and Kathryn Norberg. Stanford University Press pp. 7–66.

Sarabi, Abdul Wahed. 2002. Afghanistan. In *Elections in Asia and the Pacific: A Data Handbook. Volume 1: Middle East, Central Asia, and South Asia,* ed. Dieter Nohlen, Florian Grotz and Christof Hartmann. Oxford University Press pp. 503–514.

Saunders, Christopher. 2010. The Expansion of British Liberties: The South African Case. In *Exclusionary Empire: English Liberty Overseas, 1600–1900,* ed. Jack P. Greene. Cambridge University Press pp. 269–288.

Savary, Alan. 1952. "The French Union: Centralism or Federalism?" *International Journal* 7(4):258–264.

Scarritt, James R. and Shaheen Mozaffar. 1999. "The Specification of Ethnic Cleavages and Ethnopolitical Groups for the Analysis of Democratic Competition in Contemporary Africa." *Nationalism and Ethnic Politics* 5(1):82–117.

Schapera, Isaac. 1940. The Political Organization of the Ngwato of Bechualanland Protectorate. In *African Political Systems,* ed. M. Fortes and E.E. Evans-Pritchard. Oxford University Press pp. 80–119.

Scheffler, Thomas. 2002. Lebanon. In *Elections in Asia and the Pacific: A Data Handbook. Volume 1: Middle East, Central Asia, and South*

Asia, ed. Dieter Nohlen, Florian Grotz and Christof Hartmann. Oxford University Press pp. 169–198.

Schloss, Rebecca Hartkopf. 2009. *Sweet Liberty: The Final Days of Slavery in Martinique*. University of Pennsylvania Press.

Schmidt, Siegmar. 1999. Uganda. In *Elections in Africa*, ed. Dieter Nohlen, Bernard Thibaut and Michael Krennerich. Oxford University Press.

Schultz, Kirsten. 2000. "Royal Authority, Empire and the Critique of Colonialism: Political Discourse in Rio de Janeiro (1808–1821)." *Luso-Brazilian Review* 37(2):7–31.

Schwartzberg, J.E. 1992. *A Historical Atlas of South Asia*. Oxford University Press.

Scott, James C. 1998. *Seeing Like a State: How Certain Schemes to Improve the Human Condition Have Failed*. Yale University Press.

Seekins, Donald M. 2017. *Historical Dictionary of Burma (Myanmar)*. Rowman & Littlefield.

Shortt, Adam and Thomas Chapais. 1913. The Colony in its Political Relations. In *Canada and its Provinces: A History of the Canadian People and Their Institutions by One Hundred Associates, Volume II*, ed. Adam Shortt and Arthur G. Doughty. Edinburgh University Press pp. 315–378.

Simon, Joshua. 2017. *The Ideology of Creole Revolution: Imperialism and Independence in American and Latin American Political Thought*. Cambridge University Press.

Simpson, Lesley Byrd, Gordon Griffiths and Woodrow Borah. 1956. "Representative Institutions in the Spanish Empire of the Sixteenth Century." *The Americas* 12(3):223–257.

Sims, Richard. 2019. *Japanese Political History Since the Meiji Restoration, 1868–2000*. Springer.

Singh, Naunihal. 2014. *Seizing Power: The Strategic Logic of Military Coups*. Johns Hopkins.

Sinha, Mrinalini. 1999. "Suffragism and Internationalism: The Enfranchisement of British and Indian Women Under an Imperial State." *The Indian Economic & Social History Review* 36(4):461–484.

Sires, Ronald V. 1955. "The Experience of Jamaica with Modified Crown Colony Government." *Social and Economic Studies* 4(2):150–167.

Sisson, Richard and Stanley A. Wolpert. 1988. *Congress and Indian Nationalism: The Preindependence Phase*. University of California Press.

Skidmore, Thomas E. and Peter H. Smith. 2005. *Modern Latin America*. 6th ed. Oxford University Press.

Sklar, Richard L. and C.S. Whitaker, Jr. 1964. Nigeria. In *Political Parties and National Integration in Tropical Africa*, ed. James S. Coleman and Jr. Carl G. Rosberg. University of California Press pp. 597–564.

Slater, Dan. 2010. *Ordering Power: Contentious Politics and Authoritarian Leviathans in Southeast Asia*. Cambridge University Press.

Smith, James Patterson. 1994. "The Liberals, Race, and Political Reform in the British West Indies, 1866–1874." *Journal of Negro History* 79(2):131–146.

Sokoloff, Kenneth L. and Stanley L. Engerman. 2000. "History Lessons: Institutions, Factors Endowments, and Paths of Development in the New World." *Journal of Economic Perspectives* 14(3):217–232.

Spence, J.E. 1964. "British Policy Towards the High Commission Territories." *The Journal of Modern African Studies* 2(2):221–246.

Spieler, Miranda Frances. 2009. "The Legal Structure of Colonial Rule during the French Revolution." *William and Mary Quarterly* 66(2):365–408.

Spruyt, Hendrik. 2005. *Ending Empire: Contested Sovereignty and Territorial Partition*. Cornell University Press.

Squire, Peverill. 2012. *The Evolution of American Legislatures: Colonies, Territories, and States, 1619–2009*. University of Michigan Press.

Staniland, Martin. 1973. "The Three-party System in Dahomey: I, 1946–56." *The Journal of African History* 14(2):291–312.

Stasavage, David. 2011. *States of Credit: Size, Power, and the Development of European Polities*. Princeton University Press.

Stasavage, David. 2020. *The Decline and Rise of Democracy*. Princeton University Press.

Stearns, Peter N., Stephen S. Gosch and Erwin P. Grieshaber. 1988. *Documents in World History*. Pearson Longman.

Steinberg, S.H. 1952. *The Statesman's Year-book: Statistical and Historical Annual of the States of the World for the Year 1952*. Macmillan.

Steinberg, S.H. 1962. *The Statesman's Year-book: Statistical and Historical Annual of the States of the World for the Year 1962*. Macmillan.

Stengers, Jean. 1982. Precipitous Decolonization: The Case of the Belgian Congo. In *The Transfer of Power in Africa: Decolonization, 1940–1960*, ed. Prosser Gifford and W.M. Roger Louis. Yale University Press pp. 305–335.

Stevens, Richard P. 1963. "Swaziland Political Development." *The Journal of Modern African Studies* 1(3):327–350.

Stockwell, Sarah and L.J. Butler. 2013. Introduction. In *The Wind of Change: Harold MacMillan and British Decolonization*, ed. L.J. Butler and Sarah Stockwell. Palgrave MacMillan pp. 1–19.

Sulaiman, Yohanes. 2008. The Banteng and the Eagle: Indonesian Foreign Policy and the United States During the Era of Sukarno 1945-1967. Ph.D. thesis, The Ohio State University.

Sullivan, Mark P. 1989. The Northern Islands: The Bahamas. In *Islands of the Commonwealth Caribbean: A Regional Study*, ed. Sandra W. Meditz and Dennis M. Hanratty. Federal Research Division, Library of Congress pp. 519–560.

Svolik, Milan W. 2013. "Contracting on Violence: The Moral Hazard in Authoritarian Repression and Military Intervention in Politics." *Journal of Conflict Resolution* 57(5):765–794.

Symington, Joan and Neville Symington. 2002. *The Clinical Thinking of Wilfred Bion*. Routledge.

Tai, Hue-Tam Ho. 1984. "The Politics of Compromise: The Constitutionalist Party and the Electoral Reforms of 1922 in French Cochinchina." *Modern Asian Studies* 18(3):371–391.

Tamuno, Tekena N. 1966. *Nigeria and Elective Representation, 1923–1947*. Heinemann.

Tamuno, Tekena N. 1972. *The Evolution of the Nigerian State: The Southern Phase, 1898–1914*. Humanities Press.

Tan, Tai Yong. 2009. *The Garrison State: The Military, Government and Society in Colonial Punjab 1849–1947*. SAGE Publications.

Tarling, N. 2001. *A Sudden Rampage: The Japanese Occupation of Southeast Asia, 1941-1945*. University of Hawaii Press.

Tarrade, Jean. 1963. "L'administration coloniale en France à la fin de l'Ancien Régime: Projets de réforme." *Revue Historique* 1(229):103–122.

Taylor, Alan. 2002. *American Colonies: The Settling of North America*. Penguin Books.

Teele, Dawn Langan. 2018. *Forging the Franchise*. Princeton University Press.

Thompson, Elizabeth F. 2020. *How the West Stole Democracy from the Arabs: The Syrian Arab Congress of 1920 and the Destruction of Its Historical Liberal-Islamic Alliance*. Atlantic Monthly Press.

Thompson, I.A.A. 1994*a*. Castile: Absolutism, Constitutionalism, and Liberty. In *Fiscal Crises, Liberty, and Representative Government 1450–1789*, ed. Philip T. Hoffman and Kathryn Norberg. Stanford University Press pp. 181–225.

Thompson, I.A.A. 1994*b*. Castile: Polity, Fiscality, and Fiscal Crisis. In *Fiscal Crises, Liberty, and Representative Government 1450–1789*, ed. Philip T. Hoffman and Kathryn Norberg. Stanford University Press pp. 140–180.

Thompson, Leonard. 1971. The Compromise of Union. In *The Oxford History of South Africa Vol. II, 1870–1966*, ed. Monica Wilson and Leonard Thompson. Oxford University Press pp. 325–364.

Tomlinson, Brian Roger. 1976. *The Indian National Congress and the Raj, 1929–1942: The Penultimate Phase*. Springer.

Trapido, Stanley. 1964. "The Origins of the Cape Franchise Qualifications of 1853." *Journal of African History* 5(1):37–54.

Treaty of Versailles. 1920. "Treaty of Peace with Germany (Treaty of Versailles)." Available at www.census.gov/history/pdf/treaty_of_versailles-112018.pdf.

Treisman, Daniel. 2000. "The Causes of Corruption: A Cross-national Study." *Journal of Public Economics* 76(3):399–457.

Trevelyan, George Macaulay. 1913. *The Life of John Bright*. Constable.

Tudor, Maya. 2013. *The Promise of Power: The Origins of Democracy in India and Autocracy in Pakistan*. Cambridge University Press.

Valelly, Richard M. 2009. *The Two Reconstructions: The Struggle for Black Enfranchisement*. University of Chicago Press.

Valenzuela, J. Samuel. 1996. Building Aspects of Democracy before Democracy: Electoral Practices in Nineteenth Century Chile. In *Elections Before Democracy: The History of Elections in Europe and Latin America*, ed. Eduardo Posada-Carbó. Springer pp. 223–257.

Van Imhoff, Evert and Gijs Beets. 2004. "A Demographic History of the Indo-Dutch Population, 1930–2001." *Journal of Population Research* 21(1):47–72.

Van Zanden, Jan Luiten, Eltjo Buringh and Maarten Bosker. 2012. "The Rise and Decline of European Parliaments, 1188–1789." *The Economic History Review* 65(3):835–861.

Varshney, Ashutosh. 2022. "How India's Ruling Party Erodes Democracy." *Journal of Democracy* 33(4):104–118.

Veenendaal, Wouter. 2021. "How Instability Creates Stability: The Survival of Democracy in Vanuatu." *Third World Quarterly* 42(6): 1330–1346.

Vinogradov, Amal. 1972. "The 1920 Revolt in Iraq Reconsidered: The Role of Tribes in National Politics." *International Journal of Middle East Studies* 3(2):123–139.

Wasserman, Gary. 1976. *Politics of Decolonization: Kenya Europeans and the Land Issue 1960–1965*. Cambridge University Press.

Waterhouse, Richard. 2010. Liberty and Representative Government in Australia, 1788–1901. In *Exclusionary Empire: English Liberty Overseas, 1600–1900*, ed. Jack P. Greene. Cambridge University Press pp. 220–247.

Watson, Richard Lyness. 1990. *The Slave Question: Liberty and Property in South Africa*. Wesleyan University Press.

Webb, Stephen Saunders. 1979. *The Governors-General: The English Army and the Definition of the Empire, 1569–1681*. University of North Carolina Press.

Weiner, Myron. 1987. Empirical Democratic Theory. In *Competitive Elections in Developing Countries*, ed. Myron Weiner and Ergun Ozbundun. Duke University Press pp. 3–34.

Weipert-Fenner, Irene. 2020. *The Autocratic Parliament: Power and Legitimacy in Egypt, 1866–2011*. Syracuse University Press.

Wells, Robert V. 1975. *The Population of the British Colonies in America Before 1776*. Princeton University Press.

Wheare, Joan. 1949. *The Nigerian Legislative Council*. Faber and Faber Limited.

White, Stephen. 2010. Russia. In *Elections in Europe: A Data Handbook*, ed. Dieter Nohlen and Philip Stöver. Nomos pp. 1623–1668.

Whitson, Agnes M. 1929. *The Constitutional Development of Jamaica, 1660 to 1729*. Manchester University Press.

Wight, Martin. 1946a. *The Development of the Legislative Council, 1606–1945*. Faber & Faber Limited.

Wight, Martin. 1946b. *The Gold Coast Legislative Council*. Faber & Faber Limited.

Wight, Martin. 1952. *British Colonial Constitutions: 1947*. Clarendon Press.

Wilkinson, Steven. 2015. *Army and Nation: The Military and Indian Democracy Since Independence*. Harvard University Press.

Wilkinson, Steven and Massimiliano Gaetano Onorato. 2013. "Colonial Democratic Legacies." Unpublished manuscript. Yale University and IMT Lucca.

Will, Henry A 1966. "Problems of Constitutional Reform in Jamaica, Mauritius and Trinidad, 1880–1895." *English Historical Review* 81(321): 693–716.

Will, Henry A. 1970. *Constitutional Change in the British West Indies, 1880–1903: With Special Reference to Jamaica, British Guiana, and Trinidad*. Clarendon Press.

Wilson, Bruce G. 2009. "Loyalists in Canada." Available at www.the canadianencyclopedia.ca/en/article/loyalists.

Winnacker, Rudolph A. 1938. "Elections in Algeria and the French Colonies under the Third Republic." *American Political Science Review* 32(2): 261–277.

Woodberry, Robert D. 2012. "The Missionary Roots of Liberal Democracy." *American Political Science Review* 106(2):244–274.

Wright, Joseph and Abel Escribà-Folch. 2012. "Authoritarian Institutions and Regime Survival: Transitions to Democracy and Subsequent Autocracy." *British Journal of Political Science* 42(2): 283–309.

Wright, Mary Clabaugh. 1968. *China in Revolution: The First Phase, 1900–1913*. Yale University Press.

Wright, Teresa. 2010. *Accepting Authoritarianism: State-society Relations in China's Reform Era*. Stanford University Press.

Wrong, Hume. 1923. *Government of the West Indies*. Clarendon Press.

Wyse, Akintola. 2003. *HC Bankole-Bright and Politics in Colonial Sierra Leone, 1919–1958*. Cambridge University Press.

Zisser, Eyal. 2002. Syria. In *Elections in Asia and the Pacific: A Data Handbook. Volume 1: Middle East, Central Asia, and South Asia*, ed. Dieter Nohlen, Florian Grotz and Christof Hartmann. Oxford University Press pp. 213–232.

Index